2+.99

Nelso

AVAILABLE NOW!

A FIRST COURSE IN
Psychology

NICKY HAYES

ONLY
£6.95

FULLY
REVISED
EDITION

Nicky Hayes' **A First Course in Psychology** is the essential text for a wide range of courses, including GCSE and Standard Grade. It is also ideal as a general reference book for anyone interested in psychology.

Includes new chapters on environmental psychology, abnormal psychology and play. It also has coverage of ethical issues in psychology and further develops other topics from the first edition.

A First Course in Psychology   0-17-448166-7   £6.95

Order your copy by telephoning our **Customer Services** Department on **0932 246133**

TEACHING PSYCHOLOGY:
A HANDBOOK OF RESOURCES

TEACHING PSYCHOLOGY
A HANDBOOK OF RESOURCES

BPS
BOOKS

Published by
The British Psychological Society

First published in 1990 by The British Psychological Society, St Andrews House, 48 Princess Road East, Leicester, LE1 7DR, UK.

Distributed by The Distribution Centre, Blackhorse Road, Letchworth, Herts SG6 1HN, UK.

British Library Cataloguing in Publication Data

Teaching Psychology : a handbook of resources.
1. Psychology. Teaching aids
I. British Psychological Society
150.78

ISBN 1-85433-024-1

Typeset by Litho Link Ltd., Welshpool, Powys, Wales.
Printed and bound in Great Britain by BPCC Wheatons Ltd., Exeter.
Whilst every effort has been made to ensure the accuracy of the contents of this publication, the publishers and authors expressly disclaim responsibility in law for negligence or any other cause of action whatsoever.

CONTENTS

FOREWORD

In 1984 The British Psychological Society published *Psychology Teaching: Information and resources*, which was we believe the first such handbook in this country, and which we had conceived, planned, and edited. We had always envisaged that such a book would require to be updated periodically if it were to remain useful, and in due course suggested to the Society how this might be done. In the event the Society decided on the present volume, which it felt would not require editors as such. (In fact, many of the editorial functions have been ably carried out in-house by Cassy Spearing.) We were asked to revise our individual chapters from the first book, which we have done, in each case with the collaboration of Deana Smith, and to write a Foreword.

As before, the range of the book is wide – from audiovisual aids and microcomputers to laboratory equipment and careers and courses. The primary purpose is to be of *practical* use to teachers of psychology at all levels. In this regard it will be most useful if users of the book, or indeed those who have failed to find anything of value in it, will make their views known. A third version may well be planned in due course. This volume follows the general plan of its predecessor, with individual chapters on different sorts of resource.

That such a book ought to be of use, and ought to be among the Society's publications, follows from facts which are fairly well known. There is first the steady growth in demand for courses in psychology – about ten per cent per year in the case of GCE A-level, for example. It is almost impossible to estimate total numbers of students taking some significant element of psychology at any one time, but it can hardly be far short of 100,000, if the inclusion of psychology in numerous professional training courses is taken into account. There is the consequent fact that more graduates are embarking on careers wholly or partly as teachers of their subject. There is the fact that many of these, particularly at the pre-degree levels, may well be working in relative isolation from other psychologists, and may also be in the position of starting up or developing courses. And then there are wider issues such as the changing nature both of psychology itself and of the student population. Psychology has perhaps always been a subject in which there is emphasis on the latest material, but in the last few years new challenges have arisen from the circumstance that an ever greater proportion of students are not going to become professional psychologists. Psychology is seen more and more as a general education, fitting students, it is to be hoped, for a very wide range of future options. Another significant development, with consequences hard to predict, is that the student population, from being notably male dominated, is now overwhelmingly female. Having, fortunately, succeeded in becoming attractive to women, psychology must ask itself whether, and why, it is losing the allegiance of men.

As we have said elsewhere, perhaps *ad nauseam*, psychologists, as self-proclaimed students of human behaviour, ought to be foremost in thinking about what they do, in this case what and how they teach. We, with many others, have tried to contribute to this through organizations such as the Association for the Teaching of Pyschology, and the Society's Group of Teachers. All concerned with teaching the subject ought, we suggest, to belong to one if not both of these. Similarly, we have tried to stimulate discussion through papers and books. In *The Teaching of Pyschology: Method, content, and context* (Wiley, 1980) we considered as it were tactical matters; the first version of the present book was at the practical level of resources; while in *A Liberal Science: Psychology education past, present and future* (OU/SRHE, 1989) we have attempted to say something about wider matters of policy.

The present book continues the effort to provide useful information, and we very much hope it succeeds.

John Radford
David Rose

AUDIOVISUAL AIDS

Rosemary Westley

❏ *off-air recording* ● *video formats* ● *information sources and publications* ● *films and videos: (a) distributors and libraries (b) societies and associations* ● *selected audiovisual materials* ● *addresses* ● *subject index*

Audiovisual materials are extensively used by teachers of psychology at all levels. All institutions have limited facilities for producing their own materials, overhead transparencies being the most popular, while some have fully-equipped television studios and are able to produce films for their teaching staff. However most teachers will at some time need to hire or purchase audiovisual aids.

Whether you need films, videos or cassette tape/slide programmes, there is a very wide range of commercial material available to suit all budgets. The growing popularity of videos has considerably reduced the cost of showing films. Many libraries transfer new films onto video cassettes, keep the film copy as the original and hire out the video version with savings on handling and postage. Video cassettes can also be purchased at a reasonable cost, and this is a realistic alternative to hiring them.

The main problem posed by the use of commercial products is the time it can take to find the right material. Because a range of subject areas is relevant to psychology courses, useful material may be catalogued under a number of headings. The main ones are children and child development, psychology, social psychology, medicine, mental health, social problems, health and safety, education, mental and physical handicap. However, there is a great deal of overlap in the criteria used for the classification of materials in distributors' catalogues and it is very easy to miss suitable items.

This chapter is designed to save time and effort in locating material by providing a guide to what is currently available.

There is information on where to get advice and assistance; video formats and off-air recording, distributors and their range of topics, charities that have audiovisual programmes and a selection of relevant materials from current catalogues. The chapter ends with a comprehensive subject index for easy reference and a list of the names, addresses and telephone numbers of the companies and organizations that are referred to. (Note also the chapter in this volume on psychology and cinema, which illustrates different ways in which feature films can be used in the teaching of psychology.)

OFF-AIR RECORDING

Until recently, institutions have had to confine their recording to programmes by the Open University and Channel 4, who operate licensing schemes. However, the Copyright, Design and Patents Act 1988 was brought into effect in the autumn of 1989, and allows educational institutions to record broadcasts 'off-air' for use in teaching. Section 35(i) of the Act states: 'Rights owners will no longer have an absolute right to refuse to allow recording. Instead they will have the right to receive payment through a licensing scheme. If they fail to put their copyright materials into such a scheme they will lose their right to sue for infringement.'

A new licensing scheme organized by a group of rights owners, which include the BBC and the ITV companies, has been set up by forming a new company called Educational Recording Agency Ltd (ERA). Details of the scheme and the scale of fees were not known at the time of writing, but it is clear that in the future educational users will have access to a very wide range of broadcast material, including radio.

VIDEO FORMATS

Three video cassette formats are used by distributors in education. Before hiring or purchasing video tapes check which format your video recorder uses. It will be one of the following:

Betamax

Originally designed by Sony, though manufactured under licence by a number of companies, the Betamax system uses cassettes which contain ½in. tape.

VHS

VHS (Video Home System) is now the dominant video-cassette system in the UK.

U-matic (low band)

High quality video cassette which holds ¾in. tape. This system, which is now used in a variety of modes for production purposes, was originally designed by Sony. Companies which produce U-matic machines include NEC, HVC, Sony and National. Please note: *high* band U-matic is an incompatible production format which is unlikely to be used for general distribution.

INFORMATION SOURCES AND PUBLICATIONS When selecting audiovisual material it can be difficult to decide on its suitability for your teaching need when the only information available is an uncritical description in a distributor's catalogue. Although you may be able to get recommendations from other teachers on suitable materials, there are also several organizations that can provide help in locating materials, that publish reviews and appraisals and can provide preview facilities.

British Film Institute The BFI holds the nation's film archives. It has production, distribution and information divisions.

PUBLICATIONS:
British Film Institute Film and Television Yearbook lists all production companies, exhibitions and distribution organizers, and gives general information on the film industry and BFI services.

British National Film and Video Catalogue provides a complete record of short non-fiction films, video cassettes and 16mm. feature films released for non-theatric distribution in the UK. The catalogue has been published since 1963 in quarterly issues with annual cumulated volumes.

Films and Videograms for Schools is a subject listing of films and video cassettes available for screening in primary and secondary schools within the UK.

British Universities & Video Council BUFVC exists to promote the production, study and use of films, television and related media in higher education and research. The Council provides the following facilities:

INFORMATION SERVICE: deals with enquiries by members relating to the production, availability, and use of audiovisual materials in higher education. It has a small reference library, catalogues of over 500 UK and 100 foreign distributors and a file of appraisals on audiovisual materials currently available in the UK. Membership is by subscription.

AUDIOVISUAL REFERENCE CENTRE: holds audiovisual materials produced in institutions of higher education which can be previewed in the BUFVC offices.

HIGHER EDUCATION FILM AND VIDEO LIBRARY: contains specialized films and video cassettes in all subjects. This material would not normally be available in the UK (for example films made in the course of research). The films and video cassettes are suitable for degree-level and research work. Distribution is handled on the Council's behalf by the Scottish Central Film Library.

PUBLICATIONS:
BUFVC *Catalogue* (annual) Edited by Olwen Terris comprises seven microfiches with a 48-page booklet. Some 6,000 video

cassettes, films, tape/slide programmes, audio cassettes, slide sets, computer programs and videodiscs are fully described, with subject and title indexes. Many of the programmes were produced in institutions of higher education; others have been recommended for use in degree-level teaching and research. Television programmes and sound tapes from new Open University courses are now included. Appraised items are marked, as are those available for preview at the BUFVC's Audiovisual Reference Centre. The booklet lists the addresses and telephone numbers of more than 500 UK distributors.

Interpersonal Skills: A guide to film and video resources (1987). Edited by Olwen Terris, this 40-page booklet lists 170 programmes which demonstrate counselling and communication techniques. An appendix lists organizations that provide training and advisory services.

Higher Education Film and Video Library Catalogue. Some 400 films and videos for use in degree-level teaching are listed in this 80-page booklet. They include materials produced abroad, and research and teaching materials produced in institutions of higher education which would not otherwise be easily available to teachers elsewhere. Hire and sale.

View Finder is the BUFVC magazine that is published three times a year, once each term. It contains information and reviews on audiovisual materials and publications and articles on recent developments in the film and television industry.

Health Education Council

The HEC has an information service on teaching resources.

PUBLICATIONS:

Health Education Council Resource Lists. Subject lists containing publications and audiovisual materials from many sources. Topics covered by individual booklets include cancer education, child development, environmental health, health education for ethnic minorities, alcohol education, drugs, smoking and health, teenage smoking, handicap, heart disease, obesity, relationships, family planning, dental health, mental health, pregnancy, sexually transmitted diseases, AIDS, and health in old age. Each booklet is periodically updated.

Films and Videos for Health Education (1986) lists programmes on health education topics. Hire from CFL Vision or Concord Video and Film Council, sales from the HEC. All programmes can be previewed at the HEC.

Publications and Teaching Aids. Source lists of films, videos, filmstrips and audiotapes available from a variety of distributors. Separate booklets on mental health, personal relationships, and handicap.

**Mental Health
Film Council**

MHFC is an educational charity founded in 1963 to promote the making and use of films in mental health training and education. The Council provides the following facilities:

FILM FORUMS AND WORKSHOPS: organized by the Council.

INFORMATION SERVICE: For an annual subscription fee membership offers information on a variety of films and entitles members to the MHFC catalogue, quarterly newsletter, access to the MHFC enquiry service, viewing sessions and additional workshops.

PUBLICATIONS: *Mental Health Film Council Catalogue* (annual). Hundreds of films and videos from over 60 distributors are listed alphabetically. Entries give production and distribution details and brief synopses of content. The subject index contains three main categories: mental handicap, mental health and mental disorder. Other subjects include professional training, conflict and violence, legal and statutory aspects and self-help.

**Other
Information
Sources**

Other publications that include reviews or appraisals are:
   Audio Visual Directory (1990) published by EMAP Vision, PO Box 109, 19 Scarbrook Road, Croydon CR9 1QH.
   Independent Media published monthly by DVA, 7 Campbell Court, Bramley, Basingstoke RG26 5EG.

*FILMS AND
VIDEOS:
DISTRIBUTORS
AND
LIBRARIES*

The following pages list the main distributors and film libraries that supply materials relevant to psychology. The range of topic areas covered is listed in each case, so as to help teachers decide which companies are worth contacting. The entries are numbered and these numbers are used instead of page references in the index at the end of this chapter. For titles, descriptions, prices and running times, individual catalogues should be consulted. Alongside each entry the type of media they supply is indicated as shown below:

Video	– Video cassettes
Film	– 16mm film
Slide	– Slide sets
Audio	– Audiotapes
Tape/Slide	– Audiotape and slide programmes
OHT	– Overhead transparencies
Filmstrips	– Filmstrips
Film loops	– Film loops
Learning packages	– Learning packages

Availability (i.e. hire, sale, loan) is also indicated.

1 — Aleph One

PUBLICATION: Data sheet of audio cassettes on lifestyle training recorded by Dr Robert Sharpe.

Audio
Sale

TOPICS:

assertiveness	relaxation
fear	sleep
interviewing	smoking
phobias	

2 — British Broadcasting Corporation

The BBC has more than 2,000 programmes available for educational and institutional use.

CATALOGUES: BBC *Enterprises Programmes for Education and Training Central Reference Catalogue*

Video
Film
Hire & Sale

TOPICS:

addiction	mental handicap
ageing	obesity
birth	physical handicap
the brain	police and judicial
child development	issues
death	religion
health services	social issues

3 — British Medical Assn

The BMA has over 1,000 titles suitable for medical and allied audiences, including health educators. As well as contemporary programmes, the library holds many rare archival films.

CATALOGUES: BMA *Film Library*
BMA *Videocassette Library*

Video
Film
Hire & Sale

TOPICS:

abortion	mental illness
ageing	nervous system
alcohol abuse	neurology
bereavement	paediatrics
child assessment	personal relationships
child development	physiology
child welfare	psychiatry
drug abuse	residential care
epilepsy	smoking
handicap	stress

4 — BSIP ARS Magna

The BSIP produces educational audiovisual material in sciences dealing with brain and behaviour for teaching and research. Topics listed below such as perception include subtopics, for example depth perception (visual cliff), optical illusions (ambiguous figures) and the biological basis of behaviour.

Video
Film
Slide
Audio

TOPICS:

brain damage	perception
learning	sleep
nervous system	

Tape/Slide
Hire & Sale

5 — Central Independent Television	The Video Resources Unit has films available for educational institutions and individuals.

Video
Sale

TOPICS:

child abuse	mental illness
crime	physical handicap
mental handicap	rape

6 — CFL Vision CFL Vision has a wide variety of films for education.

CATALOGUES: *Films and Videos for Education and General Interest*

Video
Film
Hire & Sale

TOPICS:

alcohol abuse	education
biology	paediatrics
blindness	parenting
child development	rehabilitation
deafness	smoking
delinquency	young people

Chiltern Consortium See Herts Media

7 — Concord Video & Film Council Now the largest educational film library in the UK, its list covers documentaries, animated films and feature-length productions concerned with contemporary issues. It is registered as a charity and distributes films for over 350 other bodies (see next section on societies and organizations). The films are selected primarily to promote discussion for instruction and training.

CATALOGUES: *Main Film and Video Catalogue* (1985/87, and supplements for 1986, 1987, 1988, 1989) Over 3,000 titles.
Video catalogue (1989–1991)
Films and Videos on Mental Handicap (1985)

Video
Film
Hire & Sale

TOPICS:

abortion	family planning
adolescence	health education
alcohol abuse	human rights
blindness	medical subjects
child development	mental health
communication	personal relationships
community care	psychology
deafness	rehabilitation
drug abuse	sex education
ecology	smoking
education	wildlife
encounter groups	young people

8 — **CTVC Film Library**

Holds films and videos on social problems such as stress, rape, bereavement, disablement and divorce. These include programmes from the Leonard Cheshire Foundation and the Parkinson's Disease Society.

CATALOGUES: CTVC *Film and Video Library*

Video
Film
Hire & Sale

TOPICS:

alcohol abuse	physical violence
anxiety	(effects on victims
behaviour	and their families)
bereavement	pre-school children
child welfare	rape
divorce	smoking
drug abuse	stillbirth
family problems	stress
physical handicap	

9 — **D.S. Information Systems**

Supply films from the National Audio-Visual Aids Library. The company provides a subscription scheme for institutions that enable films to be hired at a reduced rate.

CATALOGUE: *16mm Films in the National Audio-Visual Aids Library*

Video
Film
Hire & Sale

TOPICS:

aggression	intelligence
child development	language
child psychology	learning
cognition	sociology
dyslexia	

10 — **Edward Patterson Assn**

CATALOGUES: *Health and Safety Catalogue* (inc. medical)(1989/90) lists films and videos.
Slide/Tape Multimedia Programmes Catalogue (1989) lists slides, tapes and slide/tape programmes on health, communications, human behaviour, social studies, sciences. Preview service for sales.
Education Film and Video Catalogue

Video
Film
Slide
Audio
Tape/Slide
Hire & Sale

TOPICS:

abnormal psychology	family planning
acceptance	family problems
adolescence	genetics
ageing/dying	human development
aggression	mental handicap
alcohol abuse	mental health
animal behaviour	occupational therapy
anxiety	parenting
attitudes	peer groups
behaviour therapy	personal conflict
brain and behaviour	personal construct
child care	therapy

child development
children
child behaviour
communication
conformity and
  individualism
deafness
decision making
depression
disability
divorce
drug abuse

personality
physical handicap
Piaget
prejudice
retirement
self-image
shoplifting
smoking
stress
teenage
  communication

11— Focal Point Audio-Visual

CATALOGUES: *Art, Design and Social Studies Catalogue*
Sciences-Geography Catalogue

Video
Slide
Tape/Slide
Sale

TOPICS: addiction
community care
crime
health education
nervous system

psychiatric centres
rehabilitation
stress
wildlife

12 — Glenbuck Films

Glenbuck has a large selection of documentaries covering a wide range of contemporary and educational titles. There is a preview service for sales.

CATALOGUES: *Film Hire Library Catalogue*
Video for Sale Catalogue, and leaflets on specific topics, including health and safety, social and legal studies.

Video
Film
Hire & Sale

TOPICS: alcohol abuse
apartheid
black culture
children and their
  relationships with
  each other
communal life

drug abuse
juvenile delinquency
marriage
suicide
welfare
women's liberation

13 — Graves Medical Audio-Visual Library

Graves is a non-profit making educational charity which produces audiovisual material for use in medical education.

CATALOGUES: *Graves Medical Audio-Visual Library Catalogue* contains videos, tape/slide programmes, slide sets, audio tapes, computer software and booklets on all medical subjects. Entries arranged under more than 50 subject headings, from accidents and emergencies, addictions and alternative medicine to tropical medicine and urogenital system. Each entry includes technical details, a brief description, author, producer, date and an indication of audience level. There are subject, title, author and numerical indexes.

| *Video*
Slide
Audio
Tape/Slide
Hire | TOPICS: | abortion
addiction
adolescence
adoption
ageing
aggression
alcohol abuse
anxiety
autism
battered wives
bereavement
child abuse
child development
child welfare
communication
deafness
death
dementia
depression
drug abuse
dyslexia
examination fears
family problems
geriatric psychiatry
handicap
homosexuality
hysteria
menopause
mental illness
nervous system | neuroticism
occupational
  psychology
occupational therapy
parenting
phobias
psychiatry
psychology
psychosexual
  problems
psychosomatism
rape
rehabilitation
relaxation
residential care
schizophrenia
shock
sleep and sleep
  disorders
social problems
speech and speech
  disorders
stress
strokes
suicide
terminal care
tranquillizers and
  antidepressants
violence
vision and voice |

| *14 –* **Griffin &**
George
Slide
Audio
OHT
Sale | TOPICS: | health education
nutrition
sex education |

15 – **Guild**
Sound & Vision

Distributes all the Open University Educational Enterprises (OUEE) films and videos (see OUEE entry for details). It also deals with videos and films for higher education.

CATALOGUES: *Guild Film and Video Programmes* (1986) contains hundreds of programmes arranged by subject. Headings include commerce and business, educational studies, health and safety, medical studies and social studies. Programmes from the BBC and Thames Television are included.
    Education Video Catalogue
    Free Loan Video Catalogue

Video
Film
Hire & Sale
	TOPICS:	addiction
		adolescence
		aggression
		assertiveness
		biology
		child development
		cognitive
		  development
		communication and
		  memory
		conformity and
		  independence
		counselling
		deafness
		death
			family relationships
			handicap
			infancy
			intelligence
			language
			  development
			learning
			parenting
			Piaget
			play
			social skills training
			social workers
			stress
			visual illusion

16 – Herts Media

Specializes mainly in the production of teaching materials for higher education. Chiltern Consortium merged with Herts Media, and programmes were originally produced by lecturers and advisers working for colleges. There is a preview service.

CATALOGUES: *Chiltern Video Catalogue*

Video *Sale*	TOPICS:	assessment child development concept formation education handicap	interaction language literacy remedial assessment study skills

17 – National Film Board of Canada

CATALOGUES: *Film Loan Library Catalogue: Films available from the Film Board* Lists over 1,000 films available from a variety of distributors.

Video
Film
Sale
	TOPICS:	addiction
		adolescence
		ageing
		aggression
		alcohol abuse
		attitudes and
		  prejudice
		battered wives
		behaviour (emotional,
		  social, sexual,
		  violent)
		child development
		cognition
		communication
		crime
		death
		depression
			genetics
			greed
			institutional care
			learning
			love
			mental illness
			mental and
			  physical handicap
			mother – child
			  interaction
			perception
			personality
			prostitution
			rape
			relationships
			  (social and
			  interpersonal)

dreams	self-respect
education	sexual behaviour
fear	social control
friendship	social psychology
gambling	

18—Open University Educational Enterprises

Video
Audio
Sale

The OUEE produces films to back up its university courses. Videos for hire are distributed by Guild Sound and Vision.

CATALOGUES: *The Open University Course Material 1988/9 Complete Listing*

TOPICS: Biology of brain and behaviour (11 programmes)
Cognitive development (4 programmes)
Introduction to psychology (7 programmes)
Genetics (10 programmes)
Personality, development and learning
(9 programmes)
Social science: A foundation course
(22 programmes)
Special needs in education (9 programmes)

19—Oxford Educational Resources

Video
Tape/Slide
Hire & Sale

CATALOGUES: *Title List of Audio-Visual Programmes*

TOPICS:

adoption	health education
alcohol abuse	mental health
anxiety	neurology
battered wives	phobias
care for the elderly	psychiatry
child abuse	social problems
deafness	violence
drug abuse	zoology
epilepsy	

20—Philip Harris

Slide
OHT
Learning packages
Sale

Slides and learning packages are supplied from their Avon office; overhead transparencies from Staffordshire.

TOPICS:

addiction	genetics
animal behaviour	human biology
drugs and health	smoking

21— Psychology News

Video
Sale

Makes documentaries for ITV and Channel 4 which are often of interest to psychologists and their students.

PUBLICATIONS: *Psychology News* appears four times a year.

TOPICS:

apartheid	psychiatric hospitals
mental health care	(Soviet)
	stress

22—Scottish Central Film & Video Library Part of the Scottish Council for Educational Technology, the Library supplies educational and documentary films for hire and purchase. It acts as a distributor for a number of societies including the Mental Health Film Council and the British Universities Film and Video Council (Higher Education Film and Video Library). For further details see other entries in the Information Sources and Publications section in this chapter.

CATALOGUES: *Health Education Films and Video Catalogue* contains hundreds of films and videos listed by subject, i.e. alcohol education, child development and care, drugs, elderly, human physiology, mental health/handicap/ disability, personal relationships, smoking.
Social Subjects on 16mm. Film and Video Catalogue Mainly suitable for social sciences.
Science Catalogue includes wildlife and biology films.

Video
Film
Hire & Sale

TOPICS:

addiction	mental health
age	mother–infant
alcohol abuse	interaction
aggression	nursery schools
animal behaviour	perception
behaviour	physiology (nervous
child behaviour	system and the
child care	senses)
child development	smoking
genetics	social problems
handicap	sociology
learning	therapy
marriage problems	wildlife

23—Tavistock Videotapes Provides video cassettes which address issues encountered by medical practitioners, nurses, psychiatrists and therapists.

CATALOGUES: *Tavistock Videotapes* (1988) Lists video programmes which concentrate on the importance of interpersonal skills in medical practice. Sale only.

Video
Hire & Sale

TOPICS:

behavioural	psychiatry
psychotherapy	

24—Univ. of Aberdeen

Video
Hire & Sale

TOPICS:

anxiety	children's thought
aptitude	intelligence
child assessment	personality
children's problem	phobias
solving	psycholinguistics

25—Univ. of Birmingham

The University's Television and Film Unit produces programmes designed to teach some of the elementary principles of medical interviewing to undergraduates in psychiatry and the behavioural sciences.

CATALOGUES: *Videotapes in Psychiatry* (1985) Details of programmes produced by Dr Tim Belts dealing with interviewing and assessment techniques, neuropsychiatry, psychosexual counselling and epilepsy.

Video
Sale

TOPICS:
assessment	psychosexual
autism	counselling
epilepsy	relaxation and
hypnosis	biofeedback
interviewing	stress
neuropsychiatry	

26—Univ. of Exeter

Produces videos on social work and psychiatry.

CATALOGUES: *Brochure from Teaching Services Centre* covers programmes for use by caring professions in training and work with specific groups of clients and patients.

Video
Hire & Sale

TOPICS:
alcohol abuse	psychiatric hospitals
counselling	physical handicap
fostering	
children with a handicap	

27—Univ. of London

Video
Sale

TOPICS:
behaviour therapy	perception and
child development	communication
infant and pre-school child	phobias

28—Univ. of Manchester

The University's Department of Psychiatry has a series of self-teaching video tapes that is relevant to psychiatry.

Video
Sale

TOPICS:
behaviour	psychotherapy
EEG	relaxation
family therapy	schizophrenia
interviewing skills	stuttering

29—Univ. of Newcastle (Medical School)

CATALOGUES: *Audio-Visual Centre Film and Video Catalogue*

Video
Film
Hire & Sale

TOPICS:
child development	medicine
infant social behaviour	

30—**Viewtech Audiovisual Media**

One of the distributors for the National Film Board of Canada (see separate entry), Indiana University Audio-Visual Centre, Gateway Educational Media, Marshfilm, Rank Aldis and Walt Disney Productions.

CATALOGUES: *Video and Film Catalogue – Educative*

Video
Film
Audio
Filmstrips
Filmloops
Learning packages
Hire & Sale

TOPICS: animal behaviour   handicap
          biology   nervous system
          brain   psychology
          care of elderly   social problems
          child abuse   (including alcohol
          child development   abuse and divorce)
          drug abuse   stress
          genetics

31—**Viscom**

Distributor for a wide variety of charities and commercial companies including BSIP (see separate entry), Golden Films, PDSA, Spastics Society, John Wiley & Sons.

Video
Film
Slide
Audio
Tape/Slide
Hire & Sale

TOPICS: animal welfare   psychiatry
          human sexuality   spasticity
          physiology   statistics

FILMS AND VIDEOS: SOCIETIES AND ASSOCIATIONS

This section lists some charitable societies and associations that produce or sponsor films and other audiovisual material in an effort to publicize their cause. Many of the films can be useful for psychology teachers. These organizations quite often supply booklets and notes to go with their audiovisual materials. They can sometimes provide a speaker if there is a branch near you. The entries are numbered, and these numbers are used instead of page references in the index at the end of this chapter.

32—**Anti-Apartheid Movement**

Video
Film
Hire

TOPICS: social issues and problems in South Africa: brutality, police violence, indoctrination of white children, history of women's resistance, stresses on death row, fighting, race and society.
DISTRIBUTION: Concord Video and Film Council.

33 — Assn for TOPICS: problems of children with hydrocephalus and spina
Spina Bifida & bifida.
Hydrocephalus DISTRIBUTION: Association for Spina Bifida and Hydrocephalus.

Film
Slide
Hire

34 — Bristol TOPICS: The victims' support scheme.
Victims' DISTRIBUTION: Concord Video and Film Council.
Support
Scheme

Film
Hire

35 — British TOPICS: guidance on adoption and fostering.
Agencies for DISTRIBUTION: Concord Video and Film Council.
Adoption &
Fostering

Video
Film
Tape/Slide
Hire & Sale

36 — British TOPICS: counselling techniques, assessment of behaviour;
Assn for psychotherapy.
Counselling DISTRIBUTION: Concord Video and Film Council.

Video
Film
Audio
Hire & Sale

37 — British TOPICS: lip-reading
Assn for the DISTRIBUTION: British Association for the Hard of Hearing.
Hard of Hearing

Film
Hire & Sale

38 — British TOPICS: medical and social aspects of epilepsy and its
Epilepsy Assn treatment.
Film DISTRIBUTION: Concord Video and Film Council.
Hire

39 — **Brook**   TOPICS: sex and the physically handicapped.
Advisory   DISTRIBUTION: Brook Advisory Centres.
Centres

Video
Hire

40 — **Camphill**   TOPICS: working communities with mentally handicapped
Village Trust   people.
Film   DISTRIBUTION: Concord Video and Film Council.
Hire

41 — **Hampstead**   TOPICS: nursery school for the blind; growing up without
Child Therapy   sight.
Clinic   DISTRIBUTION: Concord Video and Film Council.

Video
Film

42 — **Health**   TOPICS: sexual and personal relationships; child develop-
Education   ment; family relationship; smoking; parenting.
Authority   DISTRIBUTION: Concord Video and Film Council and Central
Video   Film Library.
Film
Loan & Sale

43 — **Help the**   TOPICS: working with the elderly in residential homes. (Made
Aged   in association with the Institute of Psychiatry for training
Video   professionals and volunteers.)
Tape/Slide   DISTRIBUTION: Help the Aged.
Hire

44 — **National**   TOPICS: introductory and training films on autistic children
Autistic Society   and adults.
Video   DISTRIBUTION: The National Autistic Society.
Tape/Slide
Hire

45 — **SENSE**   TOPICS: working with deaf/blind children; development of
(National Deaf,   motor skills; communication and touch in young deaf/blind
Blind & Rubella   children; communication with deaf/blind and hearing peo-
Assn)   ple, the work of SENSE.
Video   DISTRIBUTION: SENSE (The National Deaf, Blind and Rubella
Hire & Sale   Association).

46— **NSPCC**
Film
Hire

TOPICS: battered babies and child abuse.
DISTRIBUTION: NSPCC (The National Society for the Prevention of Cruelty to Children).

47— **Oxfam**
Film
Hire

TOPICS: ethnological films on family life.
DISTRIBUTION: Concord Video and Film Council.

48— **RAD**

TOPICS: one film introducing RAD's work.
DISTRIBUTION: RAD (The Royal Association in Aid of Deaf People).

49— **RNID**

TOPICS: tinnitus; problems of hearing impairment.
DISTRIBUTION: RNID (The Royal National Institute for the Deaf).

50— **MENCAP**
(Royal Society for Mentally Handicapped Children & Adults)
Video
Film
Hire & Loan

TOPICS: language simulation; mental handicap; leisure and holidays; case histories; marriage; training; institutions vs family care; drama therapy; parental stress; integration into society.
DISTRIBUTION: Concord Video and Film Council and Mencap National Centre.

51— **Spastics Society**
Video
Film
Hire & Sale

TOPICS: cerebral palsy; the need for improved maternity services to reduce the incidence of disability; preparation for parenthood.
DISTRIBUTION: Concord Video and Film Council.

SELECTED AUDIOVISUAL MATERIALS

This section contains a selection of materials collected from the catalogues used in compiling this chapter which will be of interest to most psychology teachers. Most have been selected because they have been made by teachers to demonstrate various aspects of their subject or have been widely used in courses for a number of years. Each entry gives details of the title, distributor, running times and a brief description of the programme.

▶ *Human Social Development* (1984)

Video
Sale

Resource material with teachers' notes intended for use in a psychology practical. The aim of the practical is to use a category system and develop and use a sign system appropriate for recording social participation in a group of nursery school children and to calculate their relative merits.

DISTRIBUTION: City of London Polytechnic. Media Services Dept.

▶ *Children's Development: Six weeks to four years* (1987)

Video
Sale

The five parts in this series show the average developmental progress of specific children. Fine and gross motor development, vision and hearing tests and development of speech and language are illustrated. The equipment used comes from the Stycar Assessment Systems.
  Part 1: Six weeks (30 mins)
  Part 2: Six months (30 mins)
  Part 3: One year (38 mins)
  Part 4: Two and a half years (44 mins)
  Part 5: Four years (42 mins)

DISTRIBUTION: Graves Medical Audio-Visual Library.

▶ *Young Children in Brief Separation* (1968–1976)

Video
Film
Hire & Sale

Illustrates emotional and social development in very young children, and how reactions to separation from the mother are influenced by the quality of substitute care.
  John, aged 17 months, for 9 days in residential nursery (43 mins)
  Jane, aged 17 months, in foster care for 10 days (37 mins)
  Lucy, aged 21 months, in foster care for 19 days (31 mins)
  Thomas, aged 2 years 4 months, in foster care for 10 days (39 mins)
  Kate, aged 2 years 5 months, in foster care for 27 days (23 mins)
An illustrated teaching guide is supplied when any of these films or videos are rented or bought.

DISTRIBUTION: Concord Video and Film Council.

▶ *WISC* (1980)

Video
Sale

Samples of the tests from the Wechsler Intelligence Scale for Children being administered to a nine year old by a psychologist. (25 mins)

DISTRIBUTION: Herts Media.

▶ *Voices: Psychoanalysis* (1987)

Video
Sale

A series of six programmes in which aspects of Freud's work and its influence on modern thinking are discussed.
  No 1: Freud – for or against? (52 mins)
  No 2: Psychoanalysis – the impossible profession? (52 mins)
  No 3: Psychoanalysis – truth or science? (52 mins)

No 4: Psychoanalysis – what do women want? (52 mins)
No 5: Psychoanalysis – nothing sacred? (52 mins)
No 6: Psychoanalysis after Freud (52 mins)

DISTRIBUTION: Brook Productions.

▶ *C.G. Jung: Professor C.A. Meier in conversation with Dr N.D. Minton* (1986)

*Video
Sale*

A two-part interview: Professor Meier, the Swiss psychiatrist, discusses Jung's work, the therapeutic importance of dreaming and new ideas in psychosomatic medicine. (80 mins)

DISTRIBUTION: Audio Visual Centre, University of London.

▶ *How Children Think* (1986)

*Tape/Slide
Hire & Sale*

Adults often find it hard to remember what it was like to be a child. Based on Piaget's analysis, this programme describes important conceptual developmental milestones in a way which should help adults to understand children better. It is particularly useful for anyone caring for sick children. Anatomy, physiology, neurological control mechanisms, investigative techniques and equipment are covered. (80 slides; pulsed 1000 Hz; 27 mins)

DISTRIBUTION: Graves Medical Audio-Visual Library.

▶ *Children Growing Up* (1970)

*Video
Hire*

Five films in the BBC Children Growing Up series which clearly explain aspects of child development in the first five years or so of life.
All in the Game (25 mins)
Making Sense (25 mins)
Mother and Child (25 mins)
One Step at a Time (25 mins)
Power of Speech (25 mins)

DISTRIBUTION: The Scottish Central Film and Video Library.

▶ *Rock a Bye Baby*

*Film
Hire*

Good photography of classic experiments on mothering in humans and other mammals up to 1970. Includes Harlow's experiments on monkeys with substitute mothers and Prescot's experiments with monkeys raised in isolation.

DISTRIBUTION: The Scottish Central Film and Video Library.

▶ *Careers and Courses in Psychology* (1985)

Video
Sale

A guide to careers and courses for prospective psychology students. Includes advice from professional psychologists working in clinical, educational and occupational areas. (50 mins)

DISTRIBUTION: Chester College of Higher Education.

▶ *Science Topics: Senses* (1986)

Video
Sale

Looks at the function of the human senses, and shows how they work together to give the individual information about the environment. Includes a section on visual illusions and how they are constructed to deceive the eye. (20 mins)

DISTRIBUTION: BBC TV Enterprises.

▶ *Horizon: The case of ESP* (1986)

Video
Sale

Reports on recent findings in ESP investigation, many of which appear to challenge the accepted rules of modern science. It features early ESP experiments, investigations into dream telepathy, and more recent sensory-deprivation techniques, which appear to increase telepathic signals. Includes sequences on 'remote viewing' (the ability to see things up to 5,000 miles away) and on seeing in the future. (90 mins)

DISTRIBUTION: BBC TV Enterprises.

Addresses

(The distributors, libraries, societies and associations that appear in the Films and Videos section of this chapter are numbered 'in order of appearance'. You will see in the chapter index that this numbering system is used instead of page references.)

1. Aleph One Ltd
   The Old Court House
   High Street
   Bottisham
   Cambridge CB5 9BA
   tel. (0223) 811679

32. Anti-Apartheid Movement
    40 Selous Street
    London NW1 0DW
    tel. (071) 3877966

33. Association for Spina Bifida and
    Hydrocephalus
    22 Upper Woburn Place
    London W1N 7RH
    tel. (071) 3881382

34. Bristol Victims' Support Scheme
    Flat 8
    122 Pembroke Road
    Clifton
    Bristol BS8 3ER

35. British Agencies for Adoption and
    Fostering
    11 Southwark Street
    London SE1 1RQ
    tel. (071) 4078800

36. British Association for Counselling
    37a Sheep Street
    Rugby
    Warwicks CV21 3BX
    tel. (0788) 78328/9

37. British Association for the Hard of
    Hearing
    7–11 Armstrong Road
    London W3 7JL
    tel. (081) 7431110

2. British Broadcasting Corporation
   TV Enterprises
   Film and Video Sales
   Woodlands
   80 Wood Lane
   London W12 0TT
   tel. (081) 7435588/5730202

38. British Epilepsy Association
    Anstay House
    40 Hanover Square
    Leeds LS3 1BE
    tel. (0532) 439393

    British Film Institute
    Film and Video Library
    21 Stephen Street
    London W1P 1PL
    tel. (071) 2551444

3. British Medical Association
   BMA Film and Video Cassette
   Library
   BMA House
   Tavistock Square
   London WC1H 9JP
   tel. (071) 3887976

   British Universities Film and Video
   Council
   55 Greek Street
   London W1V 5LR
   tel. (071) 7343687

39. Brook Advisory Centres
    Education and Publications Unit
    24 Albert Street
    Birmingham B4 7UD
    tel. (021) 4631554

    Brook Productions Ltd
    103–109 Wardour Street
    London W1V 3TD
    tel. (071) 4399871

4. BSIP Ars Magna Ltd
   96 Wimbledon Hill
   London SW19 7PB
   tel. (081) 9474069

40. Camphill Village Trust
   32 Heath Street
   Stourbridge
   W. Mid. DY8 1BB

5. Central Independent Television
   Video Resources Unit
   Broad Street
   Birmingham B1 2JP
   tel. (021) 643 9898

6. CFL Vision
   PO Box 35
   Wetherby
   Yorks LS23 7EX

   Chester College Resource Centre
   Cheyney Road
   Chester CH1 48J
   tel. (0244) 373444

   Cheyne Centre for Spastic Children
   Cheyne Walk
   Chelsea
   London SW3 5LX
   tel. (071) 3528434

   City of London Polytechnic Media
      Services
   Calcutta House Precinct
   Old Castle Street
   London E1 7NT
   tel. (071) 2831030 × 603

   Community Service Volunteers
      Advisory Service
   237 Pentonville Road
   London N1 9NJ
   tel. (071) 2786601

7. Concord Video and Films Ltd
   201 Felixstowe Road
   Ipswich
   Suffolk IP3 9BJ
   tel. (0473) 726012/715754 (bookings/
   accounts)
   (0473) 77747 (film despatch)

8. CTVC Film and Video Library
   Beeson's Yard
   Bury Lane
   Rickmansworth
   Herts WD3 1DS
   tel. (0923) 777933

9. D.S. Information Systems Ltd
   National Audiovisual Aids Library
   Arts Building, Topsite
   Normal College
   Bangor
   Gwynedd LL57 2PZ
   tel. (0248) 370144

10. Edward Patterson Association Ltd
   Treetops
   Cannongate Road
   Hythe
   Kent CT21 5PT
   tel. (0303) 264195

11. Focal Point Audio-Visual Ltd
   251 Copnor Road
   Portsmouth
   Hants PO3 5EE
   tel. (0705) 665249

12. Glenbuck Films Ltd
   Glenbuck House
   Surbiton
   Surrey KT6 6BY
   tel. (081) 3990022

13. Graves Medical Audio-Visual
      Library
   Holly House
   220 New London Road
   Chelmsford
   Essex CM2 9BJ
   tel. (0245) 283351

14. Griffin & George Ltd
   Bishop Meadow Road
   Loughborough
   Leics LE11 CRQ
   tel. (0509) 233344

15. Guild Sound and Vision Ltd
   6 Royce Road
   Peterborough PE1 5YB
   tel. (0733) 315315

41. Hampstead Child Therapy Clinic
    27 Maresfield Gardens
    London NW3 5SD
    tel. (071) 7942313/4/5

42. Health Education Authority
    Hamilton House
    Mabledon Place
    London WC1H 9TX
    tel. (081) 6510930

43. Help the Aged
    1 Princes Avenue
    London N10 6HA
    tel. (081) 8838484

16. Herts Media
    Goldings
    North Road
    Hertford
    Herts SG14 2PY
    tel. (0922) 555871

    Mental Health Film Council
    380–384 Harrow Road
    London W9 2HU
    tel. (071) 2862346

44. National Autistic Society
    276 Willesden Lane
    London NW2 5RB
    tel. (081) 4513844

45. National Deaf, Blind and Rubella
    Association (SENSE)
    311 Grays Inn Road
    London WC1X 8PT
    tel. (071) 2781005

17. National Film Board of Canada
    1 Grosvenor Square
    London W1X 0AB
    tel. (071) 6299492 × 3482

46. National Society for the Prevention
    of Cruelty to Children (NSPCC)
    67 Saffron Hill
    London EC1 8RS
    tel. (071) 2421626

18. Open University Educational
    Enterprises Ltd
    12 Cofferidge Close
    Stony Stratford
    Milton Keynes MK11 1D4
    tel. (0908) 261662

47. Oxfam
    274 Banbury Road
    Oxford OX2 7DZ
    tel. (0865) 567770

19. Oxford Educational Resources
    197 Botley Road
    Oxford OX2 OHE
    tel. (0865) 726625

20. Philip Harris Ltd
    Lynn Lane
    Shenstone
    Staffs WS14 OEE
    tel. (0543) 480077

    Philip Harris Biological Ltd
    Oldmixen
    Weston-Super-Mare
    Avon BS24 9BT
    tel. (0934) 413063

21. Psychology News Ltd
    17A Great Ormond Street
    London WC1 3RA
    tel. (071) 8313385

48. Royal Association in Aid of Deaf
    People (RAD)
    7 Old Oak Road
    London W13 7HN
    tel. (081) 7436187

49. Royal National Institute for the
    Deaf (RNID)
    105 Gower Street
    London WC1 6AH
    tel. (071) 3878033

50. Royal Society for Mentally
    Handicapped Children and
    Adults (MENCAP)
    Mencap National Centre
    123 Golden Lane
    London EC1Y ORT
    tel. (071) 2539433

Scientific Marketing Association
37 Mildmay Grove
London N1 4RH
tel. (071) 3595357

22. Scottish Central Film and Video
    Library
    Dowanhill
    74 Victoria Crescent Road
    Glasgow G12 9JN
    tel. (041) 3349314

51. Spastics Society
    12 Park Crescent
    London NW1 4EX
    tel. (071) 6365020

23. Tavistock Videotapes
    11 New Fetter Lane
    London EC4P 4EE
    tel. (071) 5839855

24. University of Aberdeen
    Department of Medical Illustration
    University Medical Buildings
    Forester Hill
    Aberdeen AB9 22D
    tel. (0224) 681818

25. University of Birmingham
    Television and Film Unit
    PO Box 363
    Birmingham B15 2TT
    tel. (021) 4143344

26. University of Exeter
    Teaching Service Centre
    Streatham Court
    Rennes Drive
    Exeter
    Devon EX4 4PU
    tel. (0392) 77911

27. University of London
    Audio Visual Centre
    The Administrator
    North Wing Studios
    Senate House
    Malet Street
    London WC1E 7JZ
    tel. (071) 6368000

28. University of Manchester
    Department of Psychiatry
    The University Hospital of South
        Manchester
    West Didsbury
    Manchester M20 8LR

29. University of Newcastle upon Tyne
    Audio-Visual Centre
    The Medical School
    Framlington Place
    Newcastle upon Tyne NE1 4HH
    tel. (091) 2328511

30. Viewtech Audiovisual Media
    161 Winchester Road
    Brislington
    Bristol BS4 3NJ
    tel. (0272) 773422/717030

31. Viscom Ltd
    Film and Video Library
    Park Hall Trading Estate
    Dulwich
    London SE21 8EL
    tel. (081) 7613035/8

Subject Index

(The numbers given below are the entry numbers of the various distributors, libraries, societies and associations that appear in the Films and Videos section of this chapter, rather than page numbers.)

PSYCHOLOGY AND CINEMA

Robert Burden

❏ *genres* ● auteur *theory: Truffaut; Loach; Hitchcock; Roeg; Bergman* ●
specific themes: psychology and psychiatry; adolescence; handicap; war ●
filmography

The purpose of this chapter is to illustrate how the use of
feature films and, beyond this, the study of cinema itself, can
become at least a useful adjunct, at best a central aspect of
the teaching of psychology. Such an approach could form
part of the earliest introduction to psychology as an
academic discipline or equally well offer an attractive and
worthwhile final-year option on any undergraduate course.
Space limitations do not allow an in-depth exploration of
these two possibilities, but an attempt will be made to
provide information and ideas which may help to transfer
each into meaningful reality.

I begin with a statement of belief – two statements, in fact,
about the nature of psychology and the nature of cinema. I
start from the premise that psychology is essentially an
attempt to understand why people think and feel and act in
the way that they do and how this affects them and others.
The art of cinema in its broadest sense involves bringing this
quest to life on celluloid so that it can be shared by a
comparatively large group of people at any one time in a
darkened auditorium. I believe this latter statement to be
true even when the films under consideration are fictional-
ized and fantastical. Films such as *Pinocchio* and *Frankenstein*
present us with as 'true' a vision of the human condition as
do documentaries or other films with apparently more
serious intent.

The advantage that cinema has over all other art forms is
its comprehensiveness. No other art form can combine sight
and sound images, can transcend the boundaries of time and
space, touch the emotions or stimulate the intellect as can a
film.

It has been argued that this very comprehensiveness is also the cinema's weakness, since at its worst it represents no one person's reality, while at its best it leaves little to the imagination. Whilst having some sympathy for the former point – after all, an awful lot of bad films have been made – I would take issue with the latter. The best films stimulate the imagination and provoke discussion in a manner that is readily accessible to all those involved as an audience.

It is difficult to find words to describe this experience appropriately because even though the images cannot be shaped by audience response, it is not one of the passive spectator, as is sometimes assumed, but is truly interactive as far as the mind and senses are concerned. In seeking to make sense of and respond to those images, however, the audience itself becomes involved in a complex set of psychological processes. It is the nature of these processes as well as those involved in making and analysing films as such that has been the concern of many so-called cinema theorists.

In his *Introduction to the Major Film Theories* Andrew (1976) helps us to see how early film pioneers were influenced by ideas from Gestalt psychology, particularly the notion that the mind provides meaning not only to our understanding of reality but even to its physical characteristics. The work of the great Soviet film-maker Sergei Eisenstein can be seen to reflect the ideas of both Pavlov and Piaget in his dialectical thinking about film montage. Later theorists encompass the phenomenological aspect of film making and attempt to develop ways of describing the processes of signification in the cinema. This latter enterprise has developed into the science of semiotics.

At the same time, others, most notably represented by Parker Tyler in his influential book *Magic and Myth of the Movies* (1971), began to explore the mythical and dreamlike quality of films, to relate these to both the individual and collective unconscious and to provide direct psychoanalytic interpretations in their critical writings.

Starting Points   It can be seen from even this brief introduction to some of the central issues relating psychology to cinema that it would be perfectly possible, indeed desirable under certain circumstances, to proceed from a study of cinema itself to considering its various psychological manifestations. However, since it is likely that most readers will find rather more straightforward approaches initially preferable, I shall now confine myself to describing ways in which films can be used to illustrate aspects of psychology.

Three potentially illuminating approaches come immediately to mind. I shall present them in order of decreasing complexity and will devote most of my space to the third as this would seem to be the most useful starting point for the newcomer to this field. These approaches can be conveniently summarized under the headings of *genre, auteur theory* and *themes*.

GENRES

The basic premise of this approach is that there is much to be gained from exploring in-depth film genres such as westerns, science fiction, comedy, horror or gangster movies. One of the key points about westerns is that they are largely about metaphors and myths, both important aspects of human cognitive experience. We have only to consider a film like *Shane* to understand that it tells us nothing about the West as it really was. What we can see in it, however, is a fairly pure enactment of some universal myths about good and evil and the inevitability of change. This theme of change and its consequences at both a personal and social level has been taken up in various ways by John Ford in *My Darling Clementine* and, most notably, in *The Searchers*, by Howard Hawks in *Red River* and Sam Peckinpah in *Ride the High Country*.

In the developing work of each of these directors and, in particular, that of Anthony Mann we can also see the genre used as a vehicle for expressing implicit psychological theories about an individual's search for meaning in life. 'A man's gotta do what a man's gotta do . . .' is not just a hoary old western cliché but an expression of just this point.

Although I know of no evidence that Mann ever read Jung's work or undertook Jungian analysis, his films are full of Jungian archetypes and symbolism. The hero in such films as *The Man From Laramie, The Bend in the River* and *The Far Country* is always faced with a series of choices, the outcome of which will lead him closer to an integration of the self or towards ultimate despair. The hero, always played by James Stewart at a finely-balanced emotional knife edge, is usually confronted by a protagonist who represents his Jungian 'shadow' – the dark side of his personality about whom he feels a great ambivalence – both attraction and repulsion. In order to achieve integration the hero must inevitably recognize his ambivalence and face up to the shadow within himself as well as his symbolic enemy. Mann's villains are at least as interesting as his heroes in their representation of men for whom the balance between 'animus' and 'anima' has never been achieved.

There are westerns which are open to Freudian interpretation (*The Last Sunset, Johnny Guitar, The Left-Handed Gun*) and those representing universal themes of racial prejudice (*Tell*

Them Willy Boy is Here, Cheyene Autumn) and genocide (*Soldier Blue*), but it is perhaps the exploration of myth and personal responsibility to which this genre lends itself best. At the same time, the western is essentially a masculine genre which would nevertheless repay an in-depth analysis of the putative role of women.

There are those who find science-fiction films just as rewarding in their reworking of universal themes. The eminent critic and theorist Raymond Durgnat (1976) makes a strong case for this even with regard to such apparently mundane science-fiction epics as *The Island Earth*. One science-fiction film which does have interesting psychological undertones is *The Forbidden Planet*. At one level this film can be seen as a fascinating reworking of *The Tempest*, but what adds to it psychologically is the director's use of Freudian psychology to make the Caliban figure a form of psychic energy directly emanating from the incestuous feelings of the highly intelligent Prospero-like central character for his daughter.

One can readily see how science fiction touches upon our interest in and fear of the unknown. The director John Carpenter is particularly adept at conveying this in such films as *Halloween, The Thing, The Fog* and even *Assault on Precinct 13*, which, though set in the South Bronx, could just as easily be a western or set on another planet. Most of Carpenter's films dwell upon our perception of the unknown as an evil force, but one of his very best, *Starman*, takes a much gentler approach to the problems faced by a visitor to an alien world.

Two other science-fiction films worth consideration are Ridley Scott's *Alien*, if only for the fact that the sole survivor is a highly intelligent woman and, possibly the greatest of all paranoia movies, Don Siegel's *Invasion of the Body Snatchers*. The latter made a highly significant allegorical statement at the time of the US un-American hearings led by the notorious senator Joe McCarthy. What is particularly interesting in retrospect is that the film can be interpreted just as easily as an indictment of communism as of McCarthyism. It would be worthwhile comparing the original black-and-white, low-budget version of *The Body Snatchers* (first distributed as a 'B' movie) with the not uninteresting remake by Philip Kaufman and a more gruesomely explicit version on the same theme, *They Live*, by John Carpenter.

AUTEUR
THEORY

A somewhat different approach which nevertheless overlaps in part with the study of film genres is one which takes up the ideas of so-called *auteur* theory. This set of ideas (it hasn't really the status of a theory), emerged from the writings of a group of young French film critics writing after the Second World War in a journal called *Cahiers du Cinéma*. Prominent amongst this group were people like François Truffaut and Jean-Luc Godard, who were to go on to become famous as film-makers in their own right.

Basically, *auteur* theory suggests that it is worth examining the films of a particular director (just as it is the literary works of individual authors), because the same themes will continue to be worked through again and again, thereby giving us access to that director's particular view of the world and his or her attempts to make sense of it. Thus, films become a kind of projective technique, the responses to which are open to interpretation by the psychologist-critic, who seeks both individual and universal insights within the work of 'important' film-makers.

It follows, therefore, that just as writers like Dostoyevsky, Proust, Hardy or P.G. Wodehouse can illustrate and help to illuminate some aspect of the human condition, so also can certain directors – provided of course that they can make the kind of films they want to make. This proviso is an important one because, in the 'golden' days of Hollywood at least, it was rare for a director ever to have full control over any film he (until recently it was a predominantly male profession) completed.

If we take a moment to make a brief comparison between the work of two great Hollywood directors, John Huston and Howard Hawks, an important aspect of *auteur* theory may become clearer. Huston was essentially only ever interested in making films of other people's stories. For him the art of the film-maker lay in finding ways of bringing the essence of such novels as *Moby Dick*, *Moulin Rouge* or *The Treasure of Sierra Madre* to the screen. In attempting to do this he experimented with various visual techniques, colour and sound, but never imposed his interpretation upon the stories. Thus one may enjoy a John Huston film or be profoundly moved by it but this will depend almost entirely upon his success in capturing the essence of the original book.

Howard Hawks, on the other hand, made essentially the same film again and again for years, almost every time centering upon the nature of friendship, trust and loyalty between males. Every Howard Hawks film says something about Howard Hawks' view of the world. If male pair-bonding is a theme which you as a psychologist find particularly interesting, then the films of Howard Hawks provide some interesting and useful insights.

In the section which follows the work of five directors will be considered from the viewpoint of *auteur* theory. Each has a unique view of humanity which finds full expression in his films, a view which any psychologist seeking to understand why people think and feel and act in the way that they do will find enlightening. Although the five have been chosen to represent a broad cross section of rich and complex viewpoints, they by no means stand alone in this regard and any one could just as easily have been replaced by Godard or Wilder or Fellini or Buñuel or a dozen others. What they do have in common is that the work of each is largely his own, relatively untampered with by others on the cutting room floor.

This final point is worth reiterating. The interested reader is referred to Peter Wollen's *Signs and Meaning in the Cinema* for a fuller description of *auteur* theory. The idea is an attractive one but has a number of important flaws, the most obvious of which is that films are *never* the work of just one person but an amalgam of many people's efforts over a long period of time. It has been argued that the screen writer's conception is just as important as that of the director and often it is not within the latter's power to select the actors. Moreover, there are some directors who claim never to have had one of their films distributed in the form in which it was conceived and completed. It was the proud boast of the Hollywood mogul Daryl F. Zannuck that any film appearing under his name had been personally edited to fit *his* conception of the world, no matter who the director was.

Such information may be of considerable interest but little practical value to the psychology teacher. In seeking to use the work of specific directors to illustrate some aspect of psychology it is not suggested that all or even many of their films are considered in detail. It would be enough in the first instance to show two or three definitive works (marked with an asterisk in the list of the five directors' main films that appears at the end of this chapter) and set the students the task of finding common themes and messages signified in ways which are unique to that particular director's use of cinematic language in its broadest sense. At the same time, a comparison of the work of any two auteurs such as Truffaut and Loach, Roeg and Bergman, would help to bring out the distinctive nature not only of *auteur* theory but of the meaning that each individual brings to the world.

François
Truffaut

Truffaut was one of the earliest adherents to the notion of director as *auteur* in his early work as a film critic and published a particularly interesting study of the films of Alfred Hitchcock based on a series of interviews with

Hitchcock. The greater part of his own early work was a series of semi-autobiographical films covering various stages of life. His first full-length feature film, *Les Quatre Cents Coups (The 400 Blows)*, remains not only a classic of the cinema but a beautiful illustration of how a fundamentally nice boy can find himself caught up in life events that propel him towards despair and delinquency. And yet, Truffaut was essentially an optimist, a lover of life, who conveyed in several of his subsequent films with the same actor (Jean-Paul Léaud), who played the boy in *The 400 Blows*, the difficulties and joys of growing up, coming to terms with warring parents, finding one's first job, falling in and out of love and getting married.

Interestingly, in *L'Enfant Sauvage (The Wild Child)*, a film apparently quite independent of his autobiographical work, Truffaut depicts the attempts of the French psychologist and educator Itard to socialize the so-called 'Wild Boy of Aveyron'. Although in some ways Truffaut's most pessimistic film in that Itard comes to see his experiment as largely a failure, *The Wild Child* is particularly fascinating in depicting with great integrity an early form of behaviour modification. This is an important point. There have been plenty of poor or exploitative films with psychology or (more usually) psychiatry as a central theme, but very few that succeed on all fronts. *The Wild Child* is one such film.

In examining the themes that keep recurring throughout Truffaut's films and the way in which he deals with them, we come to realize that his optimistic view of life is tempered by his awareness of people's limitations. In the final analysis he is essentially a fatalist who believes that we should come to accept ourselves as we are and make the most of whatever each day brings. We may not be able to play a significant part in changing the world, but each individual has a personal responsibility to be true to themselves and play out their own part, however small. This theme is perhaps most explicitly stated in his adaptation of Ray Bradbury's *Fahrenheit 451*.

Ken Loach

It is rare to leave a Truffaut film without a sense of hope and optimism. In sharp contrast, the films of the brilliant British director Ken Loach are intensely political and ultimately despairing. Loach's two finest and best-known films *Kes* and *Family Life* are both well worth serious consideration by psychologists. For Loach the roots of mental illness and all unhappiness in life originate in early childhood experiences within the family, which he sees as a microcosm for society. The principal characters of *Kes* and *Family Life* are caught up in circumstances totally beyond their control and are seen as powerless to effect their situation in any long-term meaning-ful way. In *Kes* Billy Casper's kestrel is doomed from the start because Billy's care and loving attention is not accompanied by power. School is conveyed not as an educational or even benevolent institution, but a means of controlling and suppressing its reluctant inmates. Even the benevolent interest of one of the teachers is swamped by the sadism of the egotistical sports master and the headmaster who takes it for granted that anyone standing outside his door has been sent there to be caned.

Family Life, in a complementary way, illustrates the political and sociological implications of the Laingian view of mental illness. The film is gripping, controversial and in itself highly political. Loach pulls no punches and sits on no fences. We know exactly where he stands and can thereby relate his films easily to ideology and psychological theory.

Alfred Hitchcock

One director to whom the description of *auteur* has been applied by Truffaut and others is Alfred Hitchcock. Although he constantly denied that his films had any underlying meaning, Hitchcock is nevertheless a classic example of the director-as-psychologist in the way in which he uses the medium of film to manipulate his audience, often with stunning effect. In examining his most explicitly 'psychological' films we cannot fail to be impressed by the way in which he uses the camera, colour and sound to make a psychological point or produce a required effect. In his most famous early Hollywood film, *Spellbound*, Hitchcock employed Salvador Dali to produce the symbolical dream sequence. For many years this essentially simplistic story set in a sanatorium with 'good' and 'bad' psychoanalysts provided the classic model of psychology for the film-going public. One of the most important features of this film was its commercial success and the consequent establishment of a particular image of psychology in the public conscious-ness. For all its faults, *Spellbound* is never less than fascinating and treats its audience, like its heroine, as intelligent participants in the central mystery.

In two later films, *Psycho* and *Vertigo*, Hitchcock used the camera to good effect in the role of the observer/victim and in the former film manages by means of Bernard Hermann's excellent musical score to convey and produce a variety of emotions. In an early sequence where Janet Leigh drives off with her employer's money we find ourselves caught up in her agitation at being followed by a policeman without quite realizing at first that it is the accompanying musical score which helps to convey her emotions and affect our own. Later, in the notorious shower sequence and at the time of the detective's subsequent murder, it is again the use of sound which heightens the shock and thereby removes the need to present any particularly gruesome visual image. In one of his later films, *Marnie*, ostensibly the story of a frigid kleptomaniac who preferred horses to men, Hitchcock also explores the use of colour to excellent effect to express emotions.

In one of the most convincingly accessible books on film theory, *The World in a Frame: What we see in films* (1984), Leo Braudy makes the distinction between 'open' and 'closed' films. Basically, open films teach us about the world, closed films teach us about ourselves. For Braudy, Hitchcock is a prime example of the closed film-maker because of the way in which he sees the world as a place upon which we impose meaning. The audience of a closed film is lured into the world of the characters and becomes an accomplice, even when not identifying directly with those characters. We empathize with Janet Leigh stealing her employer's money in *Psycho* or with James Stewart's voyeurism in *Rear Window* even though we would be unlikely to condone either action. We find ourselves acknowledging 'there but for the grace of God . . .'.

For Hitchcock there is a close link, a juxtaposition, between good and evil that runs right through all his films and often leads to the death of innocent bystanders. The central character is often an apparently 'cool' blonde woman who may be a victim, as in *Psycho*, *Vertigo* and *The Birds*, often for reasons of repressed sexuality, or the one sane character in an otherwise apparently insane world. In Hitchcock films nothing can be taken for granted; again and again we are shown that even the most innocuous objects can be invested with malevolence. The world, says Hitchcock, is what we make it and beneath the most innocent personal or social exterior lies a very different world as seen, for example, in *Rear Window*. In many respects he can be seen as the most psychological of all film-makers not because of his explicit psychological and psychiatric references in films like *Spellbound*, *Psycho* and *Marnie*, but because the wellspring of his films is rich with Freudian, Jungian, Kellian and other psychological connotations.

Nicholas Roeg

Nicholas Roeg is another film-maker whose films are rich in psychological references, themes and underpinnings. His first film, *Performance*, was something of a *cause célèbre* largely because of its exploration of the association between human sexuality and violence. This is a theme to which he has returned again and again, as in *Walkabout*, where awakening awareness of her sexuality by an adolescent girl in the

Australian outback causes the tragic death of an Aboriginal boy; *Bad Timing*, where the protagonist is a disturbed psychoanalyst who makes love under a portrait of Freud; and *Track 29*, where the theme of incest is explored. These and other Roeg films, like *The Man who Fell to Earth* and *Don't Look Now*, are complex, often difficult, but usually very rewarding in their exploration of fantasy, emotions and other aspects of the human condition.

Ingmar Bergman

Although *auteur* theory arose from an interest in and has mainly been applied to Hollywood film-makers, it is in many ways more applicable to Europeans such as Bergman, Buñuel, Visconti, Resnais and others from as far afield as Japan, India and Australia, partly because they have tended to have far more control over all aspects of film production. It would be a great mistake to concentrate any psychological analysis of films and film-makers entirely upon the USA, despite the greater availability of films from that country. However, space permits the examination of just one more director, Ingmar Bergman, who in some people's minds is the greatest of modern film-makers. Bergman is a true psychologist who focuses explicitly upon the human condition and has no hesitation in using his own view of life at any one time as the central theme of his work.

Many of Bergman's early films have religion as a central theme, but this is explored in terms of the meaning that it has for the central characters, as in *The Seventh Seal*, and, thereby, the symbolic meaning invested in otherwise ordinary objects and events. Braudy (1984) sees Bergman and Hitchcock as alike in that both perceive the world to be an array of otherwise disparate or even chaotic things on which meaning has to be imposed through fantasy, allegory, ritual, dream, paranoia or religion.

In his 'middle' period Bergman moves more to an exploration of human relationships, particularly with respect to breakdown. Often there are two central characters, as in *The Silence*, *Through a Glass Darkly* and *Scenes From a Marriage*, who fail notably to communicate. At its extreme form, in *Persona*, we are unsure if the two characters are really one, as the theme of schizophrenia, introduced in *Through a Glass Darkly*, is fully played out.

SPECIFIC THEMES

It has to be said that seeking connections between psychology and cinema through an exploration of genre or the work of *auteurs* requires an interest in and knowledge of films that probably goes beyond the immediate needs of most psychology teachers and lecturers. For this reason alone, the thematic approach offers a worthwhile but ultimately less rewarding alternative. It is nevertheless a useful starting point from which a deeper study of both *auteur* theory and genre could easily emerge. Here films are mainly used as illustrations rather than explorations, although even this statement need not necessarily apply. The greatest film-makers provide few answers to the questions that their films raise. In fact, the great Soviet director Tarkovsky has been quoted as saying that even the film-maker should be unaware of what his or her films are about. Thus, the use of one of his films, for example *The Awakening*, in a series selected to illustrate various views of childhood can certainly be seen as a search for meaning which is never made evident, because the director sees confusion of images as both part of the creative film-making process and of life itself.

Nevertheless, I shall now recommend half-a-dozen or so films which I consider can be usefully used to illustrate various aspects of each of four selected themes. Inevitably, there is a degree of bias in the choice of both the themes and the individual films which probably reveals as much about the author as it does about the films.

Psychology and Despite the close links between psychology and the cinema
Psychiatry discussed earlier and the obvious fascination that psychology and psychiatry have had for film-makers throughout the history of the cinema, comparatively few films have taken psychology itself as a major theme and done the topic justice. I would argue that possibly the best film to have done so is one which has received very little recognition – *Mon Oncle d'Amérique (My American Uncle)*, by the French director Alain Resnais. Here Resnais observes and seeks to explain the actions of his characters by direct reference to behaviourist theories and by intercutting scenes of rats in stress boxes to real-life situations. It is a film not to be missed.

As a supreme storyteller, John Huston presents his film *Freud: The Secret Passion* in a straightforward manner that captures the interest and provides an uncomplicated and acceptable introduction to some of the great man's ideas. The central casting of Montgomery Clift as Freud provides a more substantial portrayal than might have been expected, but one suspects that he portrays the founder of psychoanalysis in a less arrogant and more sympathetic light than may have been the case.

Two films already mentioned, Bergman's *Persona* and Loach's *Family Life*, should also be on the list along with another film about which critics are very divided, Robert Altman's *Images*. In this story of a schizophrenic girl, Altman depicts the main character as attempting to deal with her delusions by willpower and by concealment. As the film unfolds the audience itself is drawn into the girl's world by not being informed where reality ends and delusions begin. The director uses the visual images on the screen to depict confusion and 'splitting' in a very real sense, whilst the girl seeks to take control of what she sees by her use of language and reference to myth. This film has been dismissed by some as mannered and indecipherable. It can also be seen as one of the very few honest attempts by a film-maker to enable the audience to enter the world of someone mentally disturbed by making full use of the range of available techniques.

Two other films worth considering for their depictions of psychiatrists/psychotherapists are *Equus* and *Ordinary People*. The latter has been criticized by some for what they see as an inaccurate or sanitized view of the therapeutic encounter. I find this quite surprising and have to express my own prejudice in finding both the disturbed boy and his therapist totally believable. What's more, *Ordinary People* in its own way makes as valid a set of points about families, communication, relationships and coming to terms with grief as many more vaunted art movies.

A final film in this grouping well worth considering is David Mamet's *House of Games*. This is firstly of interest because the main character is a clinical psychologist who is the victim of her own obsessional nature. However, as the film unfolds like a succession of Chinese puzzle boxes, we are again brought face to face with our perceptions of reality and our need to control in order to make sense of life.

Adolescence   There are literally hundreds of films devoted to aspects of child development, most particularly adolescence. I have found it quite possible to teach courses on understanding adolescents through film over a number of years whilst rarely showing the same film twice. The following titles are examples of a rich vein to be tapped.

In some ways Elia Kazan's *Splendour in the Grass* has never been bettered as an example of the agony and some of the ecstasy of adolescence and its effects on a highly-strung girl, played superbly by Natalie Wood in an early role, as is also her boyfriend by a young Warren Beatty. Two things stand out as being of vital importance in making successful films about adolescence, both of which are well illustrated in this film. One is the director's ability to empathize with young people in a non-exploitative way; the other is the actors' ability to be themselves rather than to act a part. This is perhaps what has helped generations of adolescents to identify with James Dean in another excellent Kazan film, *East of Eden* and, more famously, in Nicholas Ray's *Rebel*

Without a Cause. With Dean such issues as the generation gap, individuation, peer-group identity and so on are well to the fore and one might be forgiven for drawing the conclusion that adolescence really is a time of storm and stress. Similar issues are dealt with in a less dramatic way in Peter Bogdanovich's *The Last Picture Show* and John Sayles's *Baby It's You*. Joseph Losey's *The Go-Between* deals delicately with pre-adolescent incomprehension of adult relationships and the corruption of innocence whilst *The Member of the Wedding* is a beautifully underplayed version of Carson McCullers's novel about the gradual changes in a young girl during puberty.

When considering adolescence as a theme, however, the teacher must be wary of presenting an angst-ridden version of what research has clearly demonstrated to be a much more relaxed and enjoyable experience for most young people. Fortunately, there are also excellent films about the joyful side of youth, an excellent example being Peter Yates's *Breaking Away*. As his later films show, George Lucas has never lost his ability to identify with adolescents, so it is hardly surprising that many people, myself included, still consider that his *American Graffiti* is a key film in capturing much of the essence of the adolescent experience.

Handicap

Films involving handicapped adults or children often have a 'hidden agenda' or use the handicapped person(s) as supplementary to the main theme or plot. As an extreme example of this, the film *Cutter's Way* has a one-eyed, one-armed war veteran as one of its main protagonists. Neither the nature of handicap nor the plight of injured war veterans is illuminated in this film or, say, in Stanley Kubrick's *The Killing*, where one of the character's paraplegia is merely incidental to the plot. On the other hand, in William Wyler's *The Best Years of Our Lives* and Hal Ashby's *Coming Home*, in which John Voigt gave a superb performance as a wheelchair-bound veteran of the Vietnam war, the actual experience of becoming handicapped is explored in considerable depth. *Coming Home* does illustrate another common theme in such films, namely the fairly conventional love-story-with-a-twist, that is, love between a 'normal' and disabled person, as here and in the excellent *Children of a Lesser God*, or between two handicapped people as in Bryan Forbes's *The Raging Moon*.

The fact that handicap has always had a fascination for Hollywood is evidenced by the fact that Cliff Robertson was also awarded an Oscar for his performance in the title role of *Charly*, a mentally retarded young man who becomes a genius as a result of a psychological experiment, the effects of which then begin to wear off. This is a difficult theme which is less successfully handled in the film than in the novel *Flowers For Algernon* on which it is based, but the two taken in conjunction make an excellent focus for psychological study. In fact, what is demonstrated here is one of the weaknesses of cinema, the need to make a disturbing theme palatable if it is to achieve commercial success. This is true of most films depicting handicapping conditions, but in itself can provide an interesting focus for discussion.

The story of Helen Keller and her teacher is powerfully presented in *The Miracle Worker*, as also are the effects of multiple sclerosis in *Duet for One*, and issues surrounding euthanasia for severely handicapped accident victims in *Whose Life is it Anyway?*. *A Day in the Death of Joe Egg* also provides a passionate and powerfully negative view of parenting a severely multiply-handicapped child. These are films to stimulate discussion and further study, not to present facts.

Problems of communication and a different form of love are beautifully handled in yet another Oscar-winning film, *Rain Man*, even though it can easily be seen as a sanitized view of autism. Ostensibly the story of a young hustler who discovers that his father's entire three-million dollar inheritance has been bequeathed to his unknown autistic, *idiot-savant* brother and his journey across America with that kidnapped brother, *Rain Man* provides a fascinating introduction to autism and its effects upon self and others whilst only slightly glamorizing the situation. An interesting but contentious issue arising from the film is the suggestion that some of the roots of autism may lie in early childhood experience.

Two other films relating to handicap worthy of serious consideration by psychologists are Peter Bogdanovich's *Mask*, which tells the apparently true story of a highly intelligent boy with lionitis who is compelled to wear a mask because of other people's reactions to his features, and David Lynch's *Elephant Man* where John Hurt manages to convey a whole range of emotions and capture our full sympathy for the hideously deformed John Merrick with only the use of his voice and eyes. This film provides a fascinating comparative piece to *My Left Foot*, in which Daniel Day Lewis gives an outstanding performance as the brilliant but severely cerebral palsied Christy Brown. Taken together, these two films can serve as an excellent introduction to a study of stigma in terms of the 'staining' effect that a disability can have upon our perceptions of all other attributes of a person. Finally, *Best Boy*, is a virtually unknown semi-documentary about a mentally handicapped adult, Philly who is referred to by his elderly parents as their 'best boy'. The film covers three years in Philly's life and concentrates on his efforts to learn simple tasks. It provides a form of *cinéma vérité* which is both moving and enlightening.

War

Although many films have been made on the topic of war, relatively few have focused on psychological rather than physical aspects. However, amongst that number are several which can rightly be termed classics. Thus, war as a psychological phenomenon lends itself to fruitful analysis with the aid of the cinema.

One profitable approach would be to begin with an historical perspective in considering the way in which attitudes towards war have changed over the years. Despite such excellent early silent anti-war films as *The Big Parade* and *All Quiet on the Western Front*, these were far outnumbered by those eulogizing violence. Even Olivier's *Henry V* can be seen as a glorification of war for propaganda purposes at the time of its production (1945).

In sharp contrast are two films by the brilliant Japanese director Kon Ichikawa, *The Burmese Harp* and *Fires on the Plain*, which both condemn the futility of war in the strongest possible manner. Another Japanese anti-war film, considered by some critics to be the greatest ever made, is Kobayashi's *The Human Condition* which is actually three films in one. It is the avowed ambition of this film to pay penance for Japanese aggression in the thirties and forties and to condemn fascism in all forms.

Rather more accessible films on the same theme are Stanley Kubrick's *Paths of Glory*, which raises deeper issues of power relationships and the manipulation of men's lives for personal glory, Peter Weir's *Gallipoli*, and Joseph Losey's *King and Country*. In all these films and Bruce Beresford's *Breaker Morant*, the injustice and hypocrisy associated with war are tellingly revealed.

The effects of involvement in war upon the human psyche and spirit are explored to good effect in Bryan Forbes's *King Rat*, John Boorman's *Hell in the Pacific*, Oshima's *Merry Christmas Mr Lawrence* and Stephen Spielberg's *Empire of the Sun*.

The issues surrounding nuclear warfare are presented in vastly different but complementary ways in Kubrick's *Dr Strangelove* and Lumet's *Fail Safe*. Whilst these films concentrate more on how easily a nuclear holocaust could be started than on the consequences, the latter are well covered by two sharply contrasting approaches in Alain Resnais's multi-layered *Hiroshima Mon Amour* and the simple but effective cartoon version of Raymond Williams's *When the Wind Blows*.

Concluding Remarks

Three potentially fruitful areas for exploration have been offered within which a close association between psychology and cinema can be found. Those interested in *auteur theory* will find their speculations enhanced by perusal of several good biographies and autobiographies on Hitchcock, Truffaut, Kazan, Huston and others. The study of *genres* has also been explored in several good books. The thematic approach is virtually limitless in its scope. Central themes within social, educational and clinical psychology in particular, such as prejudice, propaganda, alcoholism, drug abuse, self-esteem and others, have received considerable cinema coverage. This chapter has merely scratched the surface of a relatively untapped fund of potential resources.

The references and filmography which follow should provide a reasonable starting point and information base for further action. Film titles are given in chronological order for directors but in alphabetical order for themes. Country of origin, length and date of distribution are also given. As distribution arrangements do change from time to time, advice on availability and hire of films can best be gained from the British Film Institute, 21 Stethen Street, London WIP 1PL (tel. 071-255 144). An asterisk preceding a film title indicates a good and accessible introduction to a director's work. Good viewing!

References

ANDREW, J.D. (1976) *Introduction to the Major Film Theories*. Oxford: Oxford University Press.

BRAUDY, L. (1984) *The World in a Frame: What we see in films*. Chicago: University of Chicago Press.

DURGNAT, R. (1976) *Durgnat on Film*. London: Faber.

HUSTON, J. (1980) *An Open Book*. London: Butler & Tanner.

KITSES, J. (1969) *Horizons West*. London: Thames & Hudson.

TRUFFAUT, F. (1978) *Hitchcock*. London: Granada.

TYLER, P. (1971) *Magic and Myth of the Movies*. London: Secker & Warburg.

WOLLEN, P. (1972) *Signs and Meaning in the Cinema*. London: Secker & Warburg.

FILMOGRAPHY: genres

Film title	Date	Director	Country of pro- duction	Running time in mins.
WESTERNS				
The Bend of the River	1952	Anthony Mann	USA	91
Cheyenne Autumn	1964	John Ford	USA	160
The Far Country	1955	Anthony Mann	USA	97
Johnny Guitar	1954	Nicholas Ray	USA	110
The Last Sunset	1961	Robert Aldrich	USA	112
The Left-Handed Gun	1958	Arthur Penn	USA	102
The Man from Laramie	1955	Anthony Mann	USA	104
My Darling Clementine	1946	John Ford	USA	98
Red River	1948	Howard Hawks	USA	125
Ride the High Country	1962	Sam Peckinpah	USA	94
The Searchers	1956	John Ford	USA	119
Shane	1953	George Stevens	USA	118
Soldier Blue	1970	Ralph Nielson	USA	112
Tell Them Willy Boy is Here	1989	Abraham Polonsky	USA	96
SCIENCE-FICTION FILMS				
Alien	1979	Ridley Scott	USA	124
Assault on Precinct 13	1976	John Carpenter	USA	91
The Day the Earth Caught Fire	1962	Val Guest	UK	90
The Day the Earth Stood Still	1951	Robert Wise	USA	92
The Fog	1980	John Carpenter	USA	91
The Forbidden Planet	1956	Fred M. Wilcox	USA	98
Frankenstein	1931	James Whale	USA	71
Halloween	1978	John Carpenter	USA	90
The Invasion of the Body Snatchers	1956	Don Siegel	USA	80
The Invasion of the Body Snatchers	1978	Philip Kaufman	USA	114
Seconds	1966	John Frankenheimer	USA	106
Starman	1986	John Carpenter	USA	93
They Live	1989	John Carpenter	USA	100
The Thing	1985	John Carpenter	USA	93
This Island Earth	1955	Joseph Newman	USA	87

FILMOGRAPHY: directors

Film title	Date	Country of production	Running time in mins.
INGMAR BERGMAN			
*The Seventh Seal	1957	Sweden	105
Wild Strawberries	1958	Sweden	90
Through a Glass Darkly	1963	Sweden	95
The Silence	1964	Sweden	105
*Persona	1966	Sweden	81
Hour of the Wolf	1968	Sweden	90
A Passion	1970	Sweden	93
Cries and Whispers	1972	Sweden	91
Scenes from a Marriage	1973	Sweden	168
*Fanny and Alexander	1983	Sweden	197
ALFRED HITCHCOCK			
*Spellbound	1945	USA	111
Strangers on a Train	1951	USA	101
*Rear Window	1954	USA	112
The Wrong Man	1957	USA	105
*Vertigo	1958	USA	128
*Psycho	1960	USA	108
The Birds	1963	USA	120
Marnie	1964	USA	130
KEN LOACH			
*Kes	1970	UK	110
In Two Minds	1971	UK	30
*Family Life (Wednesday's Child)	1972	UK	108
Looks and Smiles	1981	UK	100
ANTHONY MANN			
Winchester '73	1950	USA	92
*Where the River Bends	1952	USA	91
The Naked Spur	1952	USA	91
*The Far Country	1954	USA	96
*The Man From Laramie	1955	USA	101
Man of the West	1958	USA	95

FILMOGRAPHY: directors *cont.*

Film title	Date	Country of pro- duction	Running time in mins.
FRANÇOIS TRUFFAUT			
Fahrenheit 451	1966	UK	111
Les Mistons (The Mischief Makers)	1957	France	23
Les Quatre Cents Coups (The 400 Blows)	1959	France	93
L'Amour à Vingt Ans (Love at Twenty) (first section)	1962	France	29
Baisers Volés (Stolen Kisses)	1968	France	90
Domicile Conjugal (Bed and Board)	1970	France	100
L'Enfant Sauvage (The Wild Child)	1970	France	83
L'Amour en Fuite (Love on the Run)	1979	France	94
NICHOLAS ROEG			
Performance	1972	UK	106
Walkabout	1972	UK	95
Don't Look Now	1973	UK	110
The Man who Fell to Earth	1976	UK	140
Bad Timing	1979	USA	109
Eureka	1983	USA	97
Track 29	1988	USA	110

FILMOGRAPHY: specific themes

Film title	Date	Director	Country of production	Running time in mins.

PSYCHOLOGY AND PSYCHIATRY

Bad Timing	1979	Nicholas Roeg	USA	109
Face to Face	1975	Ingmar Bergman	Sweden	183
L'Enfant Sauvage (The Wild Child)	1970	François Truffaut	France	84
Family Life	1972	Ken Loach	UK	108
Freud: The Secret Passion	1962	John Huston	USA	139
House of Games	1988	David Mamet	USA	100
High Anxiety	1977	Mel Brooks	USA	94
Images	1972	Robert Altman	USA	101
I Never Promised You a Rose Garden	1975	Anthony Page	USA	92
Marnie	1964	Alfred Hitchcock	USA	130
Mon Oncle d'Amérique (My American Uncle)	1980	Alain Resnais	France	110
Ordinary People	1980	Robert Redford	USA	124
Persona	1966	Ingmar Bergman	Sweden	81
Spellbound	1945	Alfred Hitchcock	USA	111
Through a Glass Darkly	1973	Ingmar Bergman	Sweden	95
Zelig	1987	Woody Allen	USA	93

ADOLESCENCE

American Graffiti	1973	George Lucas	USA	110
Aparajito (The Unvanquished)	1958	Satyajit Ray	India	113
Baby it's You	1986	John Sayles	USA	104
The Breakfast Club	1986	John Hughes	USA	97
Breaking Away	1979	Peter Yates	USA	99
East of Eden	1955	Elia Kazan	USA	115
The Getting of Wisdom	1980	Bruce Beresford	Australia	103
The Go-Between	1971	Joseph Losey	UK	116
Gregory's Girl	1985	Bill Forsyth	UK	91
Kes	1970	Ken Loach	UK	110
The Last Picture Show	1971	Peter Bogdanovich	USA	118
Le Souffle au Coeur (Murmur of the Heart)	1971	Louis Malle	France	110
My Brilliant Career	1979	Gillian Armstrong	Australia	100
Rebel without a Cause	1955	Nicholas Ray	USA	111
Sixteen Candles	1984	John Hughes	USA	96
Splendour in the Grass	1961	Elia Kazan	USA	124
Les Quatre Cents Coups (The Four Hundred Blows)	1959	François Truffant	France	93

FILMOGRAPHY: specific themes *cont.*

Film title	Date	Director	Country of production	Running time in mins.
HANDICAP				
A Day in the Death of Joe Egg	1972	Peter Medak	UK	106
Best Boy	1979	Ira Wohl	USA	104
The Best Years of our Lives	1946	William Wyler	USA	172
Birdy	1986	Alan Parker	USA	120
Charly	1968	Ralph Nelson	USA	103
Children of a Lesser God	1987	Randa Haines	USA	115
Coming Home	1978	Hal Ashby	USA	128
The Elephant Man	1980	David Lynch	UK	123
The Heart is a Lonely Hunter	1968	Robert Ellis Miller	USA	125
Mask	1986	Peter Bogdanovich	USA	120
The Miracle Worker	1962	Arthur Penn	USA	107
My Left Foot	1989	John Sheridan	UK	98
The Raging Moon	1971	Bryan Forbes	UK	111
Rain Man	1989	Barry Levinson	USA	124
Whose Life is it Anyway	1981	John Badham	USA	110
WAR				
All Quiet on the Western Front	1930	Lewis Milestone	USA	130
The Big Parade	1925	King Vidor	USA	119
Breaker Morant	1979	Bruce Beresford	Australia	107
The Burmese Harp	1956	Kon Ichikawa	Japan	116
Dr Strangelove: Or How I Learned to Stop Worrying and Love the Bomb	1963	Stanley Kubrick	USA	93
Empire of the Sun	1987	Stephen Spielberg	USA	123
Fail Safe	1964	Sidney Lumet	USA	111
Fires on the Plain	1959	Kon Ichikawa	Japan	105
Gallipoli	1981	Peter Weir	Australia	110
Hell in the Pacific	1968	John Boorman	USA	103
Henry V	1945	Laurence Olivier	UK	137
Hiroshima Mon Amour	1959	Alain Resnais	France	97
The Human Condition	1959	Masaki Kobayashi	Japan	208
King and Country	1965	Joseph Losey	UK	86
King Rat	1965	Bryan Forbes	UK	133
Merry Christmas Mr Lawrence	1983	N. Oshima	UK/Japan	105
Paths of Glory	1957	Stanley Kubrick	USA	66
When the Wind Blows	1986	J. Murakami	UK	92

LITERARY RESOURCES

John Radford and Deana Smith

❑ novels and literary extracts ● biography, autobiography and firsthand accounts ● the press ● science fiction ● religious literature ● references

Under this title can be collated several sorts of writing which do not have a primarily psychological purpose, but which can be, and have been, used in teaching the subject.

Without attempting to define either psychology or literature, it is clear that there is quite a complex relationship between the two. This relationship is discussed for example by Sederberg and Sederberg (1975), by Weatherell et al. (1983) and Potter et al. (1984), and by Lester (1987). Weatherell et al. distinguish four sorts of interaction that have existed:

1. Literature 'as an independent variable . . . exercising a causal influence . . . on readers' personalities and attitudes'.
2. Literature as a dependent variable, involving work 'on the psychological conditions which determine the make-up of a text'.
3. Psychology used to illuminate literature.
4. Literature used to illuminate psychology.

The last will be discussed in further detail.

However, two further points should first be made. One is that the first three interactions can also be of interest in teaching psychology, but are not really a 'resource' in the sense used here. The other is that the main point of the article by Weatherell et al. is to urge a new and different way of considering the relationship between psychology and literature: that is, 'as a more symmetrical interpretation which treats both areas as forms of making sense of people's action, identities, and social lives'. In support of this they quote the attack of writers such as Barthes on the notion of literature as a passive description of reality. Such attacks, they hold, undermine the approaches which treat literature as a resource for psychology, citing here Rose and Radford (1981). The present chapter derives from that article, and it is perhaps worthwhile to suggest, first, that there is more than one view of the relationship between literature and reality; for a discussion see Nuttall (1983). Second, even if the view of Barthes and others is adopted, it is not clear that this destroys the value of literature as a resource in teaching psychology.

A fuller discussion of points made in Weatherell *et al.*'s article is provided by Potter *et al.* (1984).

Rose and Radford (1981) proposed four ways in which literature might be of use in teaching psychology. First the inclusion of illustrative 'non-psychological' literature in the reading list may help to maintain the student's interest in the course. This is perhaps particularly helpful where psychology is not the student's main subject or interest. However, even for the psychology student, a relevant interruption to the usual diet of textbook and journal can be very beneficial.

Second, and more substantially, the world of literature can provide a 'social laboratory' in terms of which to examine the tenets of academic psychology. It can 'provide a kind of systematic experiencing of a social world – albeit an imaginary one – with all the parts interacting in a credible fashion' (Sederberg and Sederberg, 1975, p.194). The value of this conveniently packed 'social world' can exist at more than one level. At the most superficial level it goes little further than providing the interest value already referred to. However, at a deeper level, contrasts which may exist between the views that authors and psychologists have of different situations and events can serve to focus attention upon the validity or otherwise of the psychological viewpoint.

A third way in which reference to 'non-psychological' literature can enhance a psychology course is in counterbalancing the fragmentation involved in the scientific approach. Necessarily, objective psychology seeks on occasion to reduce the complexity of human action to the relative simplicity of constituent processes. Subjective literary description, on the other hand, readily accepts complexity and in so doing helps to redress the balance in favour of 'whole person' descriptions.

Finally, literature is often valuable in the teaching of psychology in that it can broaden the student's experience, at least vicariously, by introducing him or her to situations, states, and human types which would not otherwise normally be encountered. For example, literature has provided many vivid accounts of the subjective experience of mental disorders, disablement, disease and bereavement. This is the function of literature which Sederberg and Sederberg (1975) have designated 'transmitting the non-transmissible'. However, Bratus (1986) points out that there are limitations in the use of literature to describe psychological phenomena such as personality traits. These include bias on the part of the author in the selection of character traits that give particular meaning to the plot, and the different aims of literature and psychology in their examination of behaviour.

There are a number of published collections and annotated lists of literary works selected for their potential as teaching aids, as well as other relevant materials. These will be reviewed under the following headings:

- novels and literary extracts
- biographies, autobiographies and firsthand accounts
- popular press
- science fiction
- religious literature.

We do not attempt to be comprehensive, nor to assess the merits of the works cited.

NOVELS AND LITERARY EXTRACTS

The first collection of literary extracts intended to illustrate various psychological principles appears to be that of Schroder *et al.* (1943). Since then a number of publications have appeared in which the selection has been made to illustrate some particular aspect of psychology: abnormal personality (Stone and Stone, 1966); social psychology (Fernandez, 1972); child development (Landau *et al.*, 1972); adolescence (Burden, 1974); human development and gerontology (Wolf, 1987). Some of these include explicit discussion of relevant psychological material (for example, Landau *et al.*), while others leave this mainly to be inferred by the reader (for example, Fernandez).

Using a slightly different approach, Kellogg (1980) advocates the use of extracts from Sherlock Holmes stories to illustrate factors influencing human learning and problem solving. He incidentally illustrates the pitfalls that lie outside one's own discipline by referring to the London schools praised by Holmes as 'boarding' schools; they were, of course, 'Board' schools. Radford (1988) parallels Holmes' investigations and explanations of human behaviour with those developing simultaneously within psychology, particularly psychoanalysis. Several other writers have also compared Sherlock Holmes with Freud, the more recent being Marcus (1984) and Shepherd (1985). Sherlock Holmes stories have also been used as an independent variable in an empirical study: Mazziotta *et al.* (1982) demonstrated that the area of activation in the left hemisphere was larger than that in the right when subjects listened to the stories.

Additional sources of literary material of this type are the various published lists of 'psychological thrillers' (McCollom, 1971, 1973, 1975; Le Unes, 1974; Benel, 1975; Swain, 1977). A 'psychological thriller' is a book of demonstrated popularity which is more readable, 'softer' and 'lower key' (Le Unes, 1974) than a psychology text, but which is relevant to some aspects of a psychology course. The lists cited above include some psychology books as well as titles from non-psychological literature. Perhaps worthy of a special mention are those novels which more or less explicitly turn on some aspect of psychology and thus have a case for inclusion in the science-fiction section. The best-known are probably Huxley's *Brave New World*, Orwell's *1984* and Skinner's *Walden Two*. Foster (1988) explores a particular psychological theme over several centuries of writing in *Sex Variant Women in Literature*.

BIOGRAPHY, AUTO-BIOGRAPHY AND FIRSTHAND ACCOUNTS

So far we have been concerned with the use of fiction in teaching psychology. Equally valuable, however, are some types of non-fiction. White (1952, 1974) has reported using biographical material in the teaching of personality, and Levin (1979) adopts a biographical approach in a general introduction to psychology. In this latter case biographical details of 15 famous people are used as a way to introduce and illustrate the basics of psychology. In some instances students' own autobiographical details have also been used as illustrative material (White, 1952, 1974; Hettich, 1976), but this goes somewhat beyond the normal definition of literature. While not every published autobiography is psychologically revealing, there are in particular many by individuals brought up in very different cultures or subcultures, which give insights no alien anthropologist can (one classic example is *Beyond a Boundary* by C.L.R. James). Graham Richards, of the Polytechnic of East London, has included in a course on personality a requirement for students to read at least two biographies. He offers a list of 100 persons and suggests that 'one could adopt a number of tacks, for example it would be possible to look at several different biographies of the same person, to look at families such as the Brontës, Huxleys, Wildes, to look at several people in the same category (women novelists, generals, scientists), or simply pick a couple of figures who particularly interest you.' The aims are: to give students a view of a personality other than their own; to consider the applicability of psychological theories to an individual life; and to raise methodological issues. For discussions of autobiographical memory in general see Rubin (1986).

There are also, of course, numerous biographies and autobiographies of eminent contributors to psychology, which can add interest and insight, and some of which certainly rank as literature, for example, Hearnshaw's life of Burt (1979) and Jones's of Freud (1953). Numerous shorter accounts appear in the *History of Psychology in Autobiography* (ed. Gardner Lindzey), and some in more general works such as the *Encyclopaedia Britannica*, the *Dictionary of National Biography*, and the *Dictionary of Scientific Biography*. Other general works on the history of psychology also give biographical sketches of psychologists, for example, Hearnshaw (1987). Among subjects treated at book length are:

Bain (Bain, 1904)
Bartlett (Crampton, in press)
Ruth Benedict (Modell, 1984)
Cyril Burt (Hearnshaw, 1979)
Charcot (Owen, 1971)
Dilthey (Rickman, 1979)
Havelock Ellis (Ellis, 1940; Grosskurth, 1980)
Eysenck (Gibson, 1981)
Ferenczi (Dupont, 1989)
Anna Freud (Peters, 1985; Young-Bruehl, 1988)
Sigmund Freud (Freud, 1935; Clark, 1982; Jones, 1953); Sulloway, 1979; Sachs, 1945)
Galton (Pearson, 1984; Forrest, 1974)
Gibson (Reed, 1989)
Horney (Rubins, 1978; Quinn, 1988)
Ernest Jones (Brome, 1982)
James (Bird, 1986; Myers, 1986)

Jung (Brome, 1978; Wehr, 1985)
Klein (Grosskurth, 1986; Wright, 1988)
Laing (Laing, 1986)
Lewin (Marrow, 1968)
Lorenz (Nisbett, 1976)
Luria (Luria, 1979)
Maslow (Hoffman, 1988)
Margaret Mead (Mead, 1973; Howard, 1984)
Mesmer (Buranelli, 1975)
Pavlov (Babkin, 1949)
S.B. Sarason (Sarason, 1988)
Wilhelm Reich (Reich, 1969; Sharaf, 1983; Reich, 1988)
Rogers (Kirschenbaum, 1979)
B.F. Skinner (Skinner, 1985a, 1985b, 1985c)
Terman (Seagoe, 1975)
Thorndike (Clifford, 1984)
Vygotsky (Wertsch, 1985)
Watson (Cohen, 1979)

See also Cohen (1977) and Schellenburg (1978) who give some brief biographies of several psychologists. There are also several relevant volumes in the Fontana/Collins series 'Modern Masters' including Chomsky, Fanon, Freud, Jung, Levi-Strauss, Laing, Marcuse, Popper, Piaget, Reich, Merleau-Ponty, and Sherrington.

Other non-fictional works which are of use in psychology

courses come under the heading of 'firsthand accounts'. These are subjective accounts by individuals of their close relatives of their experiences in coping with a variety of real-life situations or events. They include accounts of coping with physical and mental diseases and handicaps, death and bereavement, delinquency, and working with children generally. The reader will find an introduction to this literature in a series of annotated bibliographies (Rippere, 1976, 1977, 1978, 1979a, 1979b, 1980; Pearson, 1977, 1980) which between them cover well over 200 separate titles. More recent accounts of coping with mental illness include Sutherland (1987), Wigoder (1987) and Read (1989). First-hand accounts certainly add interest to a course. However, much more importantly, they provide a perspective on real-life situations which no amount of objective measurement can possibly provide and which in many instances is very much more relevant to the objectives of the course than a scientific survey. Much of the firsthand account literature is perhaps primarily of value in teaching psychology in the context of the medical and paramedical professions. However, it is a rich source of reference material which merits inspection by teachers of psychology in other contexts also.

Finally, in the category of biography – though not strictly literature – mention may be made of the use of case studies. The case studies method, in which a real-life situation or event is used to focus attention upon and illustrate certain concepts and areas of information, has of course been extensively used in certain areas of applied psychology. However, its wider use in psychology teaching has been urged by Vande Kemp (1980). (See also Bertaux, 1983, and Wrightsman, 1981.) Some case studies have been presented in a rather more literary form, for example Ellis and Pitt-Aikens (1988), respectively a popular novelist and a psychiatrist, have based their book on a case study by the latter author. Also in this subcategory might be included the collections of neurological case studies by Sachs (1984, 1985), which provide interesting illustrations of a variety of neuropsychological deficits or dysfunctions.

THE PRESS   Much of the popular and quality press carries material of psychological interest on occasion, the most consistent general source in this country being probably *The Sunday Times*, closely followed by other quality newspapers as well as *Today*. In recent times it has been noted that general and women's magazines also carry psychology features on a regular basis. Some stories, however, are of course carried by virtually all the press, and a comparison of treatments can be useful. Papers and symposia included in the various conferences of The British Psychological Society receive attention in the national press and some local papers. Such material may of course not have the label 'psychology' (or 'psychiatry'; the two words are generally interchangeable in the press) attached to it. Items can, however, be of use to illustrate applications or misapplications of psychological ideas, start discussions, etc. Items can also form the basis of an individual or group collection on a particular topic (Ruble, 1975), which can usefully be accompanied by a commentary, supplied by the student on the basic of relevant knowledge.

Most of the quality daily newspapers now have a weekly section on general health matters which often includes articles on mental health, or on psychological adjustment to physical illness.

Other useful sources of information from the press include certain types of biographical material. *The Sunday Times* for example often carries items in which eminent individuals or their close relatives give short accounts of their lives, and psychologists have occasionally been included. A further type of biographical material can also be found in the obituary columns on the death of sufficiently well-known psychologists and related scientists.

A sometimes light-hearted review of stories referring to psychology in the media appears in the 'Media Watch' column of *The Psychologist* each month. Stories in both the national and local press are covered and these often provide further examples of common lay misconceptions of psychological theories.

SCIENCE
FICTION

Science fiction is often considered a branch of literature, but in the present writers' view is better regarded as a group of concepts which can be, and have been, expressed in any medium; the printed word, but also film, TV, visual art, music and so on. There have been a few attempts to classify the concepts, the most systematic probably being that of Croghan (1981). The written form is perhaps the most easily accessible for teaching purposes and there are some theoretical grounds for giving it primacy.

The numerous definitions of science fiction nearly all depend on finite sets of criteria, often only one. In fact science fiction is multi-componential and some of the features frequently found can be of particular interest to psychologists (Radford, 1985).

First is the use of psychological science as the basis, or as a background, of a work. This is often explicit, employing an actual reported finding or theory and/or some supposed extension of it. Sometimes ideas which derive directly from psychology appear without acknowledgement, and of course one cannot say just how the author acquired and developed them. In these uses, science fiction raises the questions of what psychological knowledge is now, or could shortly be, available to us, and what the implications are.

Second, science fiction deals, again both explicitly and implicitly, with two questions that are fundamental to psychology in its widest aspect: what is science, and what is human? Science fiction addresses the question of what is human in a way somewhat analogous to that of myth, by contrast with non-human entities, specifically robots (artificial simulacra of the human) and aliens (sentient, intelligent, natural, but not human). The question of what is science is raised both by speculation as to what may be scientific knowledge in worlds other than our own, and by contrast with other systems of thought, non-logical and magical, for example.

Third, it may be suggested that science fiction is itself a psychological phenomenon worthy of study, both in its subcultural aspects and in its role in individual belief systems.

Fourth, science fiction characteristically reflects back to us the way we regard ourselves. This is particularly apposite for psychology, it may be suggested, in that it is itself a reflexive science, unique in that its exponents are themselves part of their own subject-matter. In the distorting mirror of science fiction, the psychological scientist meets himself coming back.

Most of the publications on the use of science fiction in teaching psychology have concentrated on the first of these aspects, the most obvious, and on the written word. Several readers have been published of science fiction stories, pointing out the psychological lessons to be learned, for example, Jones and Roe (1974); Katz *et al.* (1974); Estrada and Estrada (1977); Katz *et al.* (1977); Melvin *et al.* (1977); Ridgway and Benjamin (1987). An unpublished reader by Radford and Kirby (1973) is available at the Science Fiction Foundation, Polytechnic of East London, which has one of the largest collections of science fiction material and publishes the leading academic journal in the field, *Foundation*. Two other relevant collections are edited by Evans (1969, 1970).

Other publications not specifically devoted to psychology include some relevant material. For example, *The Science of Science Fiction* (ed. Nicholls, 1982), includes sections on artificial intelligence, conditioning and brainwashing, psychotropic drugs, crime and punishment, telepathy and telekinesis, and feral children. The same editor's *Encyclopaedia of Science Fiction* (1979), contains an article on psychology, and his *Science Fiction at Large* (1976), one by de Bono on lateral thinking. Knight (1967), contains some psychological interpretations of science fiction, and Wingrove (1984) includes a chapter by Stableford on 'Inner Space'.

Among books that include varied speculations about psychological questions, more or less in a science fiction context, are those of Clarke, (1974), Stableford (1977), Wilson (1977), and Sagan (1978).

There are also books which those interested may like to follow up on the teaching of science fiction itself, such as Allen (1975), and Parrinder (1980), who is particularly clear. Discussions of the nature of science fiction are far too numerous to list, though perhaps Aldiss (1973), Aldiss and Wingrove (1986), Del Rey (1979), and Suvin (1979) are particularly helpful. Two useful books within a teaching context are edited by Pringle (1985) and Barron (1987): both include short summaries of plots of science fiction novels from which those of interest in psychology can be selected.

Finally, there are two earlier reviews of the science fiction approach to psychology by Saeger (1977, 1979).

RELIGIOUS
LITERATURE

The psychology of religion is a distinct area of study that is outside our remit, but the texts, scriptures and other writings of different religions are a further source of material that can be used to illustrate areas of psychological interest. These contain many life accounts of important religious figures which show the influence of early experience or emotional factors on their behaviours, beliefs or interpretations of events. Freeman (1984) provides a discussion of models of personal growth in the New Testament and compares them to the developmental models of Jung and Kohlberg.

Religious literature also provides guidelines for desirable behaviour either through explicit rules, such as the Ten Commandments or the Buddhist Precepts, or through the teachings and examples of individuals like Christ or the Buddha. A comparison of different religions might be used in a teaching context for a discussion of cross-cultural differences in social norms for behaviour, and in views of psychological adjustment. Balodhi and Keshavan (1986), for example, discuss the concept of the mentally healthy person reflected in the *Bhagavadgita* and the relevance of its teaching to current forms of psychotherapy. Approaches to the management or modification of certain emotions and behaviours are also documented in religious texts: Stafford (1986) analyses over 500 references to anger in the Bible which suggest that it is an acceptable emotion if handled in specific ways. In a review of early Buddhist literature de Silva (1984) gives examples of techniques for the treatment of many disorders, including obesity and obsessional thoughts, which appear remarkably similar to behaviour therapies used by psychologists today. Of all major religions, perhaps Zen Buddhism has made the most direct attempt to control and modify human behaviour and experience (see Kraft, 1988).

The central characters of many religious texts are often endowed with many human characteristics and therefore, like science fiction, this body of literature also reflects the qualities we perceive in ourselves. Even God is not immune to feelings of anger (Stafford, 1986). Thus it appears that man has fashioned God in his own image.

REFERENCES

ALDISS, B. (1973) *Billion Year Spree*. London: Weidenfeld & Nicholson.

ALDISS, B.W. and WINGROVE, D. (1986) *Trillion Year Spree*. New York: Atheneum.

ALLEN, L.D. (1975) *The Ballantine Teacher's Guide to Science Fiction*. New York: Ballantine.

BABKIN, B.P. (1949) *Pavlov, A Biography*. Chicago: University of Chicago Press.

BAIN, A. (1904) *Autobiography*. London: Longman.

BALODHI, J.P. and KESHAVAN, M.S. (1986) *Bhagavadgita* and psychotherapy. *NIMHANS Journal*, 4 (2), 139–143.

BARRON, N. (Ed.) (1987) *Anatomy of Wonder: A Critical Guide to Science Fiction*, 3rd ed. New York: R.R. Bowker Co.

BENEL, R.A. (1975) Psychological thrillers: Thrilling to whom? *Teaching of Psychology*, 2, 176.

BERTAUX, D. (Ed.) (1983) *Biography and Society: The life history approach in the social sciences*. London: Sage.

BIRD, G. (1986) *William James*. London: Routledge & Kegan Paul.

BRATUS, B.S. (1986) The place of fine literature in the development of a scientific psychology of personality. *Soviet Psychology*, 25(1), 91–103.

BROME, V. (1978) *Jung, Man and Myth*. London: Macmillan.

BROME, V. (1982) *Ernest Jones: Freud's alter ego*. London: Caliban Books.

BURANELLI, V. (1975) *The Wizard From Vienna: Franz Anton Mesmer*. New York: Coward, McCann & Geoghegan.

BURDEN, R. (1974) Adolescence through literature: A novel approach to an age-old problem. *Psychology Teaching*, 2, 251–258.

CLARK, R. (1982) *Freud*. London: Weidenfeld & Nicholson.

CLARKE, A.C. (1974) Profiles of the Future. London: Gollancz.

CLIFFORD, G.C. (1984) *Edward L. Thorndike: The sane positivist*. Middletown, CT: Wesleyan University Press (Originally published as *The Sane Positivist: Edward L. Thorndike*, 1968).

COHEN, D. (1977) *Psychologists on Psychology*. London: Routledge & Kegan Paul.

COHEN, D. (1979) *J.B. Watson, The Founder of Behaviourism*. London: Routledge & Kegan Paul.

CRAMPTON, C. (in press) *Sir Frederick Bartlett and the Cambridge School*. Cambridge: CUP.

CROGHAN, A. (1981) *Science Fiction and the Universe of Knowledge: The structure of an aesthetic form.* London: Coburgh.

DE SILVA, P. (1984) Buddhism and behaviour modification. *Behaviour Research and Therapy*, 22(6), 661–678.

DEL REY, L. (1979) *The World of Science Fiction.* New York: Ballantine.

DUPONT, J. (Ed.) (1989) *The Clinical Diary of Sandor Fereuczi.* Cambridge, MA: Harvard University Press.

ELLIS, A.T. and PITT-AIKENS, T. (1988) *Secrets of Strangers.* Harmondsworth: Penguin.

ELLIS, H. (1940) *My Life.* London: Spearman.

ESTRADA, A. and ESTRADA, D. (Eds) (1977) *The Future of Being Human: Psychology through science fiction.* New York: Harper & Row.

EVANS, C. (Ed.) (1969) *Mind at Bay.* London: Panther Books.

EVANS, C. (Ed.) (1970) *Minds in Chains. London: Panther Books.*

FERNANDEZ, R. (Ed.) (1972) *Social Psychology Through Literature.* New York: Wiley.

FORREST, D.W. (1974) *Francis Galton: The life and work of a Victorian genius.* London: Elek.

FOSTER, J.H. (1988) *Sex Variant Women in Literature.* London: Naiad Press (originally published by Vintage Press, 1956).

FREEMAN, A. (1984) Styles of discipleship: Personal growth models in the New Testament. *Studies in Formative Spirituality,* 5(2), 171–188.

FREUD, S. (1935) *An Autobiographical Study.* London: Hogarth Press.

GIBSON, H.B. (1981) *H.J. Eysenck.* London: P. Owen.

GRANT, L. (1987) Psychology and Literature: A survey of courses. *Teaching of Psychology,* 14(2), 86–88.

GROSSKURTH, P. (1980) *Havelock Ellis: Stranger in the world.* London: Allen Lane.

GROSSKURTH, P. (1986) *Melanie Klein: Her world and her work.* Sevenoaks: Hodder & Stoughton.

HEARNSHAW, L.S. (1979) *Cyril Burt, Psychologist.* Sevenoaks: Hodder & Stoughton.

HEARNSHAW, L.S. (1987) *The Shaping of Modern Psychology.* London: Routledge and Kegan Paul.

HETTICH, P. (1976) The journal, an autobiographical approach to learning. *Teaching of Psychology,* 3, 60–63.

HOFFMAN, E. (1988) *The Right to be Human: A biography of Abraham Maslow.* Los Angeles: Jeremy B. Tarcher.

HOWARD, J. (1984) *Margaret Mead: A life.* London: Harvill Press.

HUXLEY, A. (1932) *Brave New World.* London: Chatto & Windus.

JAMES, C.L.R. (1976) *Beyond a Boundary,* rev.ed. London: Stanley Paul.

JONES, E. (1953) *The Life and Work of Sigmund Freud.* New York: Basic Books.

JONES, R. and ROE, R.L. (Eds) (1974) *Valence and Vision: A reader in psychology.* San Francisco, CA: Rinehart Press.

KATZ, H.A., GREENBERG, M.N. and WARRICK, P. (Eds) (1977) *Psychology Through Science Fiction,* 2nd ed. Chicago: Rand McNally.

KATZ, H.A., WARRICK, P. and GREENBERG, M.N. (1974) *Introduction to Psychology Through Science Fiction.* Chicago: Rand McNally.

KELLOGG, R.L. (1980) Sherlock Holmes and the educational process. *Teaching of Psychology, 7*, 41–44.

KIRSCHENBAUM, H. (1979) *On Becoming Carl Rogers.* New York: Delacorte.

KNIGHT, D. (1967) *In Search of Wonder,* 2nd ed. Chicago: Advent.

KRAFT, K. (1988) *Zen: Tradition and transition.* London: Rider.

LAING, R.D. (1986) *Wisdom, Madness and Folly: The Making of a Psychiatrist.* London: Papermac.

LANDAU, E.D., EPSTEIN, S.L. and STONE, A.P. (Eds) (1972) *Child Development Through Literature* . Englewood Cliffs, NJ: Prentice-Hall.

LESTER, D. (1987) Psychology and literature. *Psychology: A Quarterly Journal of Human Behaviour, 24* (1–2), 25–27.

LE UNES, A. (1974) Psychology thrillers revisited. A tentative list of master thrillers. *American Psychologist, 29*, 211–213.

LEVIN, M.J. (1979) *Psychology. A biographical approach.* New York: McGraw-Hill.

LINDZEY, G. (Ed.) (1980) *A History of Psychology in Autobiography.* Oxford: W.H. Freeman.

LURIA, A.R. (1979) *The Making of Mind: A personal account of Soviet psychology.* Cambridge, MS: Harvard University Press.

McCOLLOM, I.N. (1971) Psychological thrillers: Psychology books students read when given freedom of choice. *American Psychologist, 26*, 921–927.

McCOLLOM, I.N. (1973) Let's get them to read psychology books. *Newsletter of the American Psychological Association Division on the Teaching of Psychology,* December.

McCOLLOM, I.N. (1975) Readings readers recommend. *Teaching of Psychology, 2*, 42.

MARCUS, S. (1984) *Sigmund Freud and the Culture of Psychoanalysis.* London: George Allen & Unwin.

MARROW, A.J. (1968) *The Practical Theorist. The Life and Work of Kurt Lewin.* New York: Teachers College Press.

MAZZIOTTA, J.C., PHELPS, M.E. and KUHL, D.E. (1982) Tomographic mapping of human cerebral metabolism. *Neurology, 32*, 921–937.

MEAD, M. (1973) *Blackberry Winter: My Earlier Years.* London: Angus & Robertson.

MELVIN, K.B., BRODSKY, S.L. and FOWLER, R.D.Jr. (Eds) (1977) *PsyFi One: An anthology in science fiction.* New York: Random House.

MODELL, J. (1984) *Ruth Benedict: Patterns of a life.* London: Chatto & Windus/Hogarth Press.

MYERS, G. (1986) *William James: His life and thought.* New Haven: Yale University Press.

NICHOLLS, P. (Ed.) (1976) *Science Fiction at Large.* London: Gollancz.

NICHOLLS, P. (Ed.) (1979) *The Encyclopaedia of Science Fiction.* London: Granada.

NICHOLLS, P. (Ed.) (1982) *The Science in Science Fiction.* London: Michael Joseph.

NISBETT, A. (1976) *Konrad Lorenz.* London: Dent.

NUTTALL, A.D. (1983) *A New Mimesis: Shakespeare and the representation of reality.* London: Methuen.

ORWELL, G. (1948) *1984.* Harmondsworth: Penguin.

OWEN, A.R.F. (1971) *Hysteria, Hypnosis and Healing: The work of J.M. Charcot.* London: Dennis Dobson.

PARRINDER, P. (1980) *Science Fiction: Its criticism and teaching.* London: Methuen.

PEARSON, A. (1977) More firsthand accounts of coping with handicap, illness and deviance. *Psychology Teaching, 5,* 145–148.

PEARSON, A. (1980) Summarized firsthand accounts of coping with life crises and handicap. *Psychology Teaching, 8,* 10–21.

PEARSON, K. (1914–1930) *The Life, Letters and Labours of Francis Galton.* Cambridge: Cambridge University Press.

PETERS, V.H. (1985) *Anna Freud: A life dedicated to children.* London: Weidenfeld & Nicholson.

POTTER, J., STRINGER, P. and WEATHERELL, M. (1984) *Social Text and Context: Literature and social psychology.* London: Routledge & Kegan Paul.

PRINGLE, D. (1985) *Science Fiction: The 100 best novels.* London: Xanadu.

QUINN, S. (1988) *A Mind of Her Own: The life of Karen Horney.* London: Macmillan.

RADFORD, J. (1980) Introduction. In J. Radford and D. Rose (Eds) *The Teaching of Psychology: Method, content and context.* Chichester: Wiley.

RADFORD, J. (1985) Psychology and science fiction. *Bulletin of The British Psychological Society, 38,* 113–115.

RADFORD, J. (1988) Sherlock Holmes and the history of psychology. *The Psychologist, 1*(4), 143–146.

RADFORD, J. and KIRBY, R. (Eds) (1973) *The First Anthology of Psychological Science Fiction.* (Unpublished, but available from the Science Fiction Foundation, Polytechnic of East London.)

READ, S. (1989) *Only for a Fortnight: My life in a locked ward.* London: Bloomsbury.

REED, E.S. (1989) *James J. Gibson and the Psychology of Perception.* New Haven: Yale University Press.

REICH, I.O. (1969) *Wilhelm Reich.* London: Elek.

REICH, W. (1988) *Passion in Youth: An Autobiography 1897–1922.* London: Penguin.

RICKMAN, H.P. (1979) *Wilhelm Dilthey: Pioneer of the Human Studies.* London: Paul Elek.

RIDGWAY, J. and BENJAMIN, M. (1987) *PsiFi: Psychological Theories and Science Fictions.* Leicester: BPS Books.

RIPPERE, V. (1976) First hand accounts of coping with an ill, handicapped or deviant child. A short bibliography for use in psychology teaching. *Psychology Teaching, 4,* 158–159.

RIPPERE, V. (1977) Personal accounts of mental disorder and its treatment: A short bibliography for use in psychology teaching. *Psychology Teaching, 5,* 26–29.

RIPPERE, V. (1978) Experience of illness, disability and treatment: A short bibliography of personal accounts for use in psychology teaching. *Psychology Teaching, 6,* 57–66.

RIPPERE, V. (1979a) Training and practice in the helping professions. A short bibliography of personal accounts for use in psychology teaching. *Psychology Teaching, 7,* 23–27.

RIPPERE, V. (1979b) Bereavement, grief and mourning. A short bibliography of personal accounts for use in psychology teaching. *Psychology Teaching, 7,* 143–146.

RIPPERE, V. (1980) Working with children. A short bibliography of personal accounts for use in psychology teaching. *Psychology Teaching, 8*, 35–39.

ROSE, D, and RADFORD, J. (1981) The use of literature in teaching psychology. *Bulletin of The British Psychological Society, 34*, 453–455.

RUBIN, D.C. (Ed.) (1986) *Autobiographical Memory*. Cambridge: Cambridge University Press.

RUBINS, J.K. (1978) *Karen Horney: Gentle rebel of psychoanalysis*. New York: Dial.

RUBLE, R. (1975) Spicing up an abnormal psychology course. *Teaching of Psychology, 2*, 43–44.

SACHS, H. (1945) *Freud, Master and Friend*. London: Imago.

SACHS, O. (1984) *A Leg to Stand On*. London: Duckworth.

SACHS, O. (1985) *The Man who Mistook his Wife for a Hat*. London: Duckworth.

SAEGER, W. (1977) Science fiction as a teaching tool in social and environmental psychology. *Psychology Teaching, 5*, 154–157.

SAEGER, W. (1979) Literature and learning: The art of the state. *Psychology Teaching, 7*, 3–12.

SAGAN, C. (1978) *The Dragons of Eden: Speculations on the evolution of human intelligence*. New York: Ballantine.

SARASON, S.B. (1988) *The Making of an American Psychologist: An autobiography*. San Francisco: Jossey-Bass.

SCHELLENBERG, J.A. (1978) *Masters of Social Psychology: Freud, Mead, Lewin and Skinner*. New York: Oxford University Press.

SCHRODER, C., VAN GRUNDY, J. and HUSBAND, R.W. (Eds) (1943) *Psychology Through Literature*. New York: Oxford University Press.

SEAGOE, M.V. (1975) *Terman and the Gifted*. Los Altos, CA: William Kaufmann Inc.

SEDERBERG, P.V. and SEDERBERG, N.B. (1975) Transmitting the non-transmissable. The function of literature in pursuit of social knowledge. *Philosophy and Phenomenological Research, 36*, 173.

SHARAF, M. (1983) *Fury on Earth: A biography of Wilhelm Reich*. London: André Deutsch.

SHEPHERD, M. (1985) *Sherlock Holmes and the Case of Dr Freud*. London: Tavistock.

SKINNER, B.F. (1948) *Walden Two*. New York. Collier-Macmillan.

SKINNER, B.F. (1985a) *A Matter of Consequences*. New York: New York University Press.

SKINNER, B.F. (1975b) *Particulars of My Life*. New York: New York University Press.

SKINNER, B.F. (1975c) *The Shaping of a Behaviourist*. New York: New York University Press.

STABLEFORD, B.M. (1977) *The Mysteries of Modern Science*. London: Routledge & Kegan Paul.

STABLEFORD, B.M. (1984) Inner Space. In D. Wingrove (Ed.) *The Science Fiction Sourcebook*. New York: Van Nostrand.

STAFFORD, C.H. (1986) A biblical approach to anger management training. *Journal of Psychology and Christianity, 5*(4), 5–11.

STONE, A.A. and STONE, S.S. (Eds) (1966) *The Abnormal Personality Through Literature*. Englewood Cliffs, NJ: Prentice-Hall.

SULLOWAY, F.J. (1979) *Freud, Biologist of the Mind*. New York: Basic Books.

SUTHERLAND, N.S. (1987) *Breakdown: A Personal Crisis and a Medical Dilemma*, 2nd ed. London: Weidenfeld & Nicholson.

SUVIN, D. (1979) *Metamorphoses of Science Fiction*. New Haven: Yale University Press.

SWAIN, R. (1977) Psychological Thrillers: An Irish list. *Bulletin of The British Psychological Society, 30*, 135–137.

VANDE KEMP, H. (1980) Teaching psychology through the case study method. *Teaching of Psychology, 7*, 38–40.

WEATHERELL, M., POTTER, J. and STRINGER, P. (1983) Psychology, literature and texts. *Bulletin of The British Psychological Society, 36*, 377–379.

WEHR, G. (1985) Carl Gustav Jung. Leben, Werk, Wirkung. Munich: Kösel/KNO.

WEHR, G. (1987) *Jung: A biography*. Boston: Shambhala.

WERTSCH, J.V. (1985) *Vygotsky and the Social Formation of Mind*. Cambridge, MS: Harvard University Press.

WHITE, R.W. (1975) *Lives in Progress. A study of the natural growth of personality*, 3rd ed. New York: Holt, Rinehart & Winston.

WHITE, R.W. (1974) Teaching personality through the histories. *Teaching of Psychology, 1*, 69–71.

WIGODER, D. (1987) *Images of Destruction*. London: Kegan Paul.

WILSON, R.A. (1977) *Cosmic Trigger: The final secret of the Illuminati*. New York: Simon & Schuster.

WINGROVE, D. (Ed.) (1984) *The Science Fiction Sourcebook*. New York: Van Nostrand.

WOLF, M.A. (1987) Human development, gerontology and self-development through the writings of May Sarton. *Educational Gerontology, 13*(4), 289–295.

WRIGHT, N. (1988) *Mrs Klein*. London: Walker Books.

WRIGHTSMAN, L.S. (1981) Personal documents as data: Conceptualizing adult personality development. *Personality and Social Psychology Bulletin, 7*(3), 367–385.

YOUNG-BRUEHL, E. (1988) *Anna Freud: A biography*. New York: Summit Books.

Acknowledgements The following colleagues in universities and polytechnics have kindly made suggestions, in some cases very numerous, of further works of literature with psychological significance: Rowan Bayne, Polytechnic of East London; Prue Green, Polytechnic of East London, Clive Hollin, University of Leicester; Steve Newstead, Polytechnic South West; Ian Parker, Manchester Polytechnic; Ludmilla Rickwood, Polytechnic South West. It has not been possible to incorporate most of these into this chapter, but many will be found in The British Psychological Society's Group of Teachers of Psychology Occasional Paper *The Uses of Literature in Understanding and Teaching Psychology* (Eds D. Smith and J. Radford; in press).

THE LITERATURE ON THE TEACHING OF PSYCHOLOGY

David Rose and Deana Smith

❑ *teaching contexts* ● *the UK literature* ● *subject index*

It has recently been estimated that there are in excess of 30,000 students following GCE courses in psychology and that almost 2,000 graduate in psychology each year (Radford and Rose, 1989). To this combined figure must be added those undergoing professional training in psychology, those studying psychology as a component of other academic and professional courses and those attending the numerous adult education classes in psychology simply for enjoyment. In total the number of people studying psychology in the United Kingdom is very considerable. Consequently, it is unsurprising that there is now an extensive literature on the teaching of psychology.

In preparing the present chapter we found ourselves starting with almost 700 references on the teaching of psychology in the UK. However, our aim has not been to produce a list which can lay claim to completeness. Rather we have sought to provide the reader with the means to follow up current literature on the teaching of psychology in its various contexts. In consequence, we have been somewhat selective in our inclusion of relevant British Psychological Society (BPS) reports, guidelines and statements and we have excluded all references to abstracts. A further category of literature which we have largely omitted from the present list is that concerned with counselling training. Although much of this has relevance for teachers of psychology it is a literature that spans many disciplines and is now of such proportions that it merits its own annotated bibliographies.

We have also excluded pre-1980 references. The choice of 1980 as a cut-off point was arbitrary, of course. Whatever date had been selected would have excluded some references which we would have preferred to retain. One example which illustrates this point is the work of Rippere. Whilst her 1980 paper, a bibliography of first hand accounts of working with children, appears on our list, five earlier bibliographies, all of them of great value to teachers of psychology, are omitted. We would refer those readers who would like to examine the literature from 1970 to 1980 to an earlier listing (Rose, 1984).

Teaching Contexts   The teaching context or contexts to which each reference relates is indicated by a letter code, as listed below:

PC Pre-college: teaching O-level/GCSE, AS-level and other pre-first degree psychology courses
UG Undergraduate
PG Postgraduate: MPhil, PhD and taught MSc courses other than clinical, educational and occupational psychology.
ED Educational psychology
CL Clinical psychology
OC Occupational psychology
CR Criminological and legal psychology
GR Psychology graduates entering training for professions other than psychology, e.g. teacher training.
NP Teaching psychology to non-psychologists: for example, teachers, doctors, managers, etc.
PT Training in psychological testing
GN Of relevance to several teaching contexts.

Each reference is also numbered, and there is a subject index at the back of this chapter which categorizes the references' numbers according to their teaching context. This means that if, for example, you are interested in literature on the teaching of occupational psychology, you can see that references 40, 58, 61, 77, 117, 130, 165, 193, 205, 206, 212 and 286 are particularly relevant and can immediately check these. However, it is often difficult to classify a publication in terms of the particular types and levels of psychology teaching in which it may be of value. Even where it is obviously concerned with one specific teaching context, it may well merit the attention of teachers in related contexts. In order to avoid missing potentially valuable references it is hoped the reader will have time to examine the whole list, therefore.

As will quickly become apparent, the main sources of papers on the teaching of psychology are the *Bulletin of The British Psychological Society* (now *The Psychologist*) and *Psychology Teaching*, the Bulletin of the Association for the Teaching of Psychology. Collections of relevant articles are also to be found in three books on the teaching of psychology (Radford and Rose, 1980; 1989; Rose and Radford, 1984). Our list also contains many references to newsletters of BPS Sections and Divisions. With the exception of the *Education Section Review* and the *Clinical Psychology Forum* they are available only to members of the relevant Sections or Divisions, but may be consulted by anyone in the BPS Library at Senate House, Malet Street, London WC1 7HU.

The American Literature. In addition to the UK literature listed below there is also an extensive American literature. The reader who is interested in investigating this further is recommended to consult the following series of annotated bibliographies:

DANIEL, R.S. (1981) Annotated bibliographies on the teaching of psychology: (1980). *Teaching of Psychology, 8* (4), 249–253.

MOSLEY, C.E. and DANIEL, R.S. (1982) Annotated bibliography on the teaching of psychology: 1981. *Teaching of Psychology, 9* (4), 250–254.

BERRY, K.A. and DANIEL, R.S. (1985) Annotated bibliography on the teaching of psychology: 1984. *Teaching of Psychology, 12* (4), 231–236.

WISE, P.S. and FULKERSON, F.E. (1986) Annotated bibliography on the teaching of psychology: 1985. *Teaching of Psychology, 13* (4), 223–227.

THE UK LITERATURE

CL   1   ALLEN, C. (1987) National training needs in clinical psychology: A response from the affiliates group. *Clinical Psychology Forum, 7*, 35–36.

UG   2   ANDERSON, R.J. (1980) Contextual, integrative and ethical issues. In J. Radford and D. Rose (Eds) *The Teaching of Psychology: Method, content and context.* Chichester: Wiley.

UG   3   ARNOLD, J. and NEWSTEAD, S. (1989) Working with psychology. In J. Radford and D. Rose (Eds) *A Liberal Science: Psychology education past, present and future.* Milton Keynes: Society for Research into Higher Education and Open University Press.

UG   4   ARNOLD, J., NEWSTEAD, S.E., DONALDSON, M.L., REID, F.J.M. and DENNIS, I. (1987) Skills development in undergraduate psychology courses. *Bulletin of The British Psychological Society, 40*, 469–472.

PC   5   ASSOCIATION FOR THE TEACHING OF PSYCHOLOGY

(1983) *Handbook for GCE Teachers*. Association for the Teaching of Psychology. (Available from the ATP, c/o the BPS.)

PG 6   BADDELEY, A. (1983) The working party on postgraduate education. *Bulletin of The British Psychological Society, 36*, 9–12.

NP 7   BADDELEY, H. and BITHELL, C. (1989) Psychology in the physiotherapy curriculum: A survey. *Physiotherapy, 75* (1), 17–21.

UG 8   BALL, B. and BOURNER, T. (1984) The employment of psychology graduates. *Bulletin of The British Psychological Society, 37,* 39–40.

UG 9   BANNISTER, D. (1980) The psychology of teaching psychology. *Psychology Teaching, 8* (2), 7–9.

GN 10   BANNISTER, D. (1982) Personal construct theory and the teaching of psychology. *Education Section Newsletter* (of the BPS), *6* (2), 73–79.

CL 11   BARKER, C. (1985) Interpersonal process recall in clinical training and research. In F.N. Watts (Ed) *New Developments in Clinical Psychology*. Leicester: BPS Books and Wiley.

CL 12   BARNES, B. and PILGRIM, D. (1983) Some special features of clinical psychology student T-groups. *Division of Clinical Psychology Newsletter* (of the BPS), *39,* 25–29.

GN 13   BENDER, A.P., AITMAN, J.B., BIGGS, S., COOPER, A. and JACKSON, J. (1983) Professional development and the training requirements of psychologists working in social services and other community settings. *Bulletin of The British Psychological Society, 36,* 233–236.

CL 14   BERGER, M., COLES, C., KIRK, J., MARZILLIER, J., LAVENDER, A., MORLEY, S., REVELL, J. and WATTS, F. (1988) The assessment of clinical psychologists in training: A discussion document. *Clinical Psychology Forum, 15,* 3–15.

NP 15   BIRCHMORE, T. (1987) Skilled teaching? Teaching Skills. *Clinical Psychology Forum, 12,* 7–9.

ED 16   BLOOR, M. and LOVELL, R.B. (1988) The teaching face. In H.J. Wright and J. Radford (Eds) *The Several Faces of Educational Psychology*. Group of Teachers of Psychology (of the BPS) Occasional Paper No. 2, 13–20.

NP 17   BORS, M.G. and FALZON, J.M. (1988) A comparative study of two assessment modes used in a BEd course. *Group of Teachers of Psychology Newsletter* (of the BPS), *5,* October, 5–11.

UG 18   BRANTHWAITE, A., BROWN, R., FARR, R. and FIELD-ING, G. (1982) Films and videos for social psychology. *Social Psychology Section Newsletter* (of the BPS), *10,* 37–39.

PT 19   BRITISH PSYCHOLOGICAL SOCIETY STANDING COMMITTEE ON TEST STANDARDS (1980) Notes for guidance in planning short courses in psychological testing. *Bulletin of The British Psychological Society, 33,* 244–249.

CL 20   BRITISH PSYCHOLOGICAL SOCIETY DIVISION OF CLI-
            NICAL PSYCHOLOGY (1981) Generic training in clinical
            psychology: A statement of principles and current inter-
            pretations. *Division of Clinical Psychology Newsletter* (of the
            BPS), *34*, 14–17.
CL 21   BRITISH PSYCHOLOGICAL SOCIETY PROFESSIONAL
            AFFAIRS BOARD (1981) Criteria for the assessment of
            post-qualification courses for applied psychologists in
            psychological therapy. *Bulletin of The British Psychological
            Society, 34*, 130.
CL 22   BRITISH PSYCHOLOGICAL SOCIETY PROFESSIONAL
            AFFAIRS BOARD COMMITTEE ON TRAINING IN
            CLINICAL PSYCHOLOGY (1981) Approval of clinical
            training courses by the British Psychological Society.
            (Available from the BPS.)
CL 23   BRITISH PSYCHOLOGICAL SOCIETY (1982) Training in
            clinical psychology: A statement of policy. *Bulletin of The
            British Psychological Society, 35*, 153–155.
CL 24   BRITISH PSYCHOLOGICAL SOCIETY DIVISION OF CLI-
            NICAL PSYCHOLOGY (1982) Clinical psychology man-
            power and training. Document submitted to the DHSS.
            Division of Clinical Psychology Newsletter (of the BPS), *36*,
            1–15.
CL 25   BRITISH PSYCHOLOGICAL SOCIETY BOARD OF
            EXAMINERS FOR THE DIPLOMA IN CLINICAL
            PSYCHOLOGY (1983) Preparation of candidates for The
            British Psychological Society Diploma in clinical psychol-
            ogy. *Bulletin of The British Psychological Society, 36*, 85.
UG 26   BRITISH PSYCHOLOGICAL SOCIETY SOCIAL PSYCHOL-
            OGY SECTION (1983) Social psychology in the UK: The
            Open University's new third-level social psychology
            course. *Social Psychology Section Newsletter* (of the BPS), *11*,
            25–27.
PC 27   BRITISH PSYCHOLOGICAL SOCIETY (1987) Appropriate
            qualifications for staff intending to teach psychology at
            GCSE level. (Available from the BPS.)
PG 28   BRITISH PSYCHOLOGICAL SOCIETY (1987) Code of
            practice on the supervision, preparation and examination
            of doctoral theses in departments of psychology. *Bulletin
            of The British Psychological Society, 40*, 250–254.
PG 29   BRITISH PSYCHOLOGICAL SOCIETY (1987) Postgraduate
            qualifications by courses in psychology. (Available from
            the BPS.)
CL 30   BRITISH PSYCHOLOGICAL SOCIETY PROFESSIONAL
            AFFAIRS BOARD COMMITTEE ON TRAINING IN
            CLINICAL PSYCHOLOGY (1987) Guidelines on clinical
            supervision. (Available from the BPS.)
PC 31   BRITISH PSYCHOLOGICAL SOCIETY (1988) A- and AS-
            Level subjects for a degree in psychology and a note on

degree courses. (Available from the BPS.)

GN 32   BRITISH PSYCHOLOGICAL SOCIETY (1988) *The Future of the Psychological Sciences: Horizons and opportunities for British psychology.* (Available from the BPS.)

ED 33   BRITISH PSYCHOLOGICAL SOCIETY (1988) The initial training of educational psychologists in England, Wales, Northern Ireland and Hong Kong. A policy statement. *The Psychologist, 1* (12), 508–509.

PC 34   BRITISH PSYCHOLOGICAL SOCIETY/COMMITTEE OF THE ASSOCIATION FOR THE TEACHING OF PSYCHOLOGY (1988) Psychology as a secondary examination subject. *Group of Teachers of Psychology Newsletter* (of the BPS), *4,* April, 5–9.

CL 35   BRITISH PSYCHOLOGICAL SOCIETY PROFESSIONAL AFFAIRS BOARD COMMITTEE ON TRAINING IN CLINICAL PSYCHOLOGY (1988) Criteria for the assessment of post-graduate training courses in clinical psychology. (Available from the BPS.)

CL 36   BRITISH PSYCHOLOGICAL SOCIETY (1989) Training in psychotherapy. (Available from the BPS.)

ED 37   BRITISH PSYCHOLOGICAL SOCIETY (1989) Qualifications to become a Chartered Psychologist specializing in educational psychology. (Available from the BPS.)

CL 38   BRITISH PSYCHOLOGICAL SOCIETY BOARD OF EXAMINERS FOR THE DIPLOMA IN CLINICAL PSYCHOLOGY (1989) Guidelines for the training of independent candidates. (Available from the BPS.)

PC 39   BRODY, R. (1980) Some thoughts on A-level psychology. *Education Section Newsletter* (of the BPS), *4,* 8–10.

OC 40   BROTHERTON, C. (1982) Occupational psychology at Nottingham. Teaching the intercalated training year. *Occupational Psychology Newsletter* (of the BPS), *9,* 6–8.

UG 41   BROWN, R. (1982) Social psychology in the UK: The University of Kent. *Social Psychology Section Newsletter* (of the BPS), *9,* 8–11.

UG 42   BROWN, R.J. (1985) Psychology, information technology and curriculum development. *Bulletin of The British Psychological Society, 38,* 36–40.

UG 43   BRUCE, R.L. (1980) Biological psychology. In J. Radford and D. Rose (Eds) *The Teaching of Psychology: Method, content and context.* Chichester: Wiley.

GN 44   BUCKINGHAM, M. (1980) The study of child development in higher education: An integrated approach. *Psychology Teaching, 8* (2), 24–28.

UG 45   BURTON, A.M. (1985) Computer use in British university departments of psychology. *Bulletin of The British Psychological Society, 38,* 1–5.

UG 46   BUSHNELL, I.W.R. and MULLIN, J.T. (1986) Automated laboratory classes in psychology. *Bulletin of The British*

Psychological Society, 39, 261–262.

UG 47 BUSTIN, B. (1985) What do employers want? *Psychology Teaching,* April, 71–76.

NP 48 BUTCHER, P. and de CLIVE-LOWE, S. (1985) Strategies for living: Teaching psychological self-help as adult education. In H. Davis and P. Butcher (Eds) *Sharing Psychological Skills: Training non-psychologists in the use of psychological techniques.* Leicester: the BPS.

ED 49 CAMERON, S., MYERS, M. and REASON, R. (1986) Advanced professional training for practising educational psychologists. *Division of Educational and Child Psychology Newsletter* (of the BPS), *22,* 18–21.

UG 50 CANTER, S. and CANTER, D. (1983) Professional growth and psychology education. *Bulletin of The British Psychological Society, 36,* 283–287.

PC 51 CARTER, W. (1980) A-level psychology in the school curriculum – a personal view. *Psychology Teaching, 8*(1), 37–38.

NP 52 CHAMBERLAIN, P. and WHITE, G. (1986) The psychologist as staff trainer – do we practise what we preach? *Clinical Psychology Forum, 1,* 7–11.

ED 53 CHILD, D. (1980) The educational context. In J. Radford and D. Rose (Eds) *The Teaching of Psychology: Method, content and context.* Chichester: Wiley.

NP 54 CLAXTON, G. (1983) Why the psychology in teacher training is useless. *Division of Education and Child Psychology Newsletter* (of the BPS), *10,* 18–19.

CL 55 COATE, M.A., CONBOY-HILL, S., KERFOOT, S., MALTBY, M., PARKER, S., POWELL, G. and WYCHERLY, B. (1988) A basic grade training programme. *Clinical Psychology Forum, 14,* 16–19.

UG 56 CONNOLLY, K.J. and SMITH, P.K. (1986) What makes a 'good' degree: Variations between different departments. *Bulletin of The British Psychological Society, 39,* 48–51.

GN 57 COOPER, C.L. (1980) Experiential methods. In J. Radford and D. Rose (Eds) *The Teaching of Psychology: Method, content and context.* Chichester: Wiley.

CL/ 58 COOPER, C.L. (1986) Job distress: Recent research and the
OC emerging role of the clinical occupational psychologist. *Bulletin of The British Psychological Society, 39,* 325–331.

NP 59 COX, K.M. (1984) Teaching psychology to non-psychologists. *Psychology Teaching,* April, 4–9.

GN 60 COX, M.V. and COULSON, A. (1984) The use of feature films in the teaching of psychology. In D. Rose and J. Radford (Eds) *Teaching Psychology: Information and resources.* Leicester: BPS Books.

OC 61 CRAWSHAW, M. (1988) Postgraduate occupational psychology at Hull. *The Occupational Psychologist, 5,* August, 15–17.

CL 62   CULLEN, C. (1981) Supervisors' workshops: Report of a survey conducted by the Standing Committee on Practitioner Training. *Division of Clinical Psychology Newsletter* (of the BPS), *33*, 21–22.

CL 63   CULLEN, C. (1982) Supervisors' workshops. *Division of Clinical Psychology Newsletter* (of the BPS), *36*, 37–38.

CL 64   CULLEN C. (1984) Training clinical psychologists – for what? *Division of Clinical Psychology Newsletter* (of the BPS), *43*, 40–41.

PG 65   CULLEN, C. (1988) Doctoral degrees in applied psychology. *The Psychologist, 1*, (10), 395–396.

CL 66   DAVENHILL, R., HUNT, H., PILLAY, H.M., HARRIS, A. and KLEIN, Y. (1989) Training and selection issues in clinical psychology for black and minority ethnic groups from an equal opportunities perspective. *Clinical Psychology Forum, 19*, 13–17.

NP 67   DAVIES, M. (1989) The psychology taught on social work training courses, In N. Hayes (Ed) *Teaching Psychology to Social Workers*. Group of Teachers of Psychology (of the BPS) Occasional Paper, No. 7, 6–23.

UG 68   DAVIES, P. and BENNETT, S. (1981) Laboratory classes: Education or initiation? *Bulletin of The British Psychological Society, 34*, 312–313.

NP 69   DAVIS, H. and BUTCHER, P. (1985) *Sharing Psychological Skills: Training non-psychologists in the use of psychological techniques.* Leicester: the BPS.

CL 70   DAVIS, J., DAVIS, M. and HILDEBRAND, P. (1983) Support for post-qualification training. *Division of Clinical Psychology Newsletter* (of the BPS), *40*, 23–24.

UG 71   DE ALBERDI, M. and DE ALBERDI, L. (1988) Putting psychology to work: A view of the future of the first degree from industry/commerce. In J. Radford (Ed) *The Future of the First Degree.* Group of Teachers of Psychology (of the BPS) Occasional Paper No. 4, 6–12.

UG 72   DEJONG, W. and AMABILE, T. (1980) Social psychology. In J. Radford and D. Rose (Eds) *The Teaching of Psychology: Method, content and context.* Chichester: Wiley.

GN 73   DELL, P.A. (1984) Psychology laboratory equipment. In D. Rose and J. Radford (Eds) *Teaching Psychology: Information and resources.* Leicester: BPS Books.

GN 74   DELL, P.A. and ROSE, D. (1984) Audiovisual aids in the teaching of psychology. In D. Rose and J. Radford (Eds) *Psychology Teaching: Information and resources.* Leicester: BPS Books.

ED 75   DEPARTMENT OF EDUCATION AND SCIENCE WORKING GROUP ON THE TRAINING OF EDUCATIONAL PSYCHOLOGISTS (1985) Final Report. *Division of Educational and Child Psychology Newsletter* (of the BPS), *17*, 8–17.

NP 76   EDWARDS, H. (1987) Anxiety management workshops for

GP trainees. *Clinical Psychology Forum, 12*, 30–34.

OC   77   ELLIOT, W.S. (1983) Training of occupational psychologists. *Bulletin of The British Psychological Society, 36*, A77 (A).

ED   78   FARRELL, P. (1980) Post-experience training. Developments in the North-West. *Division of Education and Child Psychology Newsletter* (of the BPS), *4*, 13–14.

UG   79   FISHER, H. (1980) Experimental methods. In J. Radford and D. Rose (Eds) *The Teaching of Psychology: Method, content and context*. Chichester, Wiley.

ED   80   FLAVAHAN, R. and KILCARDY, B. (1985) Training for educational psychologists: Towards a new model. *Scottish Division of Educational and Child Psychology Newsletter* (of the BPS), Spring.

ED   81   FLAVAHAN, R. and KILCARDY, B. (1985) Training for educational psychologists: Towards a new model – some further thoughts. *Scottish Division of Educational and Child Psychology Newsletter* (of the BPS), Autumn.

GN   82   FLETCHER, C. (1980) Industrial, commercial and public services contexts. In J. Radford and D. Rose (Eds) *The Teaching of Psychology: Method, content and context*. Chichester: Wiley.

GN   83   FLETCHER, C. (1989) Putting psychology to work. In J. Radford and D. Rose (Eds) *A Liberal Science: Psychology education past, present and future*. Milton Keynes: Society for Research into Higher Education and Open University Press.

GN   84   FONTANA, D. (1982) The study of personality. *Education Section Newsletter* (of the BPS), *6*, 97–104.

ED   85   FOSS, B.M. (1980) An academic's view. *Division of Educational and Child Psychology* (of the BPS), *Occasional Paper, 4* (3), 17–18.

UG   86   FOSTER, J.J. (1985) Assessing student learning: Psychologists in blinkers? *Bulletin of The British Psychological Society, 38*, 370–374.

NP   87   FRANCIS, H. (1985) *Learning to Teach: Psychology in teacher training*. Lewes: Falmer Press.

ED   88   FREDERICKSON, N. (1987) Post-experience views of a regional sample of principal psychologists. *Division of Educational and Child Psychology Newsletter* (of the BPS), *25*, 14–19.

UG   89   FROSH, S. (1982) Teaching Freud to psychologists. *Bulletin of The British Psychological Society, 35*, 13–14.

CL   90   FROSH, S. (1988) Race equality training in a department of clinical psychology. *Clinical Psychology Forum, 13*, 18–22.

UG   91   GALE, A. (1985) New lamps for old: Or who stole the magic from psychology courses? *Psychology Teaching*, April, 71–76.

PC   92   GALE, A. (1985) The International Baccalaureate. *Psychology Teaching*, April, 93–99.

UG   93   GALE, A. (1989) Psychology as God's gift: How ungrateful
             can you be? A critical evaluation of the psychology degree
             and its failings. In J. Radford and D. Rose (Eds) *A Liberal
             Science: Psychology education past, present and future.* Milton
             Keynes: Society for Research into Higher Education and
             Open University Press.

GN   94   GALE, A., RADFORD, J. and TAYLOR, M. (1985) Psychol-
             ogy in the 1990's. Special edition of *Psychology Teaching,*
             April.

NP   95   GOODWIN, A. (1987) On the boundaries of training.
             Clinical Psychology Forum, 12, 37–40.

UG   96   GREER, B. and SEMRAU, G. (1984) Investigating psychol-
             ogy students' conceptual problems in mathematics in
             relation to learning statistics. *Bulletin of The British Psycho-
             logical Society, 37,* 123–125.

CL   97   GRIFFITHS, D. (1987) How successful is research training on
             clinical courses? *Clinical Psychology Forum, 9,* 16–19.

CR   98   GROARK, C. and PEASE, K. (1983) The training and work of
             prison psychologists: Data and comparisons. *Division of
             Criminological and Legal Psychology Newsletter* (of the BPS),
             13, 5–8.

PC   99   GROSS, R. (1988) Making connections in the AEB 'A' level
             psychology syllabus. *Psychology Teaching,* Part 1, 12–19.

UG   100   GUEST, H. (1981) Transpersonal psychology at the City
             University. *Self and Society, 9* (4), 183–187.

UG   101   HALE, D. (1980) Computer education in psychology. *Bulle-
             tin of The British Psychological Society, 33,* 9–11.

NP   102   HALL, E., HALL, C. and WOOSTER, A. (1987) Teaching
             psychology experientially on an MEd in human relations.
             Counselling Section Review (of the BPS), 2, (3), 16–21.

NP   103   HALL, J. (1986) Teaching psychology to trainee psychiat-
             rists. *Clinical Psychology Forum, 3,* 38–42.

CL   104   HALL, J., KOCH, H., PILLING, S. and WINTER, K. (1986)
             Health services information and clinical psychology.
             Bulletin of The British Psychological Society, 39, 126–130.

NP   105   HARNETT, O., MCPHERSON, F. and SHIMMIN, S. (1987)
             On keeping psychology to ourselves. *Bulletin of The British
             Psychological Society, 40,* 321–323.

GN   106   HARTLEY, J. and MCKEACHIE, W.J. (Eds) (In preparation)
             Handbook for the Teaching of Psychology. Hillsdale, NJ:
             Erlbaum.

GN   107   HASTINGS, N. and SCHWIESO, J. (1981) Social technik:
             Reconstructing the relationship between psychological
             theory and professional training and practice. *Oxford
             Review of Education, 7* (3), 223–229.

PC   108   HAYES, N. (1983) Group activities for GCE psychology
             teaching. *Psychology Teaching,* August, 19–22.

PC   109   HAYES, N. (1987) The role of GCE psychology. *Bulletin of
             The British Psychological Society, 40,* 63–64

NP 110 HAYES, N. (Ed) (1989) *Teaching Psychology to Social Workers.* Group of Teachers of Psychology (of the BPS), Occasional Paper No. 7.

UG 111 HAYES, N. (1989) The skills acquired in psychology degrees. *The Psychologist, 2* (6), 238–239.

NP 112 HAWKES, G. (1978) An inward look at sharing psychological methods. *Clinical Psychology Forum, 12,* 45–46.

NP 113 HEGARTY, J. R. (1987) On not teaching psychology in staff training. *Clinical Psychology Forum, 12,* 9–15.

NP 114 HEGARTY, J.R. and DECANN, R.W. (1986) *Psychology in Radiography.* Stoke-on-Trent: Change Publications.

CL 115 HENSLEY, V.R. (1980) A university-based teaching clinic. *Bulletin of The British Psychological Society, 33,* 322–323.

NP 116 HERBERT, M. (1988) The teaching of psychology in British medical schools. *Group of Teachers of Psychology Newsletter* (of the BPS), 5, October, 14–17.

OC 117 HERRIOT, P. (1985) Occupational psychology. *Psychology Teaching,* April, 45–50.

GN 118 HIGGINS, L.T. (1983) The Association for the Teaching of Psychology. *Northern Branch Newsletter* (of the BPS), *1,* 10–11.

PC 119 HIGGINS, L.T. (1989) Psychology in secondary and further education. In J. Radford and D. Rose (Eds) *A Liberal Science: Psychology education past, present and future.* Milton Keynes: Society for Research into Higher Education and Open University Press.

CL 120 HODGETTS, D. (1986) Skills: A personal approach. *Clinical Psychology Forum, 6,* 36–37.

CL 121 HOLLAND, J. (1982) Mental handicap teaching in Lancashire. *Division of Clinical Psychology Newsletter* (of the BPS), *36,* 32–34.

CL 122 HOLLAND, J. (1984) The placement component. *Division of Clinical Psychology Newsletter* (of the BPS), *43,* 38–40.

NP 123 HOLLIN, C. (1989) Teaching psychology to social workers: Summary and reflection. In N. Hayes (Ed) *Teaching Psychology to Social Workers.* Group of Teachers of Psychology (of the BPS) Occasional Paper No. 7, 45–47.

CL 124 HOOPER, J. (1988) Clinical supervision: Guidelines from trainees. *Clinical Psychology Forum, 15,* 20–26.

CL 125 HOUSTON, J., REVELL, J. and WOOLLETT, S. (1989) The need for a basic grade training programme: Results of a survey from basic grade psychologists in the SW Thames region. *Clinical Psychology Forum, 19,* 29–32.

GN 126 HOWE, M.J.A. (1980) Conventional methods. In. J. Radford and D. Rose (Eds) *The Teaching of Psychology: Method, content and context.* Chichester: Wiley.

GN 127 HOWE, M.J.A. (1982) The psychology of learning and the learning of psychology. *Education Section Newsletter* (of the BPS), *6* (2), 66–72.

CL 128   HUMPHREY, M. and HAWARD, L. (1981) Sex differences in clinical psychology recruitment. *Bulletin of The British Psychological Society, 34,* 413–414.

GN 129   ILEA (1985) The production of video-observation of individual children as a teaching resource. *Developmental Psychology Section Newsletter* (of the BPS), *10,* 21–24.

OC 130   JACKSON, C. (1988) Occupational psychology in Cardiff. *The Occupational Psychologist, 5,* August, 8–11.

CL 131   JONES, B. (1983) Training meetings for basic grades. *Division of Clinical Psychology Newsletter* (of the BPS), *39,* 32–33.

CL 132   JONES, R.B. (1983) Further training for clinical psychologists. In E. Karas (Ed) *Current Issues in Clinical Psychology.* New York: Plenum.

GN 133   JORDAN, D. and SANDERS, P. (1984) Do-it-yourself laboratory equipment. In D. Rose and J. Radford (Eds) *Teaching Psychology: Information and resources.* Leicester: BPS Books.

NP 134   KAGAN, C. (1987) Teaching interpersonal skills. In D. Müller (Ed) *Teaching Psychological Skills to Nurses.* Group of Teachers of Psychology (of the BPS), Occasional Paper No. 1, 29–38.

GN 135   KAGAN, C. (1989) Personal and social skills. In J. Radford and D. Rose (Eds) *A Liberal Science: Psychology education past, present and future.* Milton Keynes: Society for Research into Higher Education and Open University Press.

CL 136   KAT, B. (1981) Training policy. *Division of Clinical Psychology Newsletter* (of the BPS), *32,* 32–35.

CL 137   KENDRICK, D. and TAYLOR, I. (1986) The Humberside clinical psychology training course. *Clinical Psychology Forum, 6,* 21–24.

NP 138   KENT, G. and CLARKE, P. (1981) Psychology and medical teaching. *Bulletin of The British Psychological Society, 34,* 174–175.

PC 139   KIRKWOOD, J. (1988) G.C.S.E. – Already time for change. *Psychology Teaching, 1,* 20–23.

PC 140   KIRTON, M., HOLLIN, C. and RADFORD, J. (1985) School pupils' image of psychology: General knowledge and opinions. *Psychology Teaching,* April, 7–14.

CL 141   KOCH, H. (1982) Psychodynamic clinical supervision. *Division of Clinical Psychology Newsletter* (of the BPS), *35,* 35–41.

NP 142   KOPELMAN, M.D. (1986) Psychiatrists' education in psychology: Jackdaw or sponge? *Psychological Medicine, 16* (1), 13–17.

UG 143   KORNBROT, D.E. (1981) A computer system for running psychology experiments. *Behaviour Research Methods and Instrumentation, 13* (3), 351–359.

UG 144   KORNBROT, D.E. (1987) Science and psychology degree performance. *Bulletin of The British Psychological Society, 40,* 409–417.

NP 145 KYRIACOU, C. (1984) A consideration of the psychology input in teacher training. *Education Section Newsletter* (of the BPS), *8* (1), 3–6.

UG 146 LEE, M.P. SOPER, J.B. (1986) Using spreadsheets to teach statistics in psychology. *Bulletin of The British Psychological Society, 39,* 365–367.

UG 147 LEE, S. and FIELDING, G. (1982) Films and videos for social psychology. *Social Psychology Newsletter* (of the BPS), *9,* 29–30.

UG 148 LEGGE, D. (1980) Cognitive psychology. In J. Radford and D. Rose (Eds) *The Teaching of Psychology: Method, content and context.* Chichester: Wiley.

UG 149 LEGGE, D. (1981) Trends in assessment in psychology. *Assessment and Evaluation in Higher Education, 6* (2), 165–174.

GN 150 LEGGE, D. (1987) Modelling a seamless robe. *Bulletin of The British Psychological Society, 40,* 241–249.

UG 151 LEGGE, D. (1989) Psychology at degree level. In J. Radford and D. Rose (Eds) *A Liberal Science: Education in Psychology past, present and future.* Milton Keynes: Society for Research into Further Education and Open University Press.

CL 152 LEIPER, R. (1980) The revision of The British Psychological Society Diploma: A PGCC response. *Division of Clinical Psychology Newsletter* (of the BPS), *30,* 17–19.

NP 153 LEMON, N. (1989) Theoretical and experiential approaches to social work training. In N. Hayes (Ed) *Teaching Psychology to Social Workers.* Group of Teachers of Psychology (of the BPS), Occasional Paper No. 7, 38–44.

NP 154 LEWIS, P. (1984) The teaching of clinical psychology skills to non-psychologists. *Division of Clinical Psychology Newsletter* (of the BPS), *45,* 32–35.

CL 155 LIDDELL, A. (1982) Clinical psychology training: A British perspective. *Professional Psychology, 13* (4), 536–542.

CL 156 LIDDELL, A. and BOYLE, M. (1980) Characteristics of applicants to the MSc in clinical psychology at the North East London Polytechnic. *Division of Clinical Psychology Newsletter (of the BPS), 30,* 20–25.

ED 157 LINDSAY, G.A. (1981) Full frontal psychology: Human sexuality and the training of educational psychologists. *Division of Educational and Child Psychology* (of the BPS), Occasional Paper, *5* (2), 40–45.

NP 158 LLEWELYN, S.P. and FIELDING, R.G. (1987) Teaching the teachers. What are we doing? In D. Müller (Ed) *Teaching Psychological Skills to Nurses.* Group of Teachers of Psychology (of the BPS), Occasional Paper, No 1, 19–28.

UG 159 LLOYD, P. (1982) Teaching and research: A problem of ecological validity? *Education Section Newsletter* (of the BPS), *6* (2), 80–87.

GN 160 LLOYD, P. and WELLS, E. (1985) Survey on the teaching of developmental psychology. *Developmental Psychology Section Newsletter* (of the BPS), *9*, 13–18.

UG 161 LOEWENTHAL, K. (1984) Unstructured groups in undergraduate psychology teaching. *Psychology Teaching*, April, 10–13.

PC 162 LUNT, I. (1980) The development of an O-level in psychology: Child development. *Psychology Teaching*, *8* (1), 5–9.

PC 163 LUNT, I. and MURPHY, R. (1981) Ordinary and advanced level GCE examinations in psychology. *Bulletin of The British Psychological Society*, *34*, 10–11.

NP 164 LYON, J. (1987) Trying to give psychology away. *Clinical Psychology Forum*, *12*, 21–30.

OC 165 LYONS, P. (1988) MSc in occupational psychology at Hatfield Polytechnic. *The Occupational Psychologist*, *5*, August, 11–14.

NP 166 MACKAY, D. (1980) The medical context. In J. Radford and D. Rose (Eds) *The Teaching of Psychology: Method, content and context*. Chichester: Wiley.

NP 167 McKENZIE, I.K. (1984) Psychology and police education: A reply to Taylor. *Bulletin of The British Psychological Society*, *37*, 145–147.

GN 168 McKNIGHT, C. (1984) Microcomputers in psychology teaching. In D. Rose and J. Radford (Eds) *Teaching Psychology: Information and resources*. Leicester: BPS Books.

NP 169 MACLEOD CLARK, J. (1987) Teaching psychological skills to nurses – an overview. In D. Müller (Ed) *Teaching Psychological Skills to Nurses*. Group of Teachers of Psychology (of the BPS), Occasional Paper, No. 1, 39–42.

NP 170 McWHIRTER, N.P. (1980) The social work context. In J. Radford and D. Rose (Eds) *The Teaching of Psychology: Method, content and context*. Chichester: Wiley.

CL 171 MACY, C. (1986) Supervision in clinical psychology: The what and the how. *Clinical Psychology Forum*, *6*, 31–34.

ED 172 MALIPHANT, R. (1981) Post-experience training for educational psychologists. Some data from the profession. *Division of Educational and Child Psychology* (of the BPS), Occasional Paper, *5* (2), 8–16.

CL 173 MALTBY, M., LAVENDER, T., FIELD, R., WAINWRIGHT, T. and HODSON, J. (1986) Manpower findings in the South East Thames region. *Clinical Psychology Forum*, *6*, 11–15.

GN 174 MARGOLIS, J., MANICAS, P.T., HARRE, R. and SECORD, P.F. (1986) *Psychology: Designing the discipline*. Oxford: Blackwell.

CL 175 MARZILLIER, J.S. (1986) Course accreditation. *Clinical Psychology Forum*, *6*, 4–6.

GR 176 MERRY, R. (1982) Psychology graduates in teacher training. *Bulletin of The British Psychological Society, 35*, 372–374.

GN 177 MIDDLETON, D. and EDWARDS, D. (1985) Pure and applied psychology: Re-examining the relationship. *Bulletin of The British Psychological Society, 38*, 146–150.

CL 178 MILLER, E. (1982) Availability in clinical psychology and its implications. *Division of Clinical Psychology Newsletter* (of the BPS), *37*, 16–19.

CL 179 MILNE, D. (1983) Some paradoxes and findings in the training of clinical psychologists. *Bulletin of The British Psychological Society, 36*, 281–282.

GN 180 MILNE, D. (1984) Learning to teach psychology. *Psychology Teaching*, December, 15–20.

NP 181 MILNE, D. (1984) Teaching psychological skills to non-psychologists. You only get what you give away. *Division of Clinical Psychology Newsletter* (of the BPS), *46*, 23–26.

NP 182 MILNE, D. (1986) *Training Behaviour Therapists: Methods, evaluation and implementation with parents, nurses and teachers.* London: Croom Helm.

NP 183 MONEY, M.C. (1987) Health psychology for a pharmacy degree course. *Group of Teachers of Psychology Newsletter* (of the BPS), *2*, 16–19.

PG 184 MORRIS, P.E. (1983) A British Psychological Society Diploma in research skills: A discussion document. *Bulletin of The British Psychological Society, 36*, 346–347.

PG 185 MORRIS, P.E. and EVANS, J. ST B.T. (1980) Rejuvenating the British PhD. *Bulletin of The British Psychological Society, 33*, 57–59.

PG 186 MORRIS, P.E. (1984) What is the psychology PhD for? *Bulletin of The British Psychological Society, 37*, 228–229.

PG 187 MORRIS, P.E. (1985) The psychology PhD. *Psychology Teaching*, April, 63–68.

PG 188 MORRIS, P.E. (1988) BPS code of practice for the PhD: A personal view. In S.E. Newstead (Ed) *The Future of the PhD.* Group of Teachers of Psychology (of the BPS), Occasional Paper, No.5, 7–11.

ED 189 MOSS, G. (1980) Educational psychologists and in-service training for teachers: Developing teacher workshops in behavioural psychology. *British Journal of Educational Psychology, 50*, 85.

NP 190 MÜLLER, D. (1980) Further thoughts on teaching psychology in health studies courses. *Journal of Further and Higher Education, 4*(2), 52–55.

NP 191 MÜLLER, D. (Ed) (1987) *Teaching Psychological Skills to Nurses.* Group of Teachers of Psychology (of the BPS), Occasional Paper, No.1.

GN 192 MURGATROYD, S. (1982) Experiential learning and the person in pursuit of psychology. *Education Section Newsletter* (of the BPS), *6*(2), 112–118.

OC 193   MURRELL, H. (1980) Occupational psychology through
            autobiography. *Journal of Occupational Psychology, 53*(3),
            281–290.
CL 194   NEWSON, J., NEWSON, E. and GILHAM, B. (1983) Train-
            ing in clinical psychology: A reply. *Bulletin of The British
            Psychological Society, 36*, 77-79.
UG 195   NEWSTEAD, S.E. (1988) Skills teaching in undergraduate
            psychology degrees. In J. Radford (Ed) *The Future of the
            First Degree*. Group of Teachers of Psychology (of the BPS),
            Occasional Paper, No.4, 14–17.
NP 196   NEWSTEAD, S.E. (Ed) (1988) *Teaching Psychology to Nurses:
            A collection of reviews of popular texts*. Group of Teachers of
            Psychology (of the BPS), Occasional Paper, No.3.
PG 197   NEWSTEAD, S.E. (Ed) (1988) *The Future of The Psychology
            PhD*. Group of Teachers of Psychology (of the BPS),
            Occasional Paper, No.5.
CL 198   NEWTON, S. and MERIAN, S. (1986) Basic grade training
            and support: Existing schemes and issues. *Clinical Psychol-
            ogy Forum, 2*, 19–22.
NP 199   NICHOLS, K.A. (1987) Teaching nurses psychological care.
            In D. Müller (Ed) *Teaching Psychological Skills to Nurses*.
            Group of Teachers of Psychology (of the BPS), Occasional
            Paper, No.1, 5–14.
NP 200   NICHOLSON, P. (1981) Psychology teaching for social work
            students. *Bulletin of The British Psychological Society, 34*, 6–7.
CL 201   NITSUN, M. (1980) Problems of supervision in clinical
            psychology. *Bulletin of The British Psychological Society, 33*,
            344–346.
CL 202   NITSUN, M. and CAPE, J. (1981) The role of the education
            committee in the North East Thames region. *Division of
            Clinical Psychology Newsletter* (of the BPS), 32, 42–3.
ED 203   ONIONS, C. (1981) What did I get from my training? The
            thoughts of a recently trained educational psychologist.
            Division of Educational and Child Psychology Newsletter (of
            the BPS), 7, 17–23.
ED 204   OSBORNE, E.E. (1981) Post experience training. The
            Tavistock course. *Division of Educational and Child Psychol-
            ogy Newsletter* (of the BPS), 6, 17–18.
OC 205   PARKINSON, B. (1981) Occupational psychologists: Their
            training. (Report on a symposium on training held during
            the occupational psychology conference in York, 1981.)
            Occupational Psychology Newsletter (of the BPS), 4, 12–16.
OC 206   PARNY, J. (1980) Occupational psychology through auto-
            biography. *Journal of Occupational Psychology, 53*(2), 157–
            166.
GN 207   PEARSON, A. (1980) Summarised first-hand accounts of
            coping with crises and handicap. *Psychology Teaching, 8*(1),
            10–21.
GN 208   PEARSON, A. and ROSE, D. (1980) Visual aids in the

teaching of psychology. *Psychology Teaching*, 8(2), 40–42.

GN 209 PEARSON, L. and HOWARTH, I. (1982) Training professional psychologists. *Bulletin of The British Psychological Society*, 35, 375–376.

PG 210 PHILLIPS, E.M. (1988) Taught doctorates: The way forward. In S.E. Newstead (Ed) *The Future of The Psychology PhD*. Group of Teachers of Psychology (of the BPS), Occasional Paper, No. 5, 19–22.

PG 211 PHILLIPS, E.M. (1989) The PhD cohort as a recommended alternative to conventional doctoral programmes. *The Psychologist*, 2(6), 226–227.

OC 212 PHILLIPS, E.M. and COOPEY, J. (1988) Birkbeck College Department of Occupational Psychology. *The Occupational Psychologist*, 5, August, 7–8.

GN 213 PHILLIPS, K. (1987) Information and resource centre for teaching psychology involving animals. *Psychobiology Section Newsletter* (of the BPS), 8, 13–14.

CL 214 PHILLIPS, P. (1986) Intervening at the organisational level. *Clinical Psychology Forum*, 6, 37–38.

ED 215 PICKARD, E. (1982) Evaluation as an educational objective. *Education Section Newsletter* (of the BPS),6(2), 88–92.

NP 216 PRATT, J. (1980) Propositions or prescriptions: A reply to Müller. *Journal of Further and Higher Education*, 4(2), 52–55.

ED 217 PUMPHREY, P.D. (1981) The Manchester training conference 1980: Some observations and reflections. *Division of Educational and Child Psychology* (of the BPS), Occasional Paper, 5(2), 3–7.

PC 218 RADFORD, J. (1982) Psychology: A new subject for the school curriculum. In B. Dufour (Ed) *New Movements in the Social Sciences and Humanities*. London: Maurice Temple Smith.

UG 219 RADFORD, J. (1982) Re-thinking what we teach. *Education Section Newsletter* (of the BPS), 6(2), 105–111.

GN 220 RADFORD, J. (1984) Literary resources. In D. Rose and J. Radford (Eds) (1984) *Teaching Psychology: Information and resources*. Leicester: BPS Books.

UG 221 RADFORD, J. (1985) Is the customer right? Views and expectations of psychology. *Psychology Teaching*, April, 7–14.

PC 222 RADFORD, J. (1985) It's a great subject: Psychology at GCE A-level. *Psychology Teaching*, April, 87–91.

UG 223 RADFORD, J. (1987) An education in psychology. *Bulletin of The British Psychological Society*, 40, 282–289.

UG 224 RADFORD, J. (1988) The other half. In J. Radford (Ed) *The Future of the First Degree*. Group of Teachers of Psychology (of the BPS), Occasional Paper, No.4, 18–21.

PC 225 RADFORD, J. (1988) The 'teaching subject' face. In H.J. Wright and J. Radford (Eds) *The Several Faces of Educational Psychology*. Group of Teachers of Psychology (of the BPS), Occasional Paper, No.2, 8–12.

GN 226   RADFORD, J. and ROSE, D. (Eds) (1980) *The Teaching of Psychology: Method, content and context.* Chichester: Wiley.

GN 227   RADFORD, J. and ROSE, D. (1989) *A Liberal Science: Psychology education past, present and future.* Milton Keynes: Society for Research into Higher Education and Open University Press.

NP 228   RANDALL, P.E. (1982) In-service training courses for teachers and other professionals. *Division of Educational and Child Psychology* (of the BPS), Occasional Paper, 6(1), 59–64.

GN 229   RICHARDSON, J.T.E. (1980) Problems and models of small-group teaching. *Psychology Teaching, 8*(1), 22–25.

UG 230   RICHARDSON, J.T.E. (1989) Cognitive skills and psychology education. In J. Radford and D. Rose (Eds) *A Liberal Science: Psychology education past, present and future.* Milton Keynes: Society for Research into Higher Education and Open University Press.

GN 231   RIPPERE, V. (1980) Working with children: A short bibliography of personal accounts for use in psychology teaching. *Psychology Teaching, 8*(2), 35–59.

ED 232   ROBERTS, M. (1988) Comments from a field educational psychologist. In H.J. Wright and J. Radford (Eds) *The Several Faces of Educational Psychology.* Group of Teachers of Psychology (of the BPS), Occasional Paper, No.2, 51–2.

UG 233   ROBSON, C. (1980) Practical psychology and statistics. In J. Radford and D. Rose (Eds) *The Teaching of Psychology: Method, content and context.* Chichester: Wiley.

CL 234   ROPE, J. (1980) Psycho-Apex. A gaming simulation approach to teaching problems and strategies of management in a department of psychology. *Division of Clinical Psychology Newsletter* (of the BPS), 30, 26–27.

GN 235   ROSE, D. (1980) Alternative methods. In J. Radford and D. Rose (Eds) *The Teaching of Psychology: Method, content and context.* Chichester: Wiley.

GN 236   ROSE, D. (1984) The literature on the teaching of psychology. In D. Rose and J. Radford (Eds) *Teaching Psychology: Information and resources.* Leicester: BPS Books.

UG 237   ROSE, D. (1988) Psychology graduates and employment: An image problem. In J. Radford (Ed) *The Future of the First Degree.* Group of Teachers of Psychology (of the BPS), Occasional Paper, No.4, 22–27.

GN 238   ROSE, D. and RADFORD, J. (1981) The use of literature in teaching psychology. *Bulletin of The British Psychological Society, 34,* 453–455.

GN 239   ROSE, D. and RADFORD, J. (1984) *Teaching Psychology: Information and resources.* Leicester: BPS Books.

UG 240   ROSE, D. and RADFORD, J. (1986) The unemployment of psychology graduates. *Bulletin of The British Psychological Society, 39,* 451–456.

NP 241   ROSEN, N.A., GEOGIADES, N.J. and McDONALD, G. (1980) An empirical test of a leadership contingency model for teaching behavioural science concepts to managers. *Journal of Occupational Psychology, 53*(1), 1–10.

UG 242   RUSHTON, J.P. and MURRAY, H.G. (1985) On the assessment of teaching effectiveness in British universities. *Bulletin of The British Psychological Society, 38*, 361–365.

PG 243   SEMEONOFF, B. (1980) Degree class and postgraduate achievement. *Bulletin of The British Psychological Society, 33*, 277–278.

CL 244   SHARROCK, R. and HUNT, S. (1986) A national survey of trainees' satisfaction with clinical supervision. *Clinical Psychology Forum, 6*, 27–31.

PC 245   SHEA, P. (1980) The liberal studies context. In J. Radford and D. Rose (Eds) *The Teaching of Psychology: Method, content and context*. Chichester: Wiley.

UG 246   SHILLITO-CLARKE, C. (1987) Experimental interpersonal skills in the psychology curriculum. 'An ounce of practice is worth a pound of theory'. *Counselling Psychology Section Review* (of the BPS), 2(1), 6–10.

GN 247   SIMMONS, C. (1980) Teaching transactional analysis through role play and video-recording. *Psychology Teaching, 8*(2), 10–14.

GN 248   SIMMONS, C. (1982) The use of transactional analysis in the teaching of psychology (or games tutors play). *Education Section Newsletter* (of the BPS), 6(2), 93–96.

PC 249   SMITH, P.K. and CASBOLT, D. (1984) Sixth-formers and psychology: Fifteen years on. *Bulletin of The British Psychological Society, 37*, 334–337.

GN 250   SOLSO, R.L. (1980) Twenty-five years of recommended readings in psychology. *Psychology Teaching, 8*(1), 39–42.

NP 251   SPECTOR, K. (1987) Anxiety management groups: Disseminating psychological skills to other disciplines. *Clinical Psychology Forum, 12*, 34–37.

UG 252   STONE, V. (1980) University reform. *Bulletin of The British Psychological Society, 30*, 15–16.

ED 253   STRATFORD, R.J. (1985) Current issues in the training of educational psychologists. *Psychology Teaching*, April, 29–36.

NP 254   STRATTON, P. (1989) Can psychologists teach social workers about child abuse? In N. Hayes (Ed) *Teaching Psychology to Social Workers*. Group of Teachers of Psychology (of the BPS), Occasional Paper, No.7, 24–32.

ED 255   STRINGER, P. (1981) What did I get from my training? The thoughts of a recently trained educational psychologist. *Division of Educational and Child Psychology Newsletter* (of the BPS), 7, 13–16.

CL 256   STURMEY, P. (1986) The case for a skills-based approach. *Clinical Psychology Forum, 6*, 34–35.

UG 257   SUGARMAN, L. (1987) Interpersonal skills training in a psychology curriculum: Account of an experiment and a compromise. *Counselling Psychology Section Review* (of the BPS), 2(2), 8–13.

GN 258   SWAIN, R. (1984) The teaching of personal and social skills (PASS): A group-centred perspective. In D. Rose and J. Radford (Eds) *Teaching Psychology: Information and resources*. Leicester: BPS Books.

PC 259   TAYLOR, G. and WOODS, B. (1983) A different approach to A-level psychology. *Psychology Teaching*, August, 16–19.

NP 260   TAYLOR, I. (1984) Training non-psychologists in clinical psychology skills. *Division of Clinical Psychology Newsletter* (of the BPS), 46, 21–23.

NP 261   TAYLOR, M. (1985) Psychology in courses of professional training. *Psychology Teaching*, April, 77–82.

GN 262   THOMAS, J.B. (1983) Articles on teaching psychology 1970–82 published in other journals. *Psychology Teaching*, August, 2–6.

ED 263   THOMPSON, D. (1980) Evaluation of EP training: A view from the inside. *AEP: The Journal of the Association of Educational Psychologists*, 5(3), 53–55.

CL 264   THOMPSON, J. (1980) Clinical diploma: Whither now? *Bulletin of The British Psychological Society*, 33, 324–325.

CL 265   THOMPSON, J. (1981) Clinical diploma examinations: A revised format. *Bulletin of The British Psychological Society*, 34, 274–276.

CL 266   THOMPSON, J. (1981) Clinical diploma results 1978–1980. *Bulletin of The British Psychological Society*, 34, 462–464.

NP 267   TOMLINSON, A. (1985) The use of experiential methods in teaching interpersonal skills to nurses. In C. Kagan (Ed) *Interpersonal Skills in Nursing: Research and applications*. London: Croom Helm.

NP 268   TOMLINSON, P. (1988) Some post-chartering thoughts on psychology provision in teacher education. *Education Section Newsletter* (of the BPS), 12(2), 2–13.

GN 269   TRIGGS, P. (1984) Sources of published information. In D. Rose and J. Radford (Eds) *Teaching Psychology: Information and resources*. Leicester: BPS Books.

UG 270   TURNER, J. (1980) Developmental psychology. In J. Radford and D. Rose (Eds) (1980) *The Teaching of Psychology: Method, content and context*. Chichester: Wiley.

ED 271   TWEEDLE, D. (1982) In-service training for educational psychologists. *AEP: The Journal of the Association of Educational Psychologists*, 5(8), 11–15.

PG 272   USSER, J.M. (1986) Postgraduate training: An inside perspective. *Social Psychology Section Newsletter* (of the BPS), 15, 34–37.

NP 273   VELLEMAN, R. (1983) Teaching clinical psychology to student occupational therapists and student nurses.

Psychology Teaching, August, 13–16.

PG   274   VINCK, J. (1988) Training in health psychology in Europe. *Health Psychology Section Newsletter* (of the BPS), *1*, 18–23.

ED   275   WARD, J. (1980) Some comments on issues of role, function and training. *Division of Educational and Child Psychology* (of the BPS), Occasional Paper 4(3), 23–31.

NP   276   WATTLEY, L.A. (1987) Teaching investigative skills. In D. Müller (Ed) *Teaching Psychological Skills to Nurses*. Group of Teachers of Psychology (of the BPS), Occasional Paper No.1, 15–18.

CL   277   WATTS, F.N. (1980) Post-qualification training. *Division of Clinical Psychology Newsletter* (of the BPS), *27*, 10–12.

CL   278   WATTS, F.N. (1980) Training for clinical psychologists working with children. (A statement on behalf of the Committee on Training in Clinical Psychology.) *Division of Clinical Psychology Newsletter* (of the BPS), *29*, 10–12.

CL   279   WATTS, F.N. (1983) Training in clinical psychology: A reply to Newson *et al. Bulletin of The British Psychological Society, 36,* 80.

UG   280   WATTS, F. (Ed) (1990) *The Undergraduate Curriculum*. Group of Teachers of Psychology (of the BPS), Occasional Paper, No.9.

CL   281   WEEKS, J. (1985) Post-qualification training for basic grade clinical psychologists. *Division of Clinical Psychology Newsletter* (of the BPS), *47*, 23–27.

NP   282   WEINMAN, J. (1987) Teaching psychology to non-psychologists: Problems and possibilities. *Clinical Psychology Forum, 12,* 4–6.

NP   283   WEINMAN, J. (1988) Teaching psychology to medical students: Survey of current approaches in the UK. *Health Psychology Section Newsletter* (of the BPS), 1, July, 24–27.

NP   284   WEINMAN, J. and MEDLIK, L. (1985) Sharing psychological skills in the general practice setting. *British Journal of Medical Psychology, 58,* 223–230.

PG   285   WEINMAN, J., EDELMAN, R., MARKS, D. and WATTS, M. (1989) Training in health psychology: An overview of MSc courses in the UK. *Health Psychology Section Newsletter* (of the BPS), *3*, June.

OC   286   WEST, M. (1988) Innovations in the teaching of occupational psychology at Sheffield and the implications of chartering. *The Occupational Psychologist*, 5, August, 17–19.

GN   287   WETHERELL, M., POTTER, J. and STRINGER, P. (1983) Psychology, literature and texts. *Bulletin of The British Psychological Society, 36,* 377–379.

GN   288   WHETTON C. (1984) Psychological tests in the teaching of psychology. In D. Rose and J. Radford (Eds) *Teaching Psychology: Information and resources*. Leicester: BPS Books.

CL   289   WHITEHEAD, T. (1986) National training needs in clinical psychology. *Clinical Psychology Forum, 6,* 7–11.

CL 290 WHITLOW, D. and THOMAS, C. (1984) Postgraduate training and recruitment in mental handicap. *Division of Clinical Psychology Newsletter* (of the BPS), *43*, 38–40.

CL 291 WILLIAMS, M.J. (1981) Postgraduate dissertations in clinical psychology, 1977–1979. *Bulletin of The British Psychological Society, 34*, 176–177.

CL 292 WILLIAMS, R. and RIPPERE, V. (1980) Problems in clinical psychology teaching. 1: conceptualizing clinical skills. *Psychology Teaching, 8*(2), 15–23.

GN 293 WOOLFE, R. and MURGATROYD, S. (1980) On teaching humanistic psychology. *Self and Society, 8*(8), 264–271.

PG 294 WORKING PARTY OF THE COUNSELLING PSYCHOLOGY SECTION OF THE BPS (1986) Training in counselling psychology. *Counselling Psychology Section Review* (of the BPS), *1*(2), 5–16.

UG 295 WRIGHT, P. (Ed) (1989) *Practical Classes in Psychology*. Group of Teachers of Psychology (of the BPS), Occasional Paper, No.8.

UG 296 WRIGHT, P.L. and TAYLOR, D.S.(1981) Vignette analysis as an aid to psychology teaching. *Bulletin of The British Psychological Society, 34*, 68–70.

PG 297 VAN DEURZEN-SMITH, E. (1988) Integration of students' personal concerns and experiences in the postgraduate psychology curriculum. *Group of Teachers of Psychology Newsletter* (of the BPS), No.4, April, 10–15.

References

RADFORD, J. and ROSE, D. (Eds) (1980) *The Teaching of Psychology: Method, content and context*. Chichester: Wiley.

RADFORD, J. and ROSE, D. (Eds) (1989) *A Liberal Science: Psychology education past, present and future*. Milton Keynes: Society for Research into Higher Education and Open University Press.

ROSE, D. (1984) The literature on the teaching of psychology. In D. Rose and J. Radford (Eds) *Teaching Psychology: Information and resources*. Leicester: BPS Books.

ROSE, D. and RADFORD, J. (Eds) (1984) *Teaching Psychology: Information and resources*. Leicester: BPS Books.

Subject Index

PSYCHOLOGY BOOKS AND JOURNALS

❏ *general profiles of publishers* ● *journals and their readerships* ●
publishers and their readerships ● *publishers' addresses*

The aim of this chapter is simply stated: to help you, the
reader, to identify and locate all the useful books and
journals in your present sphere of psychological interest –
and for any future searches. But a number of decisions were
involved: What should it cover? Whom to include? How to
present the information? A short account of the methods
used and of the decisions underlying this database should
help you to make best use of the material.

The Scope of the
Database

Mindful that the readership of this book includes psychologists and non-psychologists, academics and practitioners,
and teachers of psychology from school to university level,
we cast our net wide and assessed not only psychology lists
but also medical, nursing, paramedical, social work, management and many others. The twin criteria used were
'psychological relevance' and 'usefulness'. We included
therefore only English-language publishers in the UK, or
with a UK base. Most of the latter are American originating
most of their titles in the States; we have tried to indicate
where this is the case. Other overseas publishers, who
quoted overseas addresses and non-sterling prices only,
were excluded. For journals, an exception was made for the
American Psychological Association, since many of their
journals are too important to omit.

Collecting the
Information

The information was collected by means of questionnaires
and requests for catalogues sent out to all 'significant'

psychology publishers during the first half of 1989. ('Significance' was judged by the quality of the list rather than size, and for this reason we included a number of association and society publishers.) Some publishers returned both; others responded with a catalogue only or a questionnaire only. Some questionnaires gave full answers; others the briefest details. Where we had only the latest catalogue (perhaps covering only the last three months) some degree of subjectivity was involved in characterizing the publisher's activities. Where we had only the questionnaire, some degree of *trust* (and sometimes discretion) was necessary in adapting the information supplied. Within these constraints, we aimed to make the database as comprehensive as possible.

How to Use the Lists

For ease of use and to cater for different needs, the information is presented in three separate lists. List 1 gives all the publishers in alphabetical order with a description of their scope and size. List 2 gives an alphabetical listing of journals by title and indicates their readership categories. List 3 takes the analysis one stage further with a tabular listing of the same publishers divided into six readership categories:

Reference – this includes dictionaries, encyclopaedias and the like and may be of interest to any reader;

Schools – this refers to textbooks and other materials used in the teaching of psychology in schools; also careers material;

Higher education – tertiary level material; largely textbooks and monographs in psychology;

Applied psychologists and other professionals – this includes all the practitioner areas both in psychology, such as clinical, educational etc., and other professions such as social workers, nurses, doctors, teachers and managers;

Trade – these are non-specialist books for the general public usually sold in high street bookshops;

Journals – largely learned and professional journals, but also a few significant weeklies; their readership is indicated in List 2.

There are different ways of approaching these lists, but perhaps the easiest is to turn straight to List 3 and use the column headings to identify your area of interest. Running your finger down the column will give you the names of relevant publishers and the addresses to write to for a catalogue are given at the end of the chapter. (Don't forget to state what subject area(s) you are interested in.)

A word about inspection copies (IC) and desk copies (DC)	Many publishers offer an inspection copy system on selected titles and, where this is known, it is indicated in List 1. But, judging from our experience, the rationale behind this 'generosity' of publishers is not well understood and occasionally gives rise to misunderstandings. It is, of course, part of a marketing strategy. A free copy of a particular title (usually a textbook) is offered to tutors in the hope that they will recommend it to their students for purchase. The publisher recoups the cost of the free one by the sale of 10 or 15. A comments form usually accompanies the inspection copy book stating that it should be paid for or returned if it is not recommended. Monographs more suitable for library use are not usually available as part of an inspection copy system.

The system of giving away desk copies operates in much the same way, the main difference being that the recipient does not have to recommend the book as a condition of keeping it. The underlying reasoning is the same though. This system is more popular in the States where the potential market for textbooks is ten times larger, though it is used occasionally in the UK.

You will not be surprised to learn that this book is not on IC or DC; none the less, I hope you find it useful.

LIST 1:
GENERAL
PROFILES OF
PUBLISHERS

A.B. Academic	Two journals for academics and professionals, in gifted education and adolescence.
Aberdeen University Press	A subsidiary of Pergamon Press with a small list of mainly general social psychology and mental health titles.
Academic Press	An imprint of Harcourt Brace Jovanovich (q.v.).
Addison-Wesley	A major publisher of books in psychology, originated both in the UK and the USA. Specialisms include computing and AI, cognition, linguistics, organizational and management psychology. The list caters for most readerships except schools. [IC, DC]
Airlift Book Company	Distributor for many small UK and (especially) North American publishers, notably Inner City Books (Canada), who specialize in Jungian psychology. Also a range of general-interest psychology titles, some among a substantial women's list.
Allyn & Bacon	See Harvester-Wheatsheaf.

American Psychological Assn	Publisher of 19 major journals and two databases.
Ann Arbor	Publisher and distributor of educational tests and remedial materials from the USA. [IC]
Anna Freud Centre	Publishes the *Bulletin of the Anna Freud Centre.*
Aquarian Press	A Thorsons imprint. Popular 'humanistic and transpersonal' psychology is published under the Crucible sub-imprint.
Edward Arnold	Now a division of Hodder & Stoughton. List includes books in introductory and general psychology and in social and developmental psychology, mainly for a readership of academics and undergraduate students but with some overlap into A-level studies. [IC]
Artesian Books	Publisher of the *British Journal of Psychotherapy.*
Assn for Behavioural Approaches with Children	Publisher of the journal *Behavioural Approaches with Children.*
Assn of Child Psychotherapists	Publisher of the *Journal of Child Psychotherapy.*
Assn of Educational Psychologists	Publisher (through Longman) of the journal *Educational Psychology in Practice.*
Assn of Therapeutic Communities	Publisher of the *International Journal of Therapeutic Communities.*
Avenue	Publisher of the *International Journal of Social Psychiatry.*
Baillière Tindall	An imprint of Harcourt Brace Jovanovich (q.v.).
BIMH Publications	A small and specialist list in the field of mental handicap mainly for practitioners. Also publish 3 journals: *Mental Handicap, Mental Handicap Bulletin* and *Mental Handicap Research* .
Basil Blackwell	Major publisher of psychology (50 new titles in 1988): books in most fields (except clinical psychology and psychiatry, health, criminology, and organizational/management psychology), mainly for academics, practitioners and professionals. Some reference publishing in general and educational psychology, and some trade titles in certain fields. [IC, DC] Blackwell also publish a number of psychology and

psychology-related journals, including *Mind and Language* and the *Journal of Research in Reading* (the latter aimed at teachers).

Blackwell Scientific	A list of some 45 books in the field of clinical psychology and psychiatry (with a degree of specialism in child psychiatry), addressed mainly to a readership of practitioners. [IC, DC]
Boyd & Fraser	See Chapman & Hall.
BPS Books	BPS is the book-publishing arm of The British Psychological Society (q.v.). They publish a wide-ranging list including textbooks, monographs and self-help; and cater for many different markets including social workers, managers, medics and paramedics, schools and careers literature as well as for academic and applied psychologists.
British Assn for Counselling	A range of books (especially reference) and other materials for counsellors, including trainees and trainers. Publisher of *Counselling*, the journal of the BAC.
British Assn of Psychotherapists	Publisher of the *Journal of the British Association of Psychotherapists*.
British Psychological Society	Publisher of seven major research journals, including the *British Journal of Psychology*. Also *Guidance & Assessment Review* and *The Psychologist* (the monthly bulletin of the Society), plus various newsletters from the sections and divisions of the Society. See also BPS Books.
British Society for Projective Psychology	Publisher of the *British Journal of Projective Psychology*.
Brooks/Cole	See Chapman & Hall.
W.C. Brown	US publisher of college-level psychology textbooks and ancillary materials. About 20 titles covering most fields, especially introductory and developmental psychology.
Butterworth Scientific	The Butterworth medical catalogue includes a substantial list in psychiatry and clinical psychology for practitioners. Most titles originate in the UK, many under the John Wright imprint. [IC, DC]

Cambridge University Press	One of the major UK publishers of psychology (50 new titles in 1988, and a large stock list). Books in all areas of psychology and at all levels, with many titles for practitioners and professionals, but mainly for a readership of high-level research psychologists.
	    Co-publisher of some titles with Maison des Sciences de l'Homme (Paris), and distributor for the American Psychiatric Press. [IC, DC]
	    CUP psychology journals (six in all) include *Behavioural and Brain Sciences* and *Psychology of Women Quarterly*.

Carfax	Journals publisher, with seven psychology-related titles (mainly for practitioners), including the *British Journal of Addiction* and the newly established interdisciplinary journal *AIDS Care*.
Cassell	A modest but expanding psychology list: titles in most areas but with a particular specialism in educational psychology. Aimed largely at undergraduates (especially those doing combined social science) and practitioners in various applied fields. [IC, DC]
Chambers	Best known for reference books, Chambers do publish some psychology in their 'Coping' series: essentially medical self-help books. [IC, DC]
Paul Chapman	A substantial education and educational psychology list, primarily for a readership of teachers and student teachers. [IC]
Chapman & Hall	A substantial list of student (mainly undergraduate) texts in psychology and counselling, most originating in the USA (from Boyd & Fraser, Brooks/Cole, Wadsworth, and Van Nostrand Reinhold Intl, among others). Also publish in clinical and other applied fields, with separate catalogues in health psychology, disability and handicap, therapy, nursing, and ageing and geriatrics. Most titles in these fields are originated in the UK. [IC: some titles]
Chartwell-Bratt	Apart from management books (some of interest to psychologists), C-B also have an extensive IT list which includes titles in human–computer interaction. [IC]
Children's Society	A range of books and other materials for child-care professionals, including titles of interest to clinical and educational psychologists. The Children's Society is a voluntary society of the Church of England and the Church in Wales.
Churchill Livingstone	See Longman.
Cole & Whurr	Publisher of the *British Journal of Experimental and Clinical Hypnosis*.
Collier Macmillan	The imprint for Macmillan (q.v.) titles imported from Macmillan Publishing Inc. of New York.
Columbia University Press	See University Presses of California, Columbia & Princeton.
Community Psychiatric Nurses Assn	Publisher of the *Community Psychiatric Nursing Journal*.
Constable	A small psychology list dominated by titles in counselling and therapy (particularly the works of Carl Rogers).

Croom Helm	Defunct. Now owned and distributed by Routledge (q.v.).
Current Science	Publisher of *Current Opinion in Psychiatry*.
Darton Longman & Todd	Religious publisher, with some titles in psychology and Christianity: counselling, clinical theology, pastoral care.
J. M. Dent	An imprint of Weidenfeld & Nicholson (q.v.). Small but various psychology/sociology list (not easy to characterize here). [DC]
Gerald Duckworth	Small but eclectic list in psychology and psychiatry, with a bias towards the latter. Includes books for researchers and practitioners. [IC]
Eating Disorders Assn	Publisher of the *British Review of Bulimia and Anorexia Nervosa*.
Element Books	Publisher and distributor of books on philosophy and religion, among other cognate subjects, with a certain amount of popular psychology mainly originated in the USA with a definite bias towards Jungian analysis.
Elsevier	Publishes in the UK under the North-Holland imprint. A major academic psychology publisher (25 new titles in 1988) with a bias towards cognitive psychology, but most fields are covered in the extensive 'Advances in Psychology' series. [IC] Also publisher of some 12 psychology or psychology-related journals, including *Acta Psychologica, Artificial Intelligence* and the *International Journal of Psychology*. [IC]
Lawrence Erlbaum Associates	One of the major UK publishers of books in psychology in all fields and (excepting school texts and general trade) at all levels. (Ninety new psychology titles published in 1988.) Sister company of LEA Inc. (USA), but over 50 per cent are UK-originated titles. Psychoanalysis is published under the Analytic Press imprint (a subsidiary of LEA Inc.). [IC, DC] LEA Ltd also publish nine psychology journals (including the *Quarterly Journal of Experimental Psychology*) and handle a further 16 published by LEA Inc.
Faber & Faber	No psychology list as such, but some miscellaneous psychological titles among their general non-fiction, plus some psychology-related nursing textbooks.
Falmer Press	Part of Taylor & Francis group. Specialist publisher of education books for teachers and student teachers (also academic monographs for HE), with a substantial list in educational psychology. [IC]
Family Welfare Assn	Small publisher of family-related titles of various kinds, including some psychology; of particular interest to social workers.

Fontana	Some general psychology paperbacks mainly in the fields of child development and management, plus some self-help.
Free Association Books	An expanding independent psychology publisher (15 new titles in 1988), specializing in psychoanalysis and psychotherapy, but also titles in social and developmental psychology. Books for all readerships except schools. [IC: some titles] Publisher of the journal *Free Associations* .
W.H. Freeman	The book-publishing arm of *Scientific American*, whose imprints include Scientific American Library and Computer Science Press. Also UK distributor of books published in the USA by Sinauer Associates Inc. The books in their life and behavioural sciences catalogue are mainly aimed at undergraduates, and include titles in social and developmental psychology, learning and cognition, statistics, neuroscience, and general psychology. [IC: some titles]
David Fulton	Modest but expanding psychology list, specializing particularly in educational psychology (principally for a readership of teachers and student teachers). Also some psychiatry. [IC; DC: some titles]
Gaskell	Imprint of the Royal College of Psychiatrists (q.v.).
Gateway Books	Small publisher whose list includes some popular psychology, mainly self-help.
Harcourt Brace Jovanovich	The American parent company includes the following imprints: Baillière Tindall; W.B. Saunders; Holt, Rinehart & Winston; Grune & Stratton; and Academic Press. Publishers of big general introductory and child development texts; also some personality, physiological psychology and statistics. A few British authors. Also, high level education books and conference proceedings under Academic Press imprint.
Harper & Row	US publisher whose psychology list consists mainly of textbooks (including introductory psychology) for undergraduates and student practitioners/professionals, though some titles address a graduate readership. [IC: some titles]
Harvester-Wheatsheaf	Catalogues also include titles from other publishers in the Simon & Schuster group (Allyn & Bacon, Prentice Hall, Woodhead Faulkner). Titles in general psychology, social and developmental psychology (notably the 'Developing Body and Mind' series), and cognitive science. The sociology catalogue includes titles of interest (social work and social welfare, family and marriage, criminology), as does the economics catalogue (economic psychology and behavioural economics). Most readerships catered for, but no school texts. [IC]

Harwood Academic	An imprint of Gordon & Breach Science Publishers. Titles in health psychology and behavioural medicine; also educational psychology and (in future) criminological and legal psychology. Readership mainly practitioners and professionals. [IC; DC: some titles] Harwood publish three psychology journals, including *Anxiety Research* and *Psychology and Health*.
Haverstock	Publisher of the *Journal of the Balint Society*, plus the occasional book in Balint-inspired medicine.
Hobsons	Some introductory and general psychology books for schools [IC: some titles]. Also the *British Journal of Guidance and Counselling*.
Hodder & Stoughton	Textbooks in introductory and general, educational, social and developmental psychology, maths and statistics/computing and AI: mainly for schools, but some overlap with FE and undergraduate readership and some titles for trainee professionals. [IC] See also Edward Arnold.
Hutchinson	Recently acquired by Unwin Hyman (q.v.).
IPC	Publisher of *New Scientist*.
JAI	US publisher specializing in research annuals, with particular emphasis on developmental and clinical psychology. Also three psychology journals.
Johns Hopkins University Press	US academic publisher with a list covering neuropsychology, cognition, and history and philosophy of psychology, and specializing particularly in psychoanalysis (including titles for practitioners). [IC, DC: some titles]
Jossey-Bass	Catalogue includes psychology-related titles in management and education, as well as a social and behavioural sciences list. Titles in the latter category are principally for practitioners.
H. Karnac	Specialist publisher of books in psychoanalysis, psychotherapy and analytical psychology, including titles co-published with the British Institute of Psychoanalysis and the Society of Analytical Psychology. Also distributor for various UK and overseas publishers in these fields.
Jessica Kingsley	Emphasis on psychotherapy but also a significant social work list including titles of interest to psychologists. [IC: some titles]
Kluwer	A small list in this field (some eight titles), predominantly textbooks in psychiatry and undergraduate psychology. [IC, DC: some titles]
Lifeskills	A selection of manuals, tapes and other training materials for personal and career development.

Longman	Most psychological titles published within the wide-ranging 'Longman Applied Psychology' series of paperbacks, but also some general psychology and (through the Churchill Livingstone imprint) specialized titles in clinical psychology and psychiatry. [IC: some titles]
McGraw-Hill	A substantial textbook list mainly in introductory and child development fields; some clinical psychology. Most books originated in the USA.
Macmillan	No separate psychology catalogue, but many psychology-related titles among other lists. (Ask for their academic catalogues in nursing, education, social work and social policy, and sociology.) Particular strengths in social and educational psychology, and a general bias towards applied fields. Co-publishers (with the BPS) of the 'Psychology for Professional Groups' series.
Manchester University Press	A few titles in psychology and psychiatry, with clear specialism in clinical fields. Most titles aimed at practitioners & professionals in the caring services, but some self-help books. [IC: some titles]
MCB University Press	The initials stand for Management Consultants Bradford. Publisher of more than 60 serials for professionals, including the *Journal of Managerial Psychology*.
Methuen	Defunct. Academic list now owned and distributed by Routledge (q.v.).
MIND	Ten new titles per year in the field of mental health and cognate areas, including criminological and legal psychology. Also publisher of the bi-monthly journal *Openmind*.
MIT Press	US academic publisher (MIT stands for Massachussetts Institute of Technology) with specialisms in cognitive psychology, neuroscience, AI and philosophy of mind. Eight new psychology titles in 1988. [IC: some titles] Two recently established journals: *Neural Computation* and the *Journal of Cognitive Neuroscience*.
Multilingual Matters	Specialist publisher of social psychology and psycholinguistics. Five new titles in 1988. Publisher of the *Journal of Language and Social Psychology*.
National Extension College	Publisher of open-learning materials for schools and FE colleges as well as correspondence students and adult learners, including a GCSE psychology package; some titles on health and social issues may also be of interest. [IC: some titles]
Thomas Nelson	Educational publisher whose sociology catalogue includes one introductory psychology textbook. [IC: some titles]

New York Academy of Sciences	A small academic list (about 20 titles), with a leaning towards neuropsychology and physiological psychology.
New York University Press	See University Presses of California, Columbia & Princeton.
NFER-Nelson	Leading UK publisher and supplier of testing and assessment materials for the caring professions, not least psychologists (clinical, occupational, educational) and counsellors. Also interdisciplinary training materials for practitioners and professionals. Many NFER-Nelson materials originate in the USA.
North-Holland	The European imprint of Elsevier Science Publishers (q.v.).
Norton	US-based publisher with a clear bias towards psychoanalysis and psychotherapy. Some undergraduate texts. Norton Professional Books covers titles for psychiatrists, counsellors and therapists. [IC: some titles]
Oneworld	Small publisher of general-reader psychology, particularly therapy/psychoanalysis. Distributed by Element Books (q.v.).
Open Books	Small psychology list mainly in the education field.
Open University Press	A substantial psychology list (11 new titles in 1988), principally for students and teachers in higher education: specialisms in social and development psychology and psychotherapy and counselling, but also a number of general/introductory texts. [IC, DC: some titles]
Oxford University Press	Major international publisher in the life sciences, with a 75-page psychology catalogue (a dozen new titles in 1988). Specialisms in experimental psychology, clinical psychology and psychotherapy, but with titles in most fields. Most titles for academic/undergraduate or practitioner/professional readership. [IC: some titles] See also OUP's catalogues in medicine, neurosciences, psychiatry, and philosophy. OUP also publishes various psychology-related journals, including the *Journal of Psychopharmacology* and *Brain*.
Pan Books	A dozen or so popular psychology titles, mainly general, health, and self-help; also some titles of psychological interest among the business-management list. Pan's parent company is Macmillan. [IC: some titles]
Penguin	A large and expanding psychology list, with academic titles (especially undergraduate texts) in introductory; social and developmental; experimental and cognitive psychology; maths and stats/computing and AI; psychoanalysis (inc. the Pelican Freud Library); organizational and management psychology; and history and philosophy of psychology.

	Also reference works and titles for the general reader in many of these fields. [IC, DC: some titles]
Pergamon	Major international psychology publisher (35 new titles in 1988), principally for undergraduate and graduate students, and practitioners. Titles in most fields, but especially strong in social and educational psychology, as well as in therapy and other branches of clinical practice. Pergamon's main psychology list is published from New York; the social psychology list is published from the UK office. [IC: some titles] Pergamon also publishes some 21 psychology journals, covering a wide range of research and applied fields.
Frances Pinter	Pinter's humanities catalogue includes the first titles in a new series entitled 'Communication in Artificial Intelligence'. Some of the linguistics titles may also be of interest. [DC: some titles]
Pion	Publisher of the journal *Perception*.
Plenum	US-based publisher of high-level monographs and conference proceedings for researchers and practitioners/professionals. Titles in a range of fields, but with a general bias towards behavioural psychology. Strong specialism in social and developmental psychology, also clinical psychology and neuroscience. The vast majority of Plenum's books originate in the USA. [IC, DC: some titles] Plenum publishes some 16 high-level psychology journals for researchers and practitioners.
Positive Products	Publisher of the journal *Behavioural Approaches with Children*.
Prentice-Hall	See Harvester-Wheatsheaf.
The Psychological Corporation	World's largest publisher of psychological tests for use in: clinical, educational and occupational practice; speech and language pathology; business, industry and government. American company, but since 1987 some of these materials have been designed and produced in the UK.
Psychology News	Publishes the general-interest quarterly journal *Psychology News*.
Routledge	A major UK psychology publisher (more than 40 new books in 1988), with titles in most fields, principally for a readership of undergraduates, academics and practitioners/professionals. Particularly strong in psychoanalysis, psychotherapy and analytical psychology. Routledge co-publishes and distributes a number of titles from BPS Books (q.v.). [IC: some titles] Routledge also publishes the two journals of the Institute of Psycho-Analysis, London.

Routledge & Kegan Paul	Defunct. See Routledge.
Royal College of Psychiatrists	Publishes books under the Gaskell imprint. All publications are in psychiatry, for a practitioner/professional readership. Five new books in 1988. Two journals including the *British Journal of Psychiatry*.
Royal Society	*The Proceedings of the Royal Society of London*, Series B, is a general biological research journal with occasional papers on animal psychology and behaviour. Likewise the *Philosophical Transactions*, Series B, which also occasionally publishes psychology-related conference reports.
Sage	Basically a US-based social sciences publisher. Books mainly for practitioners (and students) in various applied fields. Apart from psychology *per se*, the catalogue features psychology-related titles under other categories such as: child abuse, counselling and psychotherapy, criminology, education, family studies, gerontology, social work. UK-originated series include 'Gender and Psychology' and 'Counselling in Action'.
	Major publisher of social science journals. Apart from their 20 psychology titles, there are many psychology-related journals under other heads (as above).
SEFA Publications	In association with the British Society for the Study of Mental Subnormality, publisher of the *British Journal of Mental Subnormality*.
Self & Society	Apart from *Self & Society: European Journal of Humanistic Psychology* (organ of the Association for Humanistic Psychology in Britain), S&S also publishes a few books in related fields, principally for practitioners.
Sheldon	An imprint of the Society for Promoting Christian Knowledge. Mainly self-help books, and one general psychology textbook for A-level/undergraduates.
Simon & Schuster	See Harvester-Wheatsheaf.
Souvenir	Some 20 miscellaneous psychology titles, in various fields and at various levels. Most published under the Condor imprint.
Springer	Berlin-based international academic publisher with a 100-page classified psychology catalogue (including psychology-related titles from other disciplines). Titles in virtually every field.
	Also five English-language research journals in psychology and psychiatry, including *Psychological Research*; many psychology-related journals in other disciplines.

Tavistock	Defunct. Now owned and distributed by Routledge (q.v.).
Taylor & Francis	Major international publisher (with its New York sister company Hemisphere) in the sciences and social sciences with small psychology list mainly in neuropsychology and a few other psychology-related titles. Most books originate in the USA. [IC: some titles] Six psychology journals, plus psychology-related journals in computer science/AI, education, ergonomics/human factors, and speech/language and rehabilitation.
University Presses of California, Columbia & Princeton	A few general and various titles from Princeton, and a sizeable psychology list (about 100 titles) from Columbia (New York University Press). Columbia publishes academic and practitioner titles in clinical psychology, psychoanalysis/ therapy & Freudian analytic theory, ageing and developmental psychology, cognitive and legal psychology.
Unwin Hyman	Most psychology titles originate from the erstwhile Hutchinson list (recently acquired by Unwin Hyman), including 'Handbooks for the Caring Professions', and a clinical psychology series for practitioners and professionals. [IC: some titles]
Van Nostrand Reinhold	See Chapman & Hall.
Virago	Some psychology titles among a general non-fiction list, especially psychoanalysis; mainly for the general reader, but of possible interest to practitioners & professionals. [IC: some titles]
Wadsworth	See Chapman & Hall.
George Weidenfeld & Nicolson	A dozen or so miscellaneous psychology titles, including some general/introductory textbooks for schools. (See also Dent.) [DC: some titles]
John Wiley	A subsidiary of John Wiley & Sons Inc., New York. Major international publisher in psychology (55 new titles in 1988), especially for practitioners and professionals but also many academic and reference titles. Books in many fields, but in particular clinical. Co-publishers with BPS Books (q.v.) and Guilford Press, NY. Distributors for Ellis Horwood ('Cognitive Science' series). [IC: some titles] Also 12 psychology journals, including *Applied Cognitive Psychology* and the *European Journal of Personality*.
Williams & Wilkins	US medical publisher. A range of titles (some 16) in clinical psychiatry, textbooks as well as books for practitioners. UK distributors for Igaku-Shoin and C.V. Mosby (also US medical & health sciences publishers). Nursing texts are one of Mosby's specialisms. W&W also publish five psychiatric journals for practitioners.

Winslow	Some psychology books among a range of multi-media therapy/rehabilitation materials for various professional groups, including nurses, occupational therapists, geriatricians and social workers; also a range of special-needs materials for child-care professionals. [IC: some titles]
Women's Press	Titles in educational, health, and general psychology; also in psychotherapy. Some of interest to practitioners and professionals, and some to teachers of women's studies, but mostly addressed to general readers. [IC: some titles]
John Wright	See Butterworth Scientific.
Yale University Press	US publisher with some psychology (15 new titles in 1988), with clear specialisms in psychiatry, psychoanalysis and child development. Readership: primarily academics, psychoanalysts and other practitioners. [IC, DC: some titles]

LIST 2: *JOURNALS* *AND THEIR* *READERSHIPS*	Journals are listed in alphabetical order in the righthand column, where the publisher of each title is also given. The lefthand column gives the readership of each journal, using the category 'R' to indicate research; 'AP' to indicate applied psychologists, such as clinical or educational psychologists; and 'OP' to indicate other interested professionals, such as social workers, nurses, doctors, teachers and managers.

R	*Acta Psychologica* (Elsevier)
AP – OP	*Addictive Behaviors* (Pergamon)
R	*Advances in Behavior Research and Therapy* (Pergamon)
R – AP – OP	*AIDS Care: Psychological and Socio-Medical Aspects of AIDS/HIV* (Carfax)
AP – OP	*American Psychologist* (American Psychological Assn)
monthly newsletter of the APA	*APA Monitor* (American Psychological Assn)
R	*Aphasiology* (Taylor & Francis)
R – AP –OP	*Applied Cognitive Psychology* (John Wiley)
R – AP	*Applied Psycholinguistics* (Cambridge University Press)
R – AP – OP	*Applied Psychology: An International Review* (Lawrence Erlbaum Associates)
R	*Archives of Clinical Neuropsychology* (Pergamon)
R	*Artificial Intelligence* (Elsevier)
AP – OP	*The Arts in Psychotherapy* (Pergamon)

R – AP	*Behavior Modification* (Sage)
R – AP – OP	*Behavioral Assessment* (Pergamon)
R	*Behavioral Ecology and Sociobiology* (Springer)
R	*Behavioral Neuroscience* (American Psychological Assn)
AP – OP	*Behavioral Residential Treatment* (John Wiley)
AP – OP	*Behavioral Sciences and the Law* (John Wiley)
R	*Behaviour and Information Technology* (Taylor & Francis)
R	*Behavior Research and Therapy* (Pergamon)
R – AP	*Behavioural and Brain Sciences* (Cambridge University Press)
AP	*Behavioural Approaches with Children* (Assn for Behavioural Approaches with Children)
R	*Behavioural Brain Research* (Elsevier)
AP – OP	*Behavioural Change* (Pergamon Press)
R	*Behavioural Processes* (Elsevier)
R – AP	*Biofeedback and Self Regulation* (Plenum)
R	*Biological Psychology* (Elsevier)
R	*Brain Injury* (Taylor & Francis)
R – AP – OP	*British Journal of Addiction* (Carfax)
R – AP – OP	*British Journal of Clinical Psychology* (British Psychological Society)
R – AP – OP	*British Journal of Developmental Psychology* (British Psychological Society)
R	*British Journal of Experimental and Clinical Hypnosis* (Cole & Whurr)
AP	*British Journal of Guidance and Counselling* (Hobsons)
R	*British Journal of Mathematical and Statistical Psychology* (British Psychological Society)
R – AP – OP	*British Journal of Medical Psychology* (British Psychological Society)
AP	*British Journal of Mental Subnormality* (SEFA, for the British Society for the Study of Mental Subnormality)
R – AP	*British Journal of Projective Psychology* (British Society of Projective Psychology)
R – AP	*British Journal of Psychiatry* (Royal College of Psychiatrists)
R – AP – OP	*British Journal of Psychology* (British Psychological Society)

AP–OP	*British Journal of Psychotherapy* (Artesian Books)
R–AP–OP	*British Journal of Social Psychology* (British Psychological Society)
R–AP–OP	*British Review of Bulimia and Anorexia Nervosa* (Eating Disorders Assn)
R–AP–OP	*Bulletin of the Anna Freud Centre* (Anna Freud Centre)
AP — OP	*Changes: Journal of the Psychology and Psychotherapy Association* (Lawrence Erlbaum Associates)
AP	*Clinical Linguistics and Phonetics* (Taylor & Francis)
R–AP–OP	*Clinical Psychology Review* (Official Journal of the Division of Clinical Psychology of the American Psychological Association; incorporates 'The Clinical Psychologist') (Pergamon Press)
R	*Cognition* (Elsevier)
R	*Cognition and Emotion* (Lawrence Erlbaum Associates)
R	*Cognition Neuropsychology* (Lawrence Erlbaum Associates)
R–AP	*Cognitive Therapy and Research* (Plenum)
R–AP–OP	*Community Psychiatry Nursing Journal* (Community Psychiatric Nurses Assn)
R–AP–OP	*Computers in Human Behavior* (Pergamon)
AP–OP	*Contemporary Psychology* (American Psychological Association)
R–AP	*The Counseling Psychologist* (Journal of the Division of Counseling Psychology of the American Psychological Assn) (Sage)
AP	*Counselling* (British Assn for Counselling)
R–AP–OP	*Counselling Psychology Quarterly* (Carfax)
R–AP–OP	*Criminal Justice and Behavior* (Sage)
R–AP–OP	*Current Opinion in Psychiatry* (Current Science)
R	*Current Psychology: Research and Reviews* (Published by Transaction Periodicals; distributed by the British Psychological Society)
AP–OP	*Death Studies* (Taylor & Francis)
R–AP	*Development and Psychopathology* (Cambridge University Press)
R	*Developmental Psychobiology* (John Wiley)

R	*Developmental Psychology* (American Psychological Assn)
R	*Deviant Behaviour* (Taylor & Francis)
R–AP	*Educational Psychology* (Carfax)
AP	*Educational Psychology in Practice* (Assn of Educational Psychologists)
R	*Environment and Behavior* (Sage)
R	*Ergonomics* (Taylor & Francis)
R–AP	*European Archives of Psychiatry and Neurological Sciences* (Springer)
R	*European Journal of Cognitive Psychology* (Lawrence Erlbaum Associates)
R	*European Journal of Personality* (Journal of the European Association of Personality Psychology) (John Wiley)
R	*European Journal of Social Psychology* (John Wiley)
R–AP–OP	*Gifted Education International* (A.B. Academic)
R–AP	*Group Analysis* (Sage)
R–AP–OP	*Group and Organization Studies* (Sage)
AP	*Guidance and Assessment Review* (British Psychological Society)
R	*Hispanic Journal of Behavioral Sciences* (Sage)
R	*Human Movement Science* (Elsevier)
R–AP–OP	*International Journal of Adolescence and Youth* (A.B. Academic)
R	*International Journal of Behavioural Development* (Lawrence Erlbaum Associates)
R	*International Journal of Eating Disorders* (John Wiley)
R–AP–OP	*International Journal of Intercultural Relations* (Pergamon)
AP	*International Journal of Law and Psychiatry* (Pergamon)
R	*International Journal of Personal Construct Psychology* (Taylor & Francis)
R–AP	*International Journal of Psychoanalysis* (official journal of the International Union of Psychological Science) (Routledge)
R	*International Journal of Psychology* (Elsevier)
R	*International Journal of Psychophysiology* (Elsevier)
R–AP	*International Journal of Short-Term Psychotherapy* (John Wiley)
R–AP	*International Journal of Social Psychiatry* (Avenue)

R–AP–OP	*International Journal of Therapeutic Communities* (Assn of Therapeutic Communities)
AP–OP	*International Review of Psychiatry* (Carfax)
R–AP	*International Review of Psychoanalysis* (Routledge)
AP	*Issues in Mental Health Nursing* (Taylor & Francis)
R	*Journal for the Theory of Social Behaviour* (Basil Blackwell)
R–AP	*Journal of Abnormal Child Psychology* (Plenum)
R	*Journal of Abnormal Psychology* (American Psychological Assn)
R	*Journal of Adolescent Research* (Sage)
R	*Journal of Ageing Studies* (JAI)
AP	*Journal of Analytical Psychology* (Routledge)
R–AP	*Journal of Anxiety Disorders* (Pergamon)
R–AP	*Journal of Applied Behavioural Science* (JAI)
R–AP	*Journal of Applied Psychology* (American Psychological Assn)
R–AP	*Journal of Autism and Developmental Disorders* (Plenum)
R–AP	*Journal of Behavior Therapy and Experimental Psychiatry* (Pergamon)
R–AP	*Journal of Behavioral Medicine* (Plenum)
R–AP	*Journal of Child Language* (Cambridge University Press)
R–AP	*Journal of Child Psychology and Psychiatry and Allied Disciplines* (Pergamon)
AP–OP	*Journal of Child Psychotherapy* (Assn of Child Psychotherapists)
AP	*Journal of Clinical Psychopharmacology* (Williams & Wilkins)
R	*Journal of Cognitive Neuroscience* (MIT Press)
R	*Journal of Comparative Psychology* (American Psychological Assn)
R–AP	*Journal of Consulting and Clinical Psychology* (American Psychological Assn)
R–AP–OP	*Journal of Counseling Psychology* (American Psychological Assn)
R	*Journal of Cross-Cultural Psychology* (Sage)
AP	*Journal of Developmental and Behavioral Pediatrics* (Williams & Wilkins)
R	*Journal of Early Adolescence* (Sage)

R	*Journal of Economic Psychology* (Elsevier)
R-AP	*Journal of Educational Psychology* (American Psychological Assn)
R	*Journal of Experimental and Theoretical Artificial Intelligence* (Taylor & Francis)
R	*Journal of Experimental Psychology* (American Psychological Assn)
R	*Journal of Experimental Psychology: Animal Behavior Processes* (American Psychological Assn)
R	*Journal of Experimental Psychology: Human Perception and Performance* (American Psychological Assn)
R	*Journal of Experimental Psychology: Learning, Memory and Cognition* (American Psychological Assn)
R-AP	*Journal of Family Psychology* (Journal of the Division of Family Psychology of the American Psychological Assn) (Sage)
R-AP-OP	*Journal of Family Violence* (Plenum)
R	*Journal of Humanistic Psychology* (Sage)
R-AP-OP	*Journal of Interpersonal Violence* (Sage)
R	*Journal of Language and Social Psychology* (Multilingual Matters)
AP	*Journal of Managerial Psychology* (MCB University Press)
R-AP	*Journal of Mental Health Counseling* (Sage)
AP	*Journal of Nervous and Mental Disease* (Williams and Wilkins)
R-AP	*Journal of Occupational Psychology* (British Psychological Society)
R-AP-OP	*Journal of Pediatric Psychology* (Plenum)
R	*Journal of Personality and Social Psychology* (American Psychological Assn)
R	*Journal of Psychiatric Research* (Pergamon)
R-AP	*Journal of Psycholinguistic Research* (Plenum)
R-AP	*Journal of Psychopathology and Behavioral Assessment* (Plenum)
R	*Journal of Psychopharmacology* (Oxford University Press)
R	*Journal of Psychophysiology* (Oxford University Press)
AP	*Journal of Psychosomatic Medicine* (Williams & Wilkins)
R	*Journal of Psychosomatic Research* (Pergamon)

AP	*Journal of Reading, Writing and Learning Disabilities* (Taylor & Francis)
R	*Journal of Reproductive and Infant Psychology* (John Wiley)
AP	*Journal of Research in Reading* (Basil Blackwell)
R–AP	*Journal of School Psychology* (Pergamon)
R	*Journal of Social and Personal Relationships* (Sage)
R	*Journal of Social Issues* (Plenum)
AP–OP	*Journal of Substance Abuse Treatment* (Pergamon)
AP	*Journal of the American Academy of Child and Adolescent Psychiatry* (Williams & Wilkins)
R–AP	*Journal of the American Academy of Psychoanalysis* (John Wiley)
R–AP–OP	*Journal of the Balint Society* (Haverstock)
AP–OP	*Journal of the British Association of Psychotherapists* (British Assn of Psychotherapists)
R	*Journal of the Society for Psychical Research* (Incorporated Society for Psychical Research)
R–AP	*Journal of Traumatic Stress* (Plenum)
R–AP	*Journal of Youth and Adolescence* (Plenum)
R	*Language and Cognitive Processes* (Lawrence Erlbaum Associates)
R	*Mind and Language* (Basil Blackwell)
R–AP	*Motivation and Emotion* (Plenum)
AP–OP	*Nature* (Macmillan)
R	*Neural Computation* (MIT Press)
AP	*Neuropsychology* (Taylor & Francis)
R	*New Ideas in Psychology: An International Journal of Innovative Theory in Psychology* (Pergamon)
AP–OP	*New Scientist* (IPC)
AP	*Open Mind* (MIND)
R	*Perception* (Pion)
R	*Personality and Individual Differences* (Pergamon)
R	*Personality and Social Psychology Bulletin* (Journal of the Society for Personality and Social Psychology of the American Psychological Association) (Sage)
R–AP–OP	*Person-Centred Review* (Sage)

R	*Philosophical Psychology* (Carfax)
R	*Philosophical Transactions of the Royal Society of London, Series B* (The Royal Society)
R	*Political Psychology* (Plenum)
R	*Proceedings of the Royal Society of London, Series B* (The Royal Society)
R – AP	*Professional Psychology: Research and Practice* (American Psychological Assn)
AP	*Psychiatric Bulletin* (Royal College of Psychiatrists)
R	*Psychiatric Developments* (Oxford University Press)
R – AP – OP	*Psychological Abstracts* (American Psychological Assn)
R – AP	*Psychological Bulletin* (American Psychological Assn)
R – AP	*Psychological Medicine* (Cambridge University Press)
R	*Psychological Research: An International Journal of Perception, Learning and Communication* (Springer)
monthly bulletin of the BPS	*The Psychologist* (British Psychological Society)
R – AP	*Psychology and Developing Countries* (Sage)
R – AP	*Psychology and Marketing* (John Wiley)
AP	*Psychology News* (Psychology News)
AP – OP	*Psychology of Women Quarterly* (Cambridge University Press)
R	*Psychopharmacology* (Sage)
R – AP – OP	*PsycSCAN* (American Psychological Assn)
R	*Quarterly Journal of Experimental Psychology: Section A: Human Experimental Psychology; Section B: Comparative and Physiological Psychology* (Lawrence Erlbaum Associates)
AP – OP	*Reading Psychology* (Taylor & Francis)
R	*Research in Development Disabilities* (Pergamon)
R – AP	*School Psychology International* (Sage)
R – AP – OP	*Self and Society: European Journal of Humanistic Psychology* (Self and Society)
R – AP	*Sex Roles* (Plenum)
R – AP – OP	*Sexual and Marital Therapy* (Carfax)
R	*Small Group Behavior* (Sage)
R	*Social Behavior* (John Wiley)

R	*Social Epistemology* (Taylor & Francis)
R – AP – OP	*Social Justice Research* (Plenum)
R	*Social Network* (Elsevier)
R	*Social Psychiatry and Psychiatric Epidemiology* (Springer)
R	*Speech Communication* (Elsevier)
R	*Symbolic Interaction: Official Journal of the Society for the Study of Symbolic Interaction* (JAI)
R	*Work and Stress* (Taylor & Francis)

LIST 3: PUBLISHERS AND THEIR READERSHIPS	REFERENCE	SCHOOLS & FURTHER EDUCATION	HIGHER EDUCATION & ACADEMIC	APPLIED PSYCHOLOGISTS & OTHER PROFESSIONS	TRADE & GENERAL	JOURNALS
A.B. Academic						●
Aberdeen Univ. Press				●	●	
Academic Press			●			
Addison-Wesley	●		●	●	●	
Airlift				●	●	
Allyn & Bacon			●			
American Psychological Assn						●
Ann Arbor				●		
Anna Freud Centre						●
Aquarian Press					●	
Edward Arnold		●	●			
Artesian Books						●
Assn for Behavioural Approaches with Children						●
Assn for Child Psychotherapists						●
Assn of Educational Psychologists						●
Assn of Therapeutic Communities						●
Avenue						●
Baillière Tindall				●		
Basil Blackwell	●		●	●	●	●
BIMH Publications				●		●
Blackwell Scientific				●		
BPS Books	●	●	●	●	●	
Br. Assn for Counselling	●			●		●
Br. Assn of Psychotherapists						●
British Psychological Society						●

	REFERENCE	SCHOOLS & FURTHER EDUCATION	HIGHER EDUCATION & ACADEMIC	APPLIED PSYCHOLOGISTS & OTHER PROFESSIONS	TRADE & GENERAL	JOURNALS
Br. Soc. for Projective Psychology						●
W.C. Brown		●	●			
Butterworth Scientific				●		
Cambridge Univ. Press	●		●	●		●
Carfax						●
Cassell		●	●	●		
Chambers				●	●	
Paul Chapman			●	●		
Chapman & Hall			●	●		
Chartwell-Bratt			●	●		
Children's Society				●	●	
Churchill Livingstone				●		
Cole & Whurr						●
Community Psychiatric Nurses Assn						●
Constable				●	●	
Current Science						●
Darton Longman & Todd				●	●	
J.M. Dent				●		
Gerald Duckworth			●	●	●	
Eating Disorders Assn						●
Element Books				●	●	
Elsevier	●		●			●
Erlbaum	●		●			●
Faber & Faber				●	●	
Falmer			●	●		
Family Welfare Assn				●	●	
Fontana				●	●	
Free Association Books	●		●	●	●	●

	REFERENCE	SCHOOLS & FURTHER EDUCATION	HIGHER EDUCATION & ACADEMIC	APPLIED PSYCHOLOGISTS & OTHER PROFESSIONS	TRADE & GENERAL	JOURNALS
W.H. Freeman		●	●		●	●
David Fulton				●	●	
Gaskell			●			
Gateway				●		
Harcourt Brace Jovanovich		●	●	●		
Harper & Row			●	●		
Harvester-Wheatsheaf	●		●	●		
Harwood Academic	●			●		●
Haverstock				●		●
Hobsons		●				●
Hodder & Stoughton		●	●	●		
Hutchinson		●	●			
IPC						●
JAI	●		●	●		●
Johns Hopkins Univ. Press			●	●		
Jossey–Bass			●	●		
H. Karnac				●		
Jessica Kingsley				●		
Kluwer			●	●		
Lifeskills		●				
Longman			●	●	●	
MacGraw-Hill		●	●	●		
Macmillan			●	●		●
Manchester Univ. Press				●		
MCB Univ. Press						●
MIND				●		●
MIT			●			●
Multilingual Matters			●			●

	REFERENCE	SCHOOLS & FURTHER EDUCATION	HIGHER EDUCATION & ACADEMIC	APPLIED PSYCHOLOGISTS & OTHER PROFESSIONS	TRADE & GENERAL	JOURNALS
National Extension Coll.		•				
Thomas Nelson		•				
New York Academy of Sciences			•			
NFER-Nelson				•		
W.W. Norton			•	•		
Oneworld				•		
Open Books				•		
Open Univ. Press			•	•		
Oxford Univ. Press	•		•	•		•
Pan				•	•	
Penguin	•		•		•	
Pergamon			•	•		•
Frances Pinter			•	•		
Pion						•
Plenum			•	•		•
Positive Products				•		
Prentice-Hall			•			
Psychology Corp.				•		
Psychology News						•
Routledge		•	•	•	•	•
Royal Coll. of Psychiatrists						•
Royal Society			•			•
Sage			•	•		•
SEFA						•
Self & Society				•		•
Sheldon		•			•	
Souvenir				•	•	
Springer-Verlag			•	•		•

	REFERENCE	SCHOOLS & FURTHER EDUCATION	HIGHER EDUCATION & ACADEMIC	APPLIED PSYCHOLOGISTS & OTHER PROFESSIONS	TRADE & GENERAL	JOURNALS
Taylor & Francis			●	●		●
Univ. Presses of Columbia & Princeton			●	●		
Unwin Hyman				●	●	
Virago				●	●	
Weidenfeld & Nicolson		●			●	
John Wiley	●		●	●		●
Williams & Wilkins				●		
Winslow Press				●		
Women's Press				●	●	
Yale Univ. Press			●	●	●	

Publishers' Addresses

A.B. Academic Publishers
PO Box 42
Bicester
Oxon OX6 7NW

Aberdeen University Press
Farmers Hall
Aberdeen AB9 2XT

Academic Press Inc. (London) Ltd
24-28 Oval Road
London NW1 7DX

Addison-Wesley Publishers Ltd
Finchampstead Road
Wokingham
Berks RS11 2NZ

Airlift Book Co.
26-28 Eden Grove
London N7 8EF

American Psychological Association
1200 Seventeenth Street, NW
Washington DC 20036
USA

Ann Arbor Publishers
PO Box 1
Belford
Northumb. NE70 7JX

Anna Freud Centre
1 Maresfield Gardens
London NW3 5SH

Aquarian Press Ltd
Thorsons Publishers Ltd
Denington Estate
Wellingborough
Northants NN8 2RQ

Edward Arnold
see Hodder & Stoughton

Artesian Books
18 Artesian Road
London W2 5AR

Association for Behavioural Approaches
with Children
Centre for Child Study
School of Education
University of Birmingham
Birmingham B15 2TT

Association of Child Psychotherapists
Burgh House
New End Square
Hampstead
London NW3 1LT

Association of Educational
Psychologists
3 Sunderland Road
Durham DH1 2LH

Association of Therapeutic
Communities
14 Charterhouse Square
London EC1 M6XA

Avenue Publishing Co.
55 Woodstock Avenue
London NW11 9RG

Baillière Tindall
see Harcourt Brace Jovanovich

BIMH Publications
PO Box 1
Portishead
Bristol BS20 9EG

Basil Blackwell Publishers Ltd
108 Cowley Road
Oxford OX4 IJF

Blackwell Scientific Publications Ltd
Osney Mead
Oxford OX2 OEL

Boyd & Fraser
see Chapman & Hall

BPS Books
see The British Psychological Society

British Association for Counselling
37A Sheep Street
Rugby
War. CV21 3BX

British Association of Psychotherapists
c/o Mrs M.R. Stumpfl
28 Stratford Villas
London NW1 9SG

The British Psychological Society
St Andrews House
48 Princess Road East
Leicester LE1 7DR

British Society for Projective Psychology
Tavistock Centre
120 Belsize Lane
London NW3 5BA

Brooks/Cole
see Chapman & Hall

W.C. Brown Publishers
Merrill Publishing International
Holywell House
Osney Mead
Oxford OX2 OES

Butterworth Scientific
Westbury House
Bury Street
Guildford
Surrey GU2 5BH

Cambridge University Press
The Edinburgh Building
Shaftesbury Road
Cambridge CB2 2RU

Carfax Publishing Co.
PO Box 25
Abingdon
Oxon OX14 3UE

Cassell plc
Artillery House
Artillery Row
London SW1P 1RT

Chambers Publishers
43-45 Annandale Street
Edinburgh EH7 4AZ

Chapman & Hall Ltd
11 New Fetter Lane
London EC4P 4EE

Paul Chapman Publishing Ltd
144 Liverpool Road
London N1 1LA

Chartwell-Bratt (Publishing & Training)
 Ltd
Old Orchard
Bickley Road
Bromley
Kent BR1 2NE

The Children's Society
Edward Rudolf House
Margery Street
London WC1X OJL

Churchill Livingstone
see Longman

Cole & Whurr
19B Compton Terrace
London N1 2UN

Collier Macmillan Ltd
see Macmillan

Columbia University Press
see University Presses of California,
 Columbia & Princeton

Community Psychiatric Nurses
 Association
c/o 4 St James' Road
Sevenoaks
Kent TN13 3NH

Constable & Co. Ltd
10 Orange Street
London WC2H 7EG

Current Science
34-42 Cleveland Street
London W1P 5FP

Darton Longman & Todd Ltd
89 Lillie Road
London SW6 1UD

J.M. Dent & Sons Ltd
91 Clapham High Street
London SW4 7TA

Gerald Duckworth & Co. Ltd
The Old Piano Factory
43 Gloucester Crescent
London NW1 7DY

Eating Disorders Association
Sackville Place
44 Magdalen Street
Norwich NR3 1JE

Element Books Ltd
Longmead
Shaftesbury
Dorset SP7 8PL

Elsevier Science Publishers B.V.
PO Box 1991
1000 BZ Amsterdam
The Netherlands

Lawrence Erlbaum Associates Ltd
Palmeira Mansions
Church Road
Hove
East Sussex BN3 2FA

Faber & Faber Ltd
3 Queen Square
London WC1N 3AU

Falmer Press Ltd
Rankine Road
Basingstoke
Hants RG24 OPR

Family Welfare Association
Family Welfare Enterprises Ltd
Unit 4b
Standard Industrial Estate
2 Henley Road
North Woolwich
London E16 SEG

Fontana
8 Grafton Street
London W1X 3LA

Free Association Books
26 Freegrove Road
London N7 9RQ

W.H. Freeman & Co. Ltd
20 Beaumont Street
Oxford OX1 2NQ

David Fulton Publishers Ltd
2 Barbon Close
Great Ormond Street
London WC1N 3JX

Gaskell
see Royal College of Psychiatrists

Gateway Books
The Hollies
Mill Hill
Wellow, nr Bath BA2 8QJ

Harcourt Brace Jovanovich Ltd
1 Vincent Square
London SW1P 2PN

Harper & Row Ltd
Middlesex House
34-42 Cleveland Street
London WIP 5FP

Harvester-Wheatsheaf
Simon & Schuster International Group
66 Wood Lane End
Hemel Hempstead
Herts HP2 4RG

Harwood Academic Publishers Ltd
1 Bedford Street
London WC2E 9HD

Haverstock Publications
249 Haverstock Hill
Hampstead
London NW3 4PS

Hobsons Publishing plc
Bateman Street
Cambridge CB2 1LZ

Hodder & Stoughton Ltd
Mill Road
Dunton Green
Sevenoaks
Kent TN12 6SU

Hutchinson
see Unwin Hyman

IPC
Commonwealth House
1-19 New Oxford Street
London WC14 1NG

JAI Press
3 Henrietta Street
London WC2E 8LU

Johns Hopkins University Press
c/o Trevor Brown Associates
Suite 7B
26 Charing Cross Road
London WC2H OLN

Jossey-Bass Publishers Ltd
28 Banner Street
London EC1Y 8QE

H. Karnac (Books) Ltd
58 Gloucester Road
London SW7 4QY

Jessica Kingsley Publishers
13 Brunswick Centre
London WC1N 1AF

Kluwer Academic Publishers
PO Box 55
Lancaster LA1 IPE

Lifeskills Associates Ltd
51 Clarendon Road
Leeds LS2 9NZ

Longman Group UK Ltd
Longman House
Burnt Mill
Harlow
Essex CM20 2JE

McGraw-Hill Book Co. (UK) Ltd
Shoppenhangers Road
Maidenhead
Berks SL6 2QL

Macmillan Publishers Ltd
Macmillan Distribution
Houndmills
Basingstoke
Hants RG21 2XS

Manchester University Press
The University
Manchester M13 9PL

MCB University Press Ltd
62 Toller Lane
Bradford BD8 9BY

MIND Publications
(National Association for Mental Health)
4th Floor
24-32 Stephenson Way
London NW1 2HD

The MIT Press
126 Buckingham Palace Road
London SW1W 9SA

Multilingual Matters Ltd
Bank House
8a Hill Road
Clevedon
Avon BS21 7HH

National Extension College
18 Brooklands Avenue
Cambridge CB2 2HN

Thomas Nelson & Sons Ltd
Nelson House
Mayfield Road
Walton-on-Thames
Surrey KT12 5PL

New York Academy of Sciences
STM Distribution Ltd
Enterprise House
Ashford Road
Ashford
Middx TW15 1XB

New York University Press
see University Presses of California,
Columbia & Princeton

NFER-Nelson
Darville House
2 Oxford Road East
Windsor
Berks SL4 1DF

North-Holland Publishing Co.
see Elsevier Science Publishers

W.W. Norton & Co. Ltd
37 Great Russell Street
London WC1B 3NU

Oneworld Publications Ltd
1c Standbrook House
Old Bond Street
London W1X 3TD

Open Books Publishing Ltd
Beaumont House
New Street
Wells
Som. BA5 2LD

Open University Press
Celtic Court
22 Ballmoor
Buckingham MK18 1XW

Oxford University Press
Science, Medical & Journal Division
Walton Street
Oxford OX2 6DP

Pan Books Ltd
Houndmills
Basingstoke
Hants RG21 2YT

Penguin Books Ltd
Bath Road
Harmondsworth
Middx UB7 ODA

Pergamon Press Ltd
Headington Hill Hall
Oxford OX3 OBW

Frances Pinter Publishers Ltd
25 Floral Street
Covent Garden
London WC2E 9DS

Pion Ltd
207 Brondesbury Park
London NW2 5JN

Plenum Publishers Co. Ltd
88-90 Middlesex Street
London E1 7EZ

Positive Products
PO Box 45
Cheltenham GL52 3BBX

Prentice-Hall
see Harvester-Wheatsheaf

The Psychological Corporation Ltd
Foots Cray High Street
Sidcup
Kent DA14 5HP

Psychology News Ltd
17a Great Ormond Street
London WC1N 3RA

Routledge Ltd
11 New Fetter Lane
London EC4P 4EE

Routledge & Kegan Paul
see Routledge

Royal College of Psychiatrists
17 Belgrave Square
London SW1X 8PG

The Royal Society
6 Carlton House Terrace
London SW1Y 5AG

Sage Publications Ltd
28 Banner Street
London EC1Y 8QE

SEFA (Publications) Ltd
(British Society for the Study of Mental
    Subnormality)
The Globe
4 Great William Street
Stratford-upon-Avon

Self & Society
62 Southwark Bridge Road
London SE1 OAS

Sheldon Press
Holy Trinity Church
Marylebone Road
London NW1 4DU

Simon & Schuster Ltd
see Harvester-Wheatsheaf

Souvenir Press Ltd
43 Great Russell Street
London WC1B 3PA

Springer-Verlag London Ltd
8 Alexander Road
London SW19 7JZ

Taylor & Francis Ltd
Rankine Road
Basingstoke
Hants RG24 OPR

University Presses of California,
  Columbia & Princeton
Avonlea
10 Watlington Road
Cowley
Oxford OX4 5NF

Unwin Hyman Ltd
15-17 Broadwick Street
London W1V 1FP

Van Nostrand Reinhold Int. Co. Ltd
see Chapman & Hall

Virago Press Ltd
20-23 Mandela Street
Camden Town
London NW1 OHQ

Wadsworth
see Chapman & Hall

George Weidenfeld & Nicholson Ltd
91 Clapham High Street
London SW4 7TA

John Wiley & Sons Ltd
Baffins Lane
Chichester
W. Sussex PO19 IUD

Williams & Wilkins Ltd
Broadway House
2-6 Fulham Broadway
London SW6 1AA

Winslow Press
Telford Road
Bicester
Oxon OX6 OTS

The Women's Press Ltd
34 Great Sutton Street
London EC1V ODX

John Wright
see Butterworth Scientific

Yale University Press
23 Pond Street
London NW3 2PN

PSYCHOLOGICAL TESTS
Chris Whetton

❏ *why bother to teach about tests?* ● *what is a psychological test?* ● *test content* ● *technical properties* ● *ethical issues* ● *qualifications for test users*

WHY BOTHER
TO TEACH
ABOUT
TESTS?

There is a curious contrast in the attitude of psychologists to psychological tests. On the one hand, there is great concern about the validity and utility of the abstractions of behaviour which tests provide, to the extent that some would advocate not using tests at all. On the other hand, a great deal of the subject matter of psychology courses relies on research which has included the use of test instruments. Additionally many of the members of specialist professional groups (clinical, educational and occupational psychologists) use tests routinely. Tyler and Miller (1986) report on a survey of test use by these groups.

In psychology teaching, testing is often neglected; for example, a review of the prospectuses of 22 university psychology departments indicated that only two mentioned psychometrics and only one psychological testing. Most include topics such as 'individual differences' or 'cognitive psychology' but are not explicit about whether the measurement aspects of these are covered. A-level syllabuses make some mention of testing, either specifically in relation to intelligence tests or in contrast to school attainment tests. The 1989 report of the chief examiner for the Diploma in Clinical Psychology noted that 'candidates showed a marked reluctance to answer questions which ask for information about issues of assessment i.e. details of commonly used tests or basic psychometry and measurement issues' (Morley, 1989). According to Kline (1988) the psychometric tradition in British psychology is all but dead.

So, why bother to teach about tests? Firstly because, if students continue with psychology as a profession, it is highly likely that they will have to administer tests or, more importantly, to interpret the results. Secondly, much psychological theory and debate is reliant for its information on the measures used and these are often psychometric tests of some description. An understanding of the issues involved ought to include knowledge of the characteristics of the psychological tests used. Thirdly, a particular form of test, the intelligence test, has been the most persuasive invention of psychology and has probably exerted greater influence on the social life of the UK through its use in an educational context than any other practical application of psychology. Even after the decline of the eleven plus, tests remain one of the areas where members of the public encounter psychology, through occupational selection or other assessments.

For all these reasons, psychology students ought to be taught about tests to an appropriate extent. The depth of knowledge which they need will depend on the level at which they are studying psychology and the purposes for which they will use them. Currently, systems of qualification for the supply of tests are based on the formal qualifications of the purchaser (see below), it being assumed that the appropriate education about the administration and interpretation of tests will have been provided on the course. Thus, it is expected that postgraduate students of educational psychology will have been taught the theory and practice of using and interpreting individually administered test batteries with many sub-scales (for example, the WISC-R or BASR). Similarly, postgraduate students in clinical or occupational psychology need training in the use of the assessment techniques which they are likely to employ in their professional work. In these cases the students will need to become completely familiar with the test material, and this familiarity can only be gained by a close examination of the items and scoring procedures of the test.

At undergraduate level, however, such close familiarity may be unnecessary. Degree courses might, though, include the administration of group tests of aptitude and personality to the students themselves. Here the teaching method is primarily the administration of the test. For A-level students of psychology and for general interest courses, such a teaching method may be inappropriate (see section on ethical issues) and other methods must be considered.

WHAT IS
A PSYCHO-
LOGICAL
TEST?

A psychological test may be broadly defined as a standard assessment procedure which measures individual differences in some psychological function. Many professional groups use assessment procedures and it is sometimes difficult to decide whether or not these can be called 'psychological tests'; there is such a considerable diversity in their content and use that an all-inclusive definition is impossible. Any definition, however, would have to emphasize both the content of the tests and the procedures involved in the assessment.

Recently, a statement by The British Psychological Society [BPS] Steering Committee on Test Standards (BPS, 1989) has defined a psychological test in two ways, as:

– an instrument designed to produce a quantitative assessment of some psychological attribute or attributes;

or as:

– any procedure on the basis of which inferences are made concerning a person's capacity, propensity or liability to act, react, experience, or to structure or order thought or behaviour in particular ways.

The two crucial elements are that a test is a procedure, and that this provides a basis for inference concerning matters of psychological importance.

An earlier attempt at a legal definition (The British Psychological Society Working Party on Competence in Psychological Testing, 1983) gave a list of content areas which included tests of intelligence, ability, aptitude, language development and function, perception, personality, temperament and disposition, interests, habits, values and preferences. It excluded educational attainment tests and non-standardized attitude inventories, among other assessments. In contrast, the technical recommendations for psychological tests (The British Psychological Society Professional Affairs Board, 1980) emphasized the procedures involved in the assessment, advising that the term 'test' should be used only for techniques which yield ratings or scores derived from procedures clearly described in a manual and based on adequate standardization data. They emphasized the technical aspects of tests, their construction and item analysis, norms, reliability and validity. Both these approaches are now combined in the 1989 statement.

There are, then, two aspects to education about tests: first, their content; and secondly, their procedures. The first of these is complicated by ethical considerations, and the second necessarily involves some statistical considerations which may provide difficult for some students. The following two sections outline possible methods of education in the content of psychological tests and their technical properties.

TEST
CONTENT

Many concepts which are measured by tests form the basis of familiar debates at all levels of psychology teaching. Arguments about the heritability of intelligence or the nature of personality, for example, are often considered without reference to the characteristics of tests which have been used. Understanding of such debates can often be deepened by a knowledge of the content and technical qualities of psychological tests.

Used in this way, some tests can be valuable as instructional devices. For example, it is often easier for the student to gain an understanding of 'spatial ability' by reference to a few instances of appropriate item types than from a definition such as 'the ability to perceive patterns and to manipulate them or transform them into other arrangements'. The contrast between the formal definition and the attempt at measurement provided by the test can be illuminating to students and may provide a suitable starting point for discussion of the problems of definition in psychology.

As a concept becomes more complex, however, tests tend to become less useful in helping a student's understanding. Administering an intelligence or creativity test would probably not assist a student to understand the nature of intelligence or be helpful in relating definitions to the reasoning processes implied by the test. When a test is used to illustrate a concept, in most cases it is not necessary to administer the full version to provide instances of the types of operation involved, and a few examples of item types would serve just as well. In many ways it is wasteful of valuable teaching time to administer complete psychological tests to a group of students simply to instruct them in the content of tests. There may also be ethical objections.

One method of overcoming this is to use the versions of tests available in popular paperbacks. Some of these are:

EYSENCK, H.J. (1962) *Know Your Own IQ.*
BUTLER, E. and PIRIE, M. (1983) *Test Your IQ.*
DE CARLO, N. (1984) *Psychological games: A book of tests and puzzles to teach you more about yourself and those around you.*
EYSENCK, H.J. (1986) *Know Your Own PSI-Q.*
ANONYMOUS (1987) *Test Your Reasoning.*
SULLIVAN, N. (1988) *Test Your Intelligence.*

Older books which are out of print but are sometimes available second-hand or from libraries are:

EYSENCK, H.J. (1969) *Check Your Own IQ.*
EYSENCK, H.J. and WILSON, G.D. (1976) *Know Your Own Personality.*
BARRETT, J.S. and WILLIAMS, G.R. (1980) *Test Your Own Aptitude.*

Another ready source of such 'tests' is the press, ranging from recruitment advertisements for Mensa to fairly serious stress indicators. Often (particularly in the heavier papers and their magazines) the 'tests' are based on relatively sound research instruments with some academic support and credibility. In other cases, a few ambiguous questions have been thrown together by a journalist for some salacious purpose.

Teachers will appreciate that even the better of popular 'tests' must be used with caution; evidence of reliability or information on the derivation of the norms is seldom given. Indeed, the shortcomings of such tests would be a good subject for class discussion, or an exercise where students review one of these 'tests'.

A related approach may be for the teacher to devise a short test made up of different types of item representative of various approaches to measuring a particular concept. This could be administered to the students and followed by group discussion or review.

In the field of aptitude testing, a test battery specially produced for familiarizing psychology students and others with a variety of types of tests may be used. This is the Multi-Aptitude Test by Cureton *et al.* (1959), previously available from the Psychological Corporation. This test contains ten sub-tests, which take only 35 minutes in total to administer, but, unlike the other examples given, have been subject to proper test construction and item analysis. Its manual also gives helpful suggestions for using the test with students on courses at different levels. It may still occasionally be available in some libraries.

As a more modern British alternative, there is a Work Aptitude Practice and Profile Set available from Saville & Holdsworth. This consists of five short tests aimed at giving practice in tests to young people completing educational courses. It includes verbal reasoning, spatial, clerical, data interpretation and diagramming (logic) tests. These appear to be well-constructed and appropriate tests, but no information is given on their technical characteristics.

More rapidly used modern alternatives are the practice leaflets which are produced by test publishers to accompany certain tests or to be given to prospective test takers. For example, Saville & Holdsworth market a series of practice leaflets entitled 'Why do we use Aptitude Tests?', which provide examples of the types of item which are encountered in their technical, personnel, advanced and programmer aptitude test batteries. These leaflets have a selection of items and a mock answer sheet in the middle pages, allowing the reader to attempt the questions. The correct answers are then given on the back page of the leaflet together with general advice on taking tests. These leaflets give a limited introduction to the content of vocational aptitude tests.

Similarly, the ASE Occupational Test Series General Ability Tests (NFER-Nelson) have 'A Test Taker's Guide' which gives examples of item types and advice on taking tests. The Psychological Corporation, too, has a range of practice material available for such tests as the Differential Aptitude Tests (Orientation Booklet for Forms V and W).

Much of the current development work in psychological assessment is concerned with the production of tests for administration by computer. Computerized tests can have great advantages over pencil and paper assessments, since they can measure response times, provide dynamic displays, allow repeated attempts at an item or allow the tailoring of a test to the ability of the testee. Computers can also cope rapidly with complex scoring methods and provide statistical analyses of test results which are continuously updated after each client. For all these reasons, much of the future of psychological assessment may lie with computer-based assessments.

Initially, research in this area tended to concentrate on adaptations of existing pencil and paper tests to be administered by computer. Some of these are available from the test publishers given below. In addition some popular 'tests' are available as games software for the home computer market, and these may be used for teaching purposes. As with pencil and paper tests, they can be used to illustrate test content, but they may also be used to promote discussion of the problems of transposing a test from one medium to another. This could lead to an exercise in which an experiment is to be designed to gauge the effect of computerization on the tests' reliability, validity and norms.

The emphasis on more recent development work is on using the capabilities of the computer to a much greater extent. For students interested in this, there is *A Directory of Research into Automated Testing* (DRAT) which is compiled by and available from Sarah L. Wilson, Research Dept., The Royal Hospital and Home, Putney, West Hill, London SW15 3SW. A set of guidelines for the design of software for computer-based assessment has been adapted by the Scientific Affairs Board of the BPS. A summary is given by Bartram *et al.* (1987). For a further discussion of the use of microcomputers in the area of psychological tests see Underwood and Underwood (this volume).

TECHNICAL PROPERTIES   The level of knowledge which it is necessary for a student to attain of test theory will (like test content) depend on the particular course. There are, though, several important ideas with which all students should become familiar. These ideas are often statistical in nature, and though this can cause some difficulties, it has the advantage that some real data can be generated and analysed, giving practice in computation and interpretation.

Some of the basic ideas and suggestions for teaching them are:

1. The need for a standard procedure in administration and scoring. The result of different testing sessions run by different examiners can only be compared meaningfully when the administration instructions in the test manual have been followed exactly. Although this is nearly always accepted in theory by would-be test administrators, it is often ignored in practice. The example of a model administration and a serious attitude to the test sessions can help to make this point.

2. Students should understand the distinction between relatively objective tests and relatively subjective tests. This can be brought out in a marking exercise where a specially devised test, complete with responses, is given to the whole class. Using a common answer key they can all be asked to mark the test and give a total score. The test should consist of a variety of item types, including multiple-choice, completion format, short sentence responses and paragraphs of prose. Discussion of the diversity of results which will arise will lead to some understanding of the need for objective scoring.

3. Most psychological tests are norm-referenced, that is, they compare the individual's score with some defined population. The student should be aware of the different types of standardized score and their meanings in terms of the population. The concepts of variance and standard deviation can be reinforced in this context. The relationship between standardized scores and percentile ranks is also important and can be illustrated by the use of conversion tables.

4. The importance of the statistical concept of reliability should be stressed. There are a number of different ways of measuring this, most of which involve some form of correlation coefficient. This, therefore, lends itself well to exercises involving the use and understanding of this statistic. In order to establish the need for consistency of test results, a small test–retest exercise may be carried out. The same short test could be administered on successive weeks to the whole class. The two sets of results can then be

collated and the correlation calculated. Plotting a scatter graph of the results will provide a visual demonstration of the departures from expectations which can take place. Alternatively, if two forms of the test are available, they may be administered in the same session and the same type of exercise carried out to convey statistically the idea of parallel form reliability. If both exercises are carried out it would be expected that the two reliability coefficients would differ and this can lead to a discussion of the sources of variance in test results.

The various reliability coefficients of internal consistency (Kuder Richardson's '20', Cronbach's 'alpha') are more difficult to explain, but, with more numerate students, class exercises in their calculation may also be possible.

Discussions of reliability can serve as an introduction to the important notion of errors of measurement in tests. The idea that tests are unreliable is one of the most vital to be communicated at all levels of teaching. It is most instructive for a class to calculate the standard errors associated with tests of decreasing reliabilities and then to find a true score confidence band based on these. This can be combined with an exercise on percentile ranks, to show the great range of the population which must be included when calculating a confidence interval for an individual's score when the test is unreliable. An example of the sort of table students could be asked to draw up is shown in Table 1. The Standard Error of Measurement (SEm) is calculated from the formula:

$SEm = SD \sqrt{1-r}$
where SD = standard deviation of the test scores
r = test reliability
and the 95% confidence interval is given by
Score $\pm 1.96 \times SEm$.

For a fuller explanation see, for example, Anastasi (1988).

Table 1 illustrates that, even with a highly reliable test, the 95 per cent confidence interval is very wide in terms of the population encompassed, and, as a test becomes more unreliable, the stage may be reached where 80 per cent of the population is covered by the confidence interval. This type of reminder of the extent to which tests are fallible can prove very useful to students of psychology at all levels.

5. The concept of validity and the distinction from reliability is also important. Although perhaps the most important characteristic of a test, it is sometimes difficult to explain the many types of validity adequately. The various forms of construct and criterion validity, however, again lend themselves to small scale correlation studies.

Table 1. Examples of the confidence intervals for high, average and low scores on tests of different reliability

Reliability of test	SEm	Score	95% confidence interval	Percentiles of extremes confidence interval
.6	9.5	120	101–139	52–99
		100	81–119	11–90
		80	61–99	1–48
.7	8.2	120	104–136	60–99
		100	84–116	14–86
		80	64–96	1–40
.8	6.7	120	107–133	68–99
		100	87–113	20–80
		80	67–93	1–32
.9	4.7	120	111–129	77–97
		100	91–109	28–72
		80	71–89	3–24
.95	3.7	120	113–127	80–96
		100	93–107	32–68
		80	73–87	4–20

Calculations assume standardized scores have a mean of 100 and a standard deviation of 15. For simplicity, the calculations assume symmetrical confidence intervals, a condition that would not in fact be true.

6. A final technical issue which is increasingly important is that of test bias. The examination and removal of bias from assessments is a complex task both philosophically and technically (see Berk, 1982 for a range of approaches). It is important that students should understand that the mere demonstration of differences between groups is not sufficient to indicate bias; it is only when these differences arise from factors irrelevant to those being tested that bias can be said to be operating. There are two parallel approaches to the removal of bias: reviewing material for apparent bias and statistical examination of individual questions. Smith and Whetton (1988) give a simplified case study of these processes. The statistical analysis of tests for bias is probably beyond the needs of most students but formal reviews of the content of test items for both sex and race bias can provoke heated discussion and raise issues which ultimately are matters of personal conviction. For example, should a test for young children show 'Mummy' making the tea and shopping because these are familiar to the children and reflect much of their experience, or should stereotypes be avoided at the expense of reducing the children's under-

standing of the situation and perhaps their ability to respond?

In many ways it is a more complete educational experience to attempt to produce a psychological test than simply to use one. Such a project can be tackled as a group exercise and will provide insight into the problems of defining a psychological construct, of producing an adequate operational definition, and of justifying it, as well as providing an exercise in the use of some statistical techniques. For advanced students, this could be a computerized test.

Many different ideas for such tests could be acceptable. A verbal reasoning analogies test, or a non-verbal matrices style test are both fairly readily constructed if examples of the item types are provided. Alternatively, a more challenging task is to begin from a construct, creativity or sociability for example, and proceed from definition to test construction. The students might be allowed to select their own subject.

The stage of item writing can be rapidly tackled by asking each student to produce a proportion of the test according to some pre-determined criteria (decided by class discussion); the teacher then collates the items and produces the test and each student tries it out on a small group of friends. This should generate enough data for an item analysis. Keeping the test short and the data limited will allow this to be done by hand. The two indices of difficulty and discrimination should be found for each item, and the 'Kuder Richardson 20' reliability coefficient for the test as a whole is fairly easily calculated with limited data. Alternatively, the split-half reliability could be found, giving practice at calculating correlations.

This type of analysis, though, is much more readily tackled using a computer. Students might wish to write their own programs but many statistical software packages have the means of carrying out item analyses more efficiently. For sophisticated applications such as item response theory or item banking, powerful software is available, although often expensive (e.g. the MicroCAT Testing System from Assessment Systems Corporation, 2233, University Avenue, Suite 440, St. Paul, Minnesota 55114).

A class discussion could use the data to agree on a final version of the test and also discuss the hypothetical problems involved in obtaining norms. (The standardization of tests is one of the few areas of psychology where efforts are made to ensure that subjects are a representative sample of some larger population.) With some organization and enthusiasm this exercise can provide a valuable learning experience with illustrations of several aspects of psychology.

ETHICAL
ISSUES

Any use of a psychological test poses some ethical questions for the test administrator. When, in addition, the test is being used not for its intended purpose but as a teaching device, there are further complications. The ethical problems revolve, firstly, round the issue of the confidentiality of test material and results and, secondly, the possible psychological risk and invasion of privacy of the students.

It is the responsibility of the teacher to ensure that the confidentiality of the test material is maintained as its value soon declines if it is widely available. For this reason, tests should be locked away when not in use and students should not be allowed to keep copies of the tests or the answer key. This prevents the possibility of the tests being inexpertly administered to friends and incorrectly explained and interpreted. The sessions at which the tests are administered should be treated seriously and the reasons for the restrictions on test use and the necessity for confidentiality should be explained.

When a particular assessment procedure is to be used by the students in their professional work following completion of the course, for example, postgraduate students on educational or clinical psychology courses, it is obviously important that they receive training in marking the test and interpreting results. However, in general, it is not advisable to allow the students to mark their own tests when this involves disclosing answers to all the items. Such complete feedback will obviously affect the results if the same test is subsequently administered to the student, say as a selection device for entry to an academic course or particular occupation. In other cases, revealing the items which reflect a particular personality dimension may enable a person to fake certain characteristics when later presented with the personality inventory as part of a clinical assessment procedure. For these reasons, when tests are being used simply to educate, unless it is important for the students to practise scoring and interpretation, the tests should not be marked by them.

Even when every effort is made to make the administration of the test as accurate as possible, students will still be aware that the results have no real importance. Since the tests are being used out of context, levels of motivation may be altered to such an extent that the norms in the manual are not appropriate. The results will, therefore, be more unreliable than usual. This should be explained clearly to the students, but even after a warning, it is likely that a small proportion will take their test results very seriously. These people may be put at psychological risk.

Knowledge of the results of a personality test may have

implications for the manner in which students view themselves. For example, those with a tendency to neuroticism may worry considerably if this is revealed to them by the casual use of the Eysenck Personality Inventory. This type of consideration is strongest for personality tests, but knowledge of the results of an ability test may also have untoward effects. The discovery that an intelligence test score is below average, for example, may lead to loss of self-esteem. Conversely, a student who scores extremely highly may considerably reduce the effort being put into study. It is, therefore, important to consider the possible effects before giving students their results. If results are to be given they should be given only to the individual and not to the whole class. If the group's results are presented, they should be given without attribution to individuals.

The individual's right to privacy is extremely important and, in some cases, unthinking use of psychological tests may infringe this right. Again, personality inventories are most invasive since they ask questions which are personal and potentially revealing. They may include questions on sexual habits or relationships with other people, for example. It may be that the student would not wish to disclose such information to the teacher. Similarly, the results of an ability test may cause the teacher to reconsider the student's capabilities and performance, perhaps unconsciously. If the individual reveals information which he or she would have preferred to withold, then that person's privacy has been invaded. The students should, therefore, always be told the nature of the test, how the results will be used, and who will have access to them. When they have this information, they are in a position to give, or withold, informed consent to the administration of the test.

A formal statement of the ethical principles relating to the use of assessment techniques by psychologists can be found in Principle 8 of the *Ethical Principles of Psychologists* (American Psychological Association, 1981). The safeguards necessary in teaching tests at A-level are set out by Miller (1976).

Two codes of practice for constructing and using tests are the Standards for Educational and Psychological Testing (APA, 1985) and the Code of Fair Testing Practices in Education (Joint Committee on Testing Practices, 1988). The BPS *Guidelines for the User* (BPS, 1989) also offers helpful advice on 'quality control' in using tests. It covers administration and interpretation, emphasizing the responsibilities of providing feedback to people taking a test.

QUALIFI-
CATIONS FOR
TEST USERS

The improper use of psychological tests can cause serious damage to individuals and it is, therefore, important that they should only be supplied to people who are properly qualified to use them. This prevents the public from becoming familiar with the content of tests, thereby invalidating their use, and ensures that tests are administered and interpreted correctly.

All reputable test suppliers operate systems which examine the qualifications of a prospective buyer before allowing the purchase of a particular test. These qualification systems differ from supplier to supplier but generally depend on the categorization of tests according to the complexity of their administration and interpretation, and matching these to the qualifications of the applicant.

One simple system is to have four levels of complexity of test:

Level 1 (the lowest level of complexity) includes group tests of general ability which are straightforward to administer and interpret. Examples are attainment tests or simple general ability tests, such as AH2. Usually, these are available to anyone with a teaching qualification.

Level 2 includes group tests of single psychological abilities. These are used mainly in an occupational context. Examples are Graduate and Managerial Assessment (NFER-Nelson) the Bennett Mechanical Comprehension Test (Psychological Corporation). The necessary qualification for the supply of these tests is the completion of a recognized occupational testing course, or a degree in psychology.

Level 3 includes groups of tests of personality or attitudes and batteries of aptitude tests which include measures of several dimensions. Examples would be the Eysenck Personality Inventory or the Differential Aptitude Test. These tests often require special training before they can be properly interpreted and hence they are available only to graduates in psychology or to those who have completed special courses in their use.

Level 4 includes tests which are difficult to administer or interpret. These include individual tests of mental ability (for example Wechsler Intelligence Scale for Children – Revised, or the British Ability Scales – Revised) or clinical tests. To be qualified to receive these, users must be professional psychologists (sometimes defined by eligibility for Associate Fellowship of The British Psychological Society or as having Chartered Psychologist status).

Qualifying at a higher level normally means that tests at lower levels are also available.

This is a necessarily simplified account of a qualification system and, in practice, the rules are more complex. The system used by NFER-Nelson, for example, has nine levels and makes separate provision for ability tests, personality inventories and clinical tests so that qualifications in one area will not necessarily enable a user to obtain tests in another content area. Indeed qualifications can be so specific that a person can be qualified to obtain only a single test.

There are two relevant statements from The British Psychological Society Standing Committee on Test Standards (1980, 1981) which cover courses on psychological testing and the employment of psychological tests. The process of revising these guidelines has begun, and a committee of the BPS Steering Committee on Test Standards and test publishers has produced a new set of proposals which is undergoing a process of consultation at the time of writing. It is therefore likely that a new set of arrangements will apply to the purchase of tests in the near future. The proposals switch the emphasis from the training received to an assessment of an individual's competencies. It would mean that, for example, simply being a psychology graduate would not be sufficient to qualify for a large range of tests. Instead, a Chartered Psychologist running a course intended to qualify people to use tests would assess each individual, and their competencies would determine the tests which they could have access to. Appropriate arrangements would be made to protect existing users during the change from the prevailing systems to the competency-based system.

Test Suppliers

NFER–Nelson Publishing Company
Three separate catalogues for educational, clinical and occupational tests are available, offering a wide range of British and American tests. They also act as agents for the major American publishers, and the Australian and New Zealand Councils for Educational Research.
(*Address:* Darville House, 2 Oxford Road East, Windsor, Berks. SL4 1BN *tel.* (0753) 858961)

The Psychological Corporation Ltd
A wide range of tests for clinical, occupational and educational use. Mainly American origin, but some have British editions or norms.
(*Address:* Foots Cray High Street, Sidcup, Kent DA14 5HP *tel.* (081) 3001149)

Saville & Holdsworth Ltd	Tests (generally constructed within Saville & Holdsworth) are designed mainly for occupational use and are available singly or grouped into batteries for use with different employment groups. (*Address:* The Old Post House, 81 High Street, Esher, Surrey KT10 9QA *tel.* (0372) 686834)
Science Research Associates Ltd	The British outlet of an American supplier. Mainly established occupational tests of apitude. (*Address:* Newtown Road, Henley-on-Thames, Oxon RG9 1EW *tel.* (0491) 575959)
The Test Agency	A range of educational and industrial tests, some internally published and others published by the Agency as agents for American publishers, are supplied. (*Address:* Counswood House, North Dean, High Wycomb Bucks HP14 4NW *tel.* (024024) 3384)

American test suppliers. In some cases, where tests are not in the catalogues of British suppliers, it is quicker to obtain American tests direct from their US supplier (although there can be problems with their qualification systems). Some of the larger American publishers are:

American Guidance Service
Publishers Building
Circle Pines MN 55014

Institute for Personality and Ability Testing Inc.
PO Box 188
Champaign IL 61820

Western Psychological Services
12031 Wilshire Boulevard
Los Angeles
CA 90025

The catalogues of all these suppliers are, of course, advertising brochures and should be treated as such.

Information about tests. The principle source of (relatively) unbiased information about tests is the series of *Mental Measurements Yearbooks* edited by Buros and his successors. The ninth volume (1985) covers the years 1979 to 1985 and includes reviews of tests as well as information on their availability. A rival is now *Tests: A comprehensive reference for assessments in psychology, education and business* edited by Sweetland, R.C. and Keyser, D.J. (1986, Kansas City: Test Corporation of America), available from NFER-Nelson. A collection of reviews of British educational tests is *Tests in Education* edited by P.Levy and H. Goldstein (1984, London: Academic Press).

Books on Psychological Tests

There have been many texts on psychological testing, mostly American in origin. Two of the better ones which are available in paperback are:

ANASTASI, A. (1988) *Psychological Testing*, 6th ed. New York: Macmillan.
CRONBACH, L.J. (1984) *Essentials of Psychological Testing*, 4th ed. New York: Harper & Row.

Some recent British books are:

KLINE, P. (1986) *A handbook of test construction: introduction to psychometric design*. London: Methuen.
SHELLEY, D. and COHEN, D. (1986) *Testing Psychological Tests*. Beckenham: Croom Helm.
TOPLIS, J., DULEWICZ, V. and FLETCHER, C. (1987) *Psychological Testing: a practical guide for employers.* London: Institute of Personnel Management.

References

AMERICAN PSYCHOLOGICAL ASSOCIATION (1981) Ethical principles of psychologists. *American Psychologist*, 36, 633–638.
AMERICAN PSYCHOLOGICAL ASSOCIATION (1985) *Standards for educational and psychological testing*. Washington DC: American Psychological Association.
ANONYMOUS (1987) *Test Your Reasoning*. Glasgow: Gibson.
BARRETT, J.S. and WILLIAMS, G.R. (1980) *Test Your Own Aptitude*. London: Futura Books.
BARTRAM, D., BEAUMONT, J.G., CORNFORD, T., DANN, P.L. and WILSON, S.L. (1987) Recommendations for the design of software for computer based assessment – Summary statement. *Bulletin of The British Psychological Society*, 40, 86–87.
BERK, R.A. (Ed) (1982) *Handbook of Methods for Detecting Test Bias*. London: John Hopkins.
BRITISH PSYCHOLOGICAL SOCIETY PROFESSIONAL AFFAIRS BOARD (1980) Technical recommendations for psychological tests. *Bulletin of The British Psychological Society*, 33, 161–164.
BRITISH PSYCHOLOGICAL SOCIETY COMMITTEE ON TEST STANDARDS (1980) Notes for guidance in planning short courses in psychological testing. *Bulletin of The British Psychological Society*, 33, 244–249.
BRITISH PSYCHOLOGICAL SOCIETY COMMITTEE ON TEST STANDARDS (1981) Principles governing the employment of psychological tests. *Bulletin of The British Psychological Society*, 34, 317–318.
BRITISH PSYCHOLOGICAL SOCIETY STEERING COMMITTEE ON TEST STANDARDS (1989) *Psychological Testing: Guidelines for the User*. Leicester: The BPS.
BRITISH PSYCHOLOGICAL SOCIETY WORKING PARTY ON COMPETENCE IN PSYCHOLOGICAL TESTING (1983) Psychological tests – a legal definition. *Bulletin of The British Psychological Society*, 36, 192.
BUTLER, E. and PIRIE, M. (1983) *Test Your IQ*. London: Pan.
DE CARLO, N. (1984) *Psychological games: A book of tests and puzzles to*

teach you more about yourself and those around you. New York: Facts on File.
EYSENCK, H.J. (1962) *Know Your Own IQ*. Harmondsworth: Penguin.
EYSENCK, H.J. (1969) *Check Your Own IQ*. Harmondsworth: Penguin.
EYSENCK, H.J. and WILSON, G.D. (1976) *Know Your Own Personality*. Harmondsworth: Penguin.
EYSENCK, H.J. (1986) *Know Your Own PSI-Q*. London: Corgi.
JOINT COMMITTEE ON TESTING PRACTICES (1988) *Code of Fair Testing Practices in Education*. Washington, DC: Joint Committee on Testing Practices.
KLINE, P. (1988) The British 'cultural influence' on ability testing. In S.H. Irvine and J.W. Berry (1988) *Human Abilities in Cultural Context*. Cambridge: Cambridge University Press.
MILLER, K. (1976) Teaching tests at A-level. *Psychology Teaching, 4*, 146–147.
MORLEY, S.J. (1989) Report of Chief Examiner: Diploma in Clinical Psychology. *The Psychologist, 2*, 33–34.
SMITH, P. and WHETTON, C. (1988) Bias reduction in test development. *The Psychologist, 1*. 257–258.
SULLIVAN, N. (1988) *Test Your Intelligence*. London: Javelin.
TYLER, B. and MILLER, K. (1986) The use of tests by psychologists: Report on a survey of BPS members. *Bulletin of The British Psychological Society, 39*, 405–410.

The following tests were referred to in the text, mainly for purposes of illustration. They should not be considered to be recommendations for teaching, or any other purpose.

BENNETT, G.K. (1980) Bennett Mechanical Comprehension Test, (British Edition). Sidcup, Kent: The Psychological Corporation.
BENNETT, G.K. SEASHORE, H.G. and WESMAN, A.G. (1983) Different Aptitude Tests: Forms V and W. New York: The Psychological Corporation.
CURETON, E.E. and CURETON, L.W. and students (1955) Multi-aptitude Test. New York: The Psychological Corporation.
ELLIOTT, C.D., MURRAY, D.J. and PEARSON, L.S. (1983) British Ability Scales – Revised. Windsor: NFER-Nelson.
EYSENCK, H.J. and EYSENCK, S.B.G. (1964) Eysenck Personality Inventory. London: University of London Press.
HEIM, A.W., WATTS, K.P. and SIMMONDS, V. (1974) AH2/AH3 Group Tests of General Reasoning. Windsor: NFER-Nelson.
PSYCHOMETRIC RESEARCH UNIT, HATFIELD POLYTECHNIC. (1985) Graduate and Managerial Assessment. Windsor: NFER-Nelson.
SMITH, P. and WHETTON, C. (1988) General Ability Tests. Windsor: NFER-Nelson.
WECHSLER, D. (1976) Wechsler Intelligence Scale for Children – Anglicised Revised Edition. Sidcup, Kent: The Psychological Corporation.

PSYCHOLOGY FOR TEACHERS

Second Revised Edition

David Fontana

'*will almost certainly become the standard text for teacher training ... David Fontana details with notable clarity and lack of ambiguity the very practical relevance of the theories and issues discussed.' TES*

'*a breath of fresh air. With its simplicity and relevance, it bridges theory and practice.'*
Education Section Review

Psychology shows that no child's behaviour can be fully understood unless we also study the behaviour of others - teachers, parents, friends. This text deals with core concerns such as the practical applications of learning theory, classroom control and moral development. And in this new single-author edition, issues have been introduced concerning the home-school relationship, strategies to aid learning and personal development, children with special needs, teacher stress and counselling.

Psychology for Teachers is specially designed to meet the needs of students on BEd, PGCE and other higher degree courses, whatever their subject; experienced teachers will also find it invaluable.

2nd rev. edn 1988; 384 pp
0 333 46125 8 pb
0 333 46124 X hb

£8.50
£25.00

British Psychological Society
St Andrews House
48 Princess Road East
Leicester LE1 7DR UK

Decision Dynamics Ltd

MICROCOMPUTERS: COURSEWARE AND SOFTWARE

Geoffrey Underwood and Jean D.M. Underwood

❏ *statistical packages ● personality, psychometric and other tests ● the micro-based lab. class ● on-line control of lab. apparatus ● artificial intelligence ● micro-controlled interactive video techniques ● addresses of software agents and suppliers ● software index*

We approached this chapter by looking *principally* at what microcomputers are being used for in psychology teaching. Occasionally we have been sidetracked into suggesting useful software packages, or, in the case of interactive videodisc technology, for instance, we have mentioned a development which we confidently expect to have an impact upon teaching practices within the next few years. We have focused almost entirely upon the software that is available, mentioning hardware only in the context of which system is necessary to run a particular piece of software. On the principle that one does not need to understand the thermoelectronics of a car's ignition system in order to drive between Nottingham and Derby, we can see no argument for dwelling upon the electronic wizardry that lives beneath the microcomputer's bonnet. Hence no talk of 16-bit and 32-bit machines, or of the superiority of the 386 over the 286 processor.

However it is necessary to start by defining one term which is central to our review. A *microcomputer* here is regarded as a machine that is relatively small in terms of processing capacity, which is normally dedicated to one user who will control its input and output routines, and which normally sits on a desktop at the point of use. The next size up is a minicomputer, which, by virtue of a more sophisticated operating system, will often serve 16 or more networked users within a department or within a research group. The large, remote machine which serves an institution, and which is managed by a team of computer engineers, is likely to be a mainframe computer. One metric here is the scale of service – the desktop, the department or the institution – and another is the control available to the user. At one end of this continuum the user has total control over when the machine is switched on, as well as over which programs are available, and at the other extreme the user is served by a team of engineers whose job it is to make programs and other facilities available.

The microcomputers to be discussed here include IBM PC-compatible machines (which use the same software but which tend to cost less than the IBM PC), the BBC series, and the Apple Macintosh series. They tend to be dedicated to one user (but can be networked), tend to be located in the same room as the user (though not if networked), and tend to be supplemented by dedicated peripheral devices such as printers and external memory readers. The micros to be discussed here generally cost less than £1,000 and can be used as stand-alone machines operating upon software stored on a floppy disc installed by the person who will use the software. Costs start to escalate, of course, as soon as we want to install a hard-disc memory system so that all of our programs can be kept in one place which is convenient for machine accessibility, or when we need to install printers and graph plotters for publication-quality output.

In order to supplement our own direct experiences of how psychology teachers choose to use micros, as well as other possible ways in which they can be used, we have drawn upon published reviews of software for psychologists. Both *The Psychologist* and *Behavior Research Methods, Instruments and Computers* regularly feature software reviews, and are essential reading for anyone requiring updates and opinions on commercially available software: we have based a large number of our comments upon reviews in these journals. We also sent a questionnaire to 25 polytechnic and university psychology departments, and to 25 schools and colleges of further education that teach A-level psychology. The questionnaire asked specifically about micro and software use in teaching statistics, personality and ability testing, laboratory classes, on-line control of apparatus, AI (artificial intelligence) applications and programming, and also asked what else micros were used for. As might be expected, there is both more use and a greater range of use of micros in degree-level institutions. They simply have larger budgets, and a number of A-level teachers commented that they do not have regular access to microcomputers. But one reason given for the slight use of micros in an A-level institution was that psychology is taught in a short course, and this does not give enough time for any study which is not directly applicable in the examination. We regard this as unfortunate, and one of our aims here is to show how micros can be used with commercially available software for the enhanced presentation of materials which are of direct examination relevance.

STATISTICAL
PACKAGES

The most common use of microcomputers in undergraduate psychology courses is for the statistical analysis of data collected in experiments, and there are so many general-purpose packages available that choice will most probably be made on the basis of existing hardware. It seems that relatively few A-level courses are making use of the statistics packages which are available. Because of the huge number of statistical tests and statistics packages we have restricted our comments to the packages which current users have found to be satisfactory. We have also excluded programs which handle only one statistical test, simply because teachers and students tend to prefer a general package so that a separate command structure does not have to be learnt for each test.

The most frequently used packages at undergraduate level for IBM PC-compatible machines are SPSS PC+, UNISTAT II, and Minitab. Whereas SPSS PC+ and UNISTAT II are in the 'research-use' category, and are intended for use beyond the teaching of elementary statistics, Minitab and its BBC-based offspring can be used for A-level and introductory undergraduate support purposes. There is also a large number of statistics packages available for the Apple Macintosh, but these are generally for dedicated Macintosh users at degree level and beyond.

The 'Big Daddy' of statistical packages is SPSS, which runs on IBM PC-compatible machines in its SPSS PC+ form. It is very powerful, and the mainframe version (SPSSX) is very awkward to use. SPSS mainframe users will find the command syntax familiar, and micro users will be familiar with its use of help screens, menus, and excellent graphics. For teaching purposes, it is unnecessary to take the mainframe-SPSS route, except if students need to be introduced to the 'industry standard'. SPSS packages do come with back-up texts which can be used as the basis for an entire statistics course at degree level, and cover all of the tests that most of us could imagine using for research purposes, let alone teaching. The big problem is that mainframe-SPSS is a relic from the days of data-card punching and batch processing. Commands are written with a specific syntax, and then the data file entered. Learning the commands and their structure can be a very time-consuming excercise. Unlike the mainframe/minicomputer version, the PC version is priced in the hundreds of pounds rather than the thousands, and it is extensive enough to require a hard disc for usable running.

It is also much more usable in its PC form. This is a thorough, serious statistical package, and 'stats-junkies' will consider the expense and learning-costs to be worthwhile.

A well-used alternative to SPSS PC+ for statistics on an IBM PC-compatible is UNISTAT II (UNISTAT III has recently been released, and even this advanced package is less than half the price of SPSS PC+). Data entry is straightforward, and processing options are selected from pull-down and pop-up menus. UNISTAT II is also available in a form which will run on BBC machines. Like SPSS PC+, the UNISTAT packages are powerful enough for research use.

Minitab is the final IBM PC-compatible package which is in frequent use in degree-level teaching, and it also has a less powerful version called Microtab, which runs on the BBC machines. These two packages offer a good range of descriptive statistics, non-parametric and simple parametric tests. They are much less sophisticated than SPSS and UNISTAT, and are priced accordingly. They are very usable in introductory statistics and laboratory classes, and with non-computer literate students, as they are operated inter-actively and with good use of natural language commands. Minitab is similar to Microtab, but is less limited in terms of the amount of memory available for data storage and manipulation. Minitab and Microtab are serious contenders as support packages for pre-degree level courses in psychology and for introductory statistics classes generally.

There is an extensive range of statistical packages available for the Apple Macintosh, and the four mentioned here are in the 'research-use' category, for comparison with the PC-compatible packages discussed above. A fuller comparison of Macintosh statistics packages has been prepared by Lehman (1986), although he tested earlier packages than are now on release, and many of them have since undergone considerable development. For those who are familiar with the Macintosh environment it is diffficult to imagine wanting to use any software on another system if there is something suitable available on the Mac. The accessibility and usability of the Macintosh is well known, and the statistics packages available for this machine make good use of its user-centred interface.

CLR ANOVA is specifically designed to handle analysis of variance, and is the best program for this purpose as measured by the larger number of factors it can take, and by the range of post-analysis tests which are available. StatView and StatWorks are rather similar. They are both general packages with a wide range of parametric and non-parametric tests, with a good range of options for data handling and description, and good graphics facilities. They both have the advantage of being easy to learn how to use.

Like CLR ANOVA, DataDesk does not handle non-parametric statistics, but is particularly good for correlation and multiple regression analysis. It also has a cluster analysis and principal components analysis, and the graphics are nothing less than magnificent. This package has been designed for research applications where the manipulation of variables could otherwise be a chore. It has an extraordinary number of options available in each product window, and because these options encourage data exploration the package is useful as a teaching tool.

PERSONALITY, PSYCHO-METRIC AND OTHER TESTS

The administration of psychological tests is remarkably easy with the micro, but we have come across limited evidence of their use in A-level or undergraduate courses on questionnaire and test design, even though they could provide valuable support materials, particularly for undergraduate teaching once the essentials of testing have been dealt with. Indeed, there is quite simply little evidence of the use of commercial software packages for psychological testing. One reason might be the high prices charged for these packages which, unlike statistical packages, require the user to buy a separate package for each test.

Automated psychological tests (APTS), such as computer-based questionnaires, have two principal advantages over their pencil-and-paper parents. Administration and scoring are automatic, and are therefore both less tedious and less prone to error. Previous questionnaire responses can be easily accessed, making for simple comparison of an individual with sample norms. Discussions of the advantages of computer-based testing can be found in Beaumont (1982), Thompson and Wilson (1982) and Watts, Baddeley and Williams (1982). APTS which scale individuals on personality and ability dimensions are in wide use in clinical and industrial personnel settings. Most of them run on IBM PC-compatible machines.

Customized APTs

Many of the traditional pencil-and-paper tests have now been converted, and are listed in the DRAT directory, which is available for a small fee from Dr Sarah L. Wilson of The Royal Hospital and Home (for address see p.163). The DRAT list of origins and specifications of a large number of APTS and other psychological diagnostic tests which have been developed 'in-house' by individuals who are, in some cases, prepared to share or sell them. Tests which are mentioned include Mill Hill Vocabulary Scale, digit span, Raven's Progressive Matrices, Eysenck Personality Inventory, Bexley-Maudsley Automated Personality Screening, Cattell's 16 PF, Myers

Briggs Type Indicator, and tests of verbal reasoning and verbal fluency. The directory lists the addresses of software writers, the machines on which the software will run, the aim of the software, and research publications relating to its use.

Commercial APTS

Commercial APTS are also available. If the three that have been reviewed in the Computer Column of *The Psychologist* recently are typical, it may be worth waiting before making an investment. Not one of them received a positive review.

Charles Johnson (1988a) reviewed Test Plus, which is based on Cattell's 16PF, and concluded that he 'would not recommend it for serious use'. This package has up to 324 items in the test section, a decision-making section which allows the creation of an ideal profile against which actual profiles can be compared, and a report writing section. The test items are sometimes poorly worded ('Is it generally false that you have never been embarrassed?'), the decision-making tool is invalid for statistical reasons, and the report writer can come up with conflicting descriptions and have the 'smack of astrological prediction'! Under Johnson's pen (1988b) a test of motivation called Spectrum-1 does not fare any better. This questionnaire scales individuals on sources of motivation – accomplishment, recognition, power and affiliation – and comes from the same software house as Test Plus. It has a similar testing/decision-making/report writing format, with similar problems associated with poor wording, 'worthless' decision making, and bland descriptions produced by paragraph pasting from the report writer. Johnson's verdict on this one is that it is 'poorly thought out and underdeveloped' and that 'using this package would not advance your understanding of someone's motivation by all that much'. The producers of the Eysenck Personality Profiler (EPP) must have been quite relieved to learn that Charles Johnson was not reviewing their software, but Charles Bethall-Fox (1989) does not let them escape lightly. The EPP is an extended version of the traditional EPQ, and claims to scale individuals along extraversion, emotionality and tough-mindedness scales with a total of 630 items. There are no indications of the reliability or validity of the extended questionnaire, failings which lead Bethall-Fox to suggest rather cautiously that 'the potential purchaser must largely rely on his or her intuitive judgement as to whether the EPP should be used for practical purposes'.

A software package which is used in psychological testing and which does seem to be usable is a program called Circumgrids (Chambers and Grice, 1986). This is a repertory grid package which allows the analysis and comparison of grids, together with a number of subsidiary analyses. It is usable only by those with a sound knowledge of repertory grid techniques and has a couple of irritating features: input and output are direct, and cannot be made through a file, and secondly it imposes a strict size limitation. It could prove useful for undergraduate teaching purposes however.

A final package, again of interest to teachers in social psychology, is the SAMP Survey Sampling computer-aided learning package reviewed by Dennis Hay (1989). This package allows a survey simulation using the population of an imaginary town. Students can select which of four survey methods will be used (random sampling; clustered random sampling; stratified random sampling; quota sampling), and what sample parameters should be applied. SAMP then gives descriptive summary statistics from the selected sample, and these can be compared with summaries from different samples. Hay describes it as a package which 'is professionally presented and provides clear, concise demonstations' although it is restricted in its scope. This simple simulation tool makes good use of the data-handling capabilities of micros and could be a useful teaching aid.

THE MICRO-BASED LABORATORY CLASS

Commercial Packages

Of the recent commercial laboratory packages, the Glasgow packages are the most comprehensive (Bushnell and Mullin, 1987), and are in use in a number of UK psychology departments to support the teaching of degree-level laboratory techniques. They run on IBM PCs or Apple IIs. There are about a dozen experiments in each package, dealing with topics such as word recognition, mental imagery, memory, visual illusions, and hemispheric asymmetry. Although designed for undergraduate classes, some of the experiments and demonstrations are also appropriate for pre-degree courses in psychology. The two packages are called *Experimental Psychology: A computerized laboratory course* and *Cognitive Psychology: A computerized laboratory course* although most of the experiments could have been presented under either label. As these packages are so comprehensive, and as so many undergraduate departments are either using or evaluating them, it is appropriate for us to look at them in some detail here. They provide a good example of the range of psychology experiments that can be demonstrated on a microcomputer. Investing in these programs is a serious decision – they each cost several hundred pounds – but only one copy of each package is required for the laboratory. The supporting texts and workbooks are necessary for each student, but they are more affordable.

The two packages allow a resource-limited laboratory instructor to provide demonstrations of a large number of experiments in psychology. In the prevailing economic climate it may be that a number of undergraduate departments will be taking a serious look at the re-organization of their laboratory classes around them. The packages are designed to allow students to use each of the experiments in the role of subject, with minimal assistance from a class tutor or demonstrator.

It is possible to run the experiments on machines which have access only to floppy disc drives, but much more convenient if the programs are stored on a hard disc. Each student needs a copy of the floppy disc with the programs for each course, and so copying of the programs is explicitly authorized. It is not clear whether the programs could be used on a network, and we have a report of one disenchanted failure. Each package contains the programs and two manuals – a detailed student's workbook and a brief instructor's guide, which contains hints about installation of the programs and encouraging comments about how easy it is to teach vast numbers of students with little more than technical back-up. The student's workbook contains sections on how to use the computer and on how to write lab. reports, in addition to instructions about running each of the experiments. The chapters on each of the experiments contain background introductions, procedural instructions and results sections with blanks for entering data. Each package comes with a set of multiple-choice questions for student assessment.

Jim Mullin, one of the package authors, gives his e-mail address in the instructor's guide and was very helpful during the installation of the programs onto our PC. The experiments are listed as follows, starting with the Experimental Psychology package. They are in the order in which they appear in the packages, as complexity and student involvement are increased progressively.

Experimental Psychology package. A simple reaction-time experiment with 20 bar-press responses presents an opportunity to look at descriptive statistics and little else. The second experiment involves lexical decisions, with high and low frequency words. The response keys are 'W' and 'N' for words and non-words, and although this makes for an easy mnemonic, it is ergonomic nonsense given the position of these keys on a QWERTY keyboard. This experiment, as with many that follow, has data from so-called 'other subjects' stored with it, to allow the calculation of a t-test – this is done automatically as the experiment finishes, and the user is presented with 'the answer'. An experiment on motion aftereffects uses the waterfall illusion in a demonstration involving interocular generalization and a Müller-Lyer experiment with varying arrow angles provides the basis for an introduction to psychophysical methods. A Prisoner's Dilemma experiment is again little more than a demonstration, and is one of the few that might be better run as a person–person conflict rather than person–machine. An ESP experiment asks the user to guess which of five numbers has been selected by the program, and this brings a new meaning to the question of mind-reading. This experiment did seem to go on a long time – there were in fact 100 trials. This raises a general point about there being more than enough trials in all of the experiments. Getting out of the programs is not always easy – the escape key works with some but not others.

There are two mental imagery experiments, one which requires judgements about the relative sizes of objects depicted by their names, and one which requires judgements about the similarity between a rotated and non-rotated figure. The quality of graphics is crude, given the possibilities which exist with the graphics packages available. The rotated figures look as if they have been drawn by hand. An experiment investigating selective attention is based upon the Shaffer and LaBerge study of the effects of flanking words upon category decision responses. The experiment finishes with the presentation of a completed summary table from an analysis of variance. A 'life events' questionnaire asks a large number of questions about the user's personal health and another set of questions about stressful life events. A few of the questions are inappropriate for an undergraduate population, but this only becomes a problem if we start to take questionnaires seriously!

One of the hemispheric asymmetry experiments looks for visual field differences in world recognition (presenting data from other subjects but leaving the user to perform the statistical calculations this time), and the second experiment investigates judgements of numerosity. Either the numerosity task is hard, or fatigue from the other experiments makes it seem that way. The final experiment in this package is one of the most detailed and most carefully prepared. It is an investigation of subliminal perception, and is therefore of considerable interest to many undergraduates. All the more reason for the experiment to be designed well, and it is. It is modelled on Marcel's primed lexical decision task, with the priming word being masked by a display of nonverbal symbols. The exposure of the prime is titrated in the first stage of the experiment to ensure non-reportability. Users are left to themselves to calculate a t-test comparing the effects of related and unrelated primes. These experiments are graded in their detail of design and in the user's post-experimental involvement, and a number of them provide useful demonstrations.

The Cognitive Psychology package uses the same format as the more introductory Experimental Psychology demonstrations. A choice reaction-time task varies the number of alternatives in an investigation of Hick's Law, and a signal detection task introduces d' and ß. A visual search experiment is used to introduce multifactorial designs, and a Posner matching task can be used as the basis for discussions about stages of processing. The Stroop experiment is a little disappointing, because rather than making use of the availability of colour graphics, the experiment relies upon the conflict between the number of figures and the identity of the figures, in a figure counting task. The study of global and local processing, based on Navon's report, is straightforward enough, as is a Sperling-type iconic memory task (except there is no machine data-logging of responses here). There are no fewer than three experiments looking at the capacity of short-term memory, but again there is no data-logging. A Sternberg-type memory search task incorporates a factor posing a problem for simple interpretations of the linear increase of RT with increasing set size – the factor of serial position of the probed item within the list. An experiment investigating the different effects of elaborative and maintenance rehearsal presents the materials to be remembered, and leaves the user to follow instructions. An experiment investigating the effects of 'levels of processing' on remembering uses visual, rhyming, and semantic decisions followed by the customary surprise recognition task. Rhyme judgements received rather close scrutiny after coming across such 'correct' rhymes as soot/fruit, food/could, spot/caught and stuff/trough, until it was remembered that the materials had been prepared for students in Glasgow! It is possible to change the materials by breaking into the program, and the next version of this package might be improved by giving the instructor an option for entering words considered to be suitable for the class using the program. The final experiment in this set, on lexical search, is introduced by a confusing discussion of Collins and Quillian and the differences between procedural and declarative knowledge, but settles down eventually to a straightforward investigation of the influence of multiple meanings upon lexical decision.

Are these experiments really usable as the basis of a lab. class for undergraduate psychologists? The advertising which accompanies the packages suggests that they could serve a 'cafeteria-system' of tuition, but most teachers would regret giving up their close involvement in laboratory class management. Some of the experiments are excellent, and could certainly be used as demonstrations at the start of a class, but they provide no opportunity for students to be involved with the decisions about designing experiments. They do not invite students to ask their own questions about human behaviour, and even at an introductory level it is important that students think about the nature of a good question. Students using this package do not need to generate their own questions or their own experimental designs, and so questions and designs are not evaluated. There is a place for learning by example, but for many lab. instructors the use of these packages would place too much distance between the student and the problem of how to go about setting up an enquiry. We have small niggles with many of the experiments – unnecessary bar presses to get the next trial up, non-ergonomic key presses, poor graphics, etc – but the real objection is to the whole philosophy of teaching by cafeteria methods which take no account of individual learning difficulties and which set out to teach by example rather than by problem solving. If the philosophy does appeal, then the package might serve your purposes – as it might if you find yourself having to teach lab. classes by distance-learning or to a couple of hundred students with limited support.

Most of the demonstrations could be used for both undergraduate and A-level teaching, however, and provided that the students are not expected to work through their own experimental designs, or apply their own statistical procedures to their data, then these demonstrations will prove to be valuable. However, a number of our questionnaire respondents did indicate disappointment. One comment we received complained of 'homespun, bug-ridden software'. You would therefore be well advised to either visit a laboratory where they are already installed, or talk to the commercial suppliers about seeing a sample from the packages in operation.

Customized Programs

The alternative to a cafeteria package is customized experiments. A large number of undergraduate departments have written their own software for specific laboratory classes. To give just one example of possible kinds of application, we shall mention a small package produced locally. (It is not available for general release.) The package was produced by the laboratory steward at Nottingham, Andy Smith, using BASIC (plus assembly language) for the BBC B micro for undergraduate lab. classes. The menu-driven open program allows a large number of different experiments to be written into it. It can present words and sentences for variable intervals, and can also record the time between presentation of the stimulus and a button press or a voice switch activation. The program offers a number of menu-selections concerning number of successive stimulus fields, presentation intervals, number of trials and so on, and includes a text-editor for test materials to be written. Before it can be used the student needs to make a number of experimental design decisions, and although the package does restrict the student in the kind of experiment that can be performed, this is true of any piece of laboratory equipment. The students are left to make decisions about experimental design, unlike anyone using the Glasgow package. Open-ended laboratory programs not only give more options than the old-style box with fluorescent tubes, but also make the experimenter's life easier by logging responses as the experiment progresses. This in turn makes the subject's life easier – experiments take less time, and are less prone to interruption while the experimenter finds his or her way. The disadvantage of this approach is that any programs that are sufficiently flexible to be usable for different experiments take a long time to write – but are worth the effort. Commercial packages which offer the same flexibility, and which, most importantly, involve the student in experimental design, would be very welcome. It would be useful to have a laboratory 'authoring shell' in commercial packages such as those produced in Glasgow, rather than set-piece demonstrations and ready-to-bake statistics.

A popular source of customized programs which allow the microcomputer to be used as a laboratory is *Behavior Research Methods, Instruments, and Computers*. These programs sometimes appear as listings, but more usually it is necessary to send the author either an empty floppy disc or a small fee to cover the cost of a new disc. An example of a program available from this source allows the presentation of a text sentence-by-sentence, with the reader able to move backwards and forwards through the text, and with data logging in the form of time-on-frame and sequence of frames (Nason and Zabrucky, 1988). This comprehension monitoring program makes use of the HyperCard facility on the Macintosh, a facility which will make a great many psychology experiments more feasible in the future. HyperCard has been described as an 'object oriented programming system' (OOPS) in which the objects are buttons, fields, cards, stacks and backgrounds which are displayed on the screen. These screen metaphors are the user-friendly interface to a powerful authoring shell which lends itself to information delivery and educational training applications, but it can also be used in more dynamic ways as a laboratory tool. By 'pressing a button' on the screen (i.e. pointing at a button using the mouse) a sub-routine in the computer program is initiated, and in laboratory applications this can lead to the presentation of displays of words, sentences or graphics, and the starting of timing routines. In the Nason and Zabrucky example, the 'button' allows the reader to select earlier or later segments of the text.

A major disadvantage of the in-house approach to writing customized lab. class programs is that departments up and down the country are duplicating each other's efforts. We like our own tachistoscope program, but it is entirely likely that someone from a department down the road will now write to us to say that they have an even better one. It would make sense, at the very least, to have a centralized register and software exchange scheme. The DRAT directory of automated psychological tests, which we discussed earlier, mentions a number of standard laboratory class packages which have been produced in-house and which may be available through software exchange or sale. This directory comes the closest to a centralized register, and perhaps the new Computers in Teaching Initiative Centre for Psychology, based at the University of York, will take this on board on a formal basis. They will be providing an advice service for computer-based teaching in psychology, as well as evaluating software and courseware. Queries about the Centre should be sent to Dr N. V. Hammond, Department of Psychology, University of York YO1 5DD. For those teaching at pre-degree level, the Association for the Teaching of Psychology is currently co-ordinating information on relevant in-house software.

ON-LINE CONTROL OF LABORATORY APPARATUS

Micros are also invaluable as laboratory control devices. Non-computing equipment can be controlled by microcomputers, and data again logged through this storage medium. Most of these applications will be customized, although one or two companies (for example, Electronic Developments Company and Forth Instruments), that have traditionally supplied psychology laboratory apparatus are now supplying the same tachistoscopes and event recorders in computer-controllable forms.

Customized Devices

An alternative to these pre-designed, off-the-shelf kits is to develop a microcomputer system to meet a specific need. This takes us more into the realm of research, but it can be instructive for undergraduate students to get an understanding of the range of behavioural measures that can be taken, and of the flexibility which laboratory micros can provide. Each laboratory has its own idiosyncratic apparatus designs, and, as there is no standard here, we shall briefly describe two customizations which have been developed in the Nottingham laboratories, so as to give some indication of the kind of system which can be developed. The journal *Behavior Research Methods, Instruments, and Computers* regularly publishes hints about adapting laboratory equipment for micro-control and also provides program listings for the more popular routines such as response timing. See, for example the 'tachistoscope' program which runs timing routines on IBM PCs (Segalowitz, 1987).

One of our first attempts at a micro-controlled laboratory was in the control of commercially supplied tachistoscopes. We originally had three slide projectors which had been supplied with tachistoscope shutters and an off-the-shelf pulse generator which acted as the driver. Responses to one of the slide projectors were recorded from two-choice response keys, which illuminated one of two bulbs in the experimenter's line of sight, to indicate which key had been pressed, and also stopped a millisecond timer which had been started by the pulse generator. The slides in the carousel advanced automatically, but everything else was done by hand – pressing a button on the pulse generator to start the sequence at the beginning of each trial, making a written note of which response key had been pressed and also a note of the response time, and then resetting the pulse generator. Experimental fatigue was evident in both subject and experimenter! So we took a tiny microcomputer – a Rockwell AIM 65 – and replaced the pulse generator. The Rockwell now controls the slide projectors, and it also records which key has been pressed, and how long the response took. The Rockwell has a very small capacity (some pocket calculators have more RAM than this machine), and requires one carousel tray of responses to be emptied from the micro's memory before the next tray of slides is presented, but it does come with an integral printer and so this is not too much of a nuisance. Running our slide presentations is not only more convenient for the experimenter, and with less risk of a recording error, but it is also faster for the subjects.

The second application we have developed is to serve our research on eye movements during reading and visual search, but the principle of data recording and data logging is very general. In this case a continuously varying, analogue input has been presented to a microcomputer – we use a BBC B or a BBC Master – and this is in the form of an electrical current which varies in voltage. The voltage represents the position of the subject's eye relative to a display. This display is also produced by the micro, as part of the overall experimental control package written specifically for this application by Howard Wilkinson (a Nottingham University laboratory technician), who also built the eye movement recorder. The BBC micro has an analogue-to-digital converter which allows the transfer of our continuously varying eye movement voltages into a digital form usable and storable by the micro. Any continuous data stream, such as polygraph recordings, could be read by this system. Handling of the digital data is taken care of with a suite of post-experimental programs which give us such measures as the reading time per sentence, as well as fine-grained detail about which letters have been inspected, and for how long. The experiments could be run off-line, by putting the voltages from the eye movement recorder directly onto a polygraph recorder for instance, but analysis of the paper records is both time-consuming and inaccurate in comparison with the data-logging facility provided by the micro. The system is simple in operation – undergraduates are able to use it for project work – and it gives students an idea of what can be achieved through the on-line control of displays and data logging.

Commercial Devices An inexpensive alternative to building a customized on-line system is provided in the form of BIOGRAM II, a software and hardware package which can be used to monitor skin conductance. This package runs on BBC micro, and uses the analogue-to-digital converter in ready-built programs which can be used as demonstrations or experiments on biofeedback, on phobia investigation and on lie detection (vocally or written presentations). It has been used successfully at GCSE and A-level, and Bob Sykes (1987) gave a very positive review, the acid test being to use it in a University Open Day: 'works very well for demonstrations . . . the results were outstandingly clear . . . the reputation of psychology as an objective and exact science received a considerable boost!' The manual also gets the Sykes medal for usability – it includes clear instructions and suggestions for experiments which can be run with the package.

ARTIFICIAL INTELLIGENCE A full range of programming languages is being used on a wide variety of machines – undergraduates are being taught LISP, POP-11, POPLOG, PROLOG, PASCAL, and FORTH, mainly using IBM PC-compatible, BBC, RML Nimbus, and Apple Macintosh machines. They are also developing expert systems, and being given introductions to the possibilities available through HyperCard techniques. A-level students are less at home with artificial intelligence (AI), and very few of them choose to answer questions on AI in their exams.

Expert Systems Of the artificial intelligence applications that are finding their way into undergraduate psychology courses, expert systems have perhaps the greatest profile. As well as preparing psychology students with the information technology systems that they could be using or building after graduation, expert systems give a presentation of decision making and knowledge simulation which is both applied and formal. Fully developed, advanced courses will continue to use professional expert systems shells, but an inexpensive introductory shell which has many of the features of the full system is Knowol+, a system which has been positively reviewed by Mike Burton (1988). It comes as a shell to be developed into a domain-specific system by the user, together with a couple of example knowledge bases which give an idea of a running, interactive system. It runs on IBM PC-compatible, and has been used for demonstration purposes with advanced-course undergraduates at Nottingham with some success.

One package that looks certain to take off is the handbook plus software *Explorations in parallel distributed processing* which McClelland and Rumelhart (1988a) have produced to accompany their two volumes on parallel distributed processing (PDP) models of the microstructure of cognition. The 'Explorations' package is already a success with the Nottingham AI group, and is installed as a central part of an AI Methods course for final-year undergraduates. Strictly speaking, the programs will run on IBM PC-compatible machines, but they are ideally installed on a UNIX-handling system (they are written in C), principally on account of the amount of time required for running through the learning processes demonstrated by the programs. The handbook gives clear and extensive information on installation, and the Nottingham group have found no bugs to date. For those who want more information without commitment, a summary of the 'Explorations' package is available in a journal article by McClelland and Rumelhart (1988b).

The package should be considered as an adjunct to the two PDP books, and although each chapter gives an overview of a different program, much of the package would not be too useful without prior study of the PDP books. The reason for this is that the simulation programs are open-ended, and it would be difficult to appreciate what they are doing without a good background in PDP/connectionist theory. The programs can be viewed as straightforward demonstrations, or they can be used interactively, through the modification of the learning parameters, and can be used as the basic toolkit for the development of new PDP models. The programs on the two floppy discs which come with the handbook deal with such models as interactive activation and competition, auto-association, pattern association, back propagation and constraint satisfaction. The package is currently priced at less than £20, and is an essential basis for a hands-on course on connectionism. Each chapter deals with a different aspect of PDP architecture, and there are excercises at the end of each chapter for students and instructors not totally familiar with PDP concepts.

Two other packages deserve mention here, on the grounds that they also offer environments for AI explorations. These are the MicroCODIL and AlpahPOP packages.

MicroCODIL is Chris Reynolds's development of the 1960s mainframe-based language CODIL, and which allows users to build introductory but useful expert systems and knowledge bases with a BBC micro. It is probably most usable by A-level and early undergraduate students. The extensive documentation starts with an outline of the theoretical underpinnings of the system. In essence, MicroCODIL employs a data structure which simulates a model of human memory and human information processing. It works on the premise that humans can only cope with a limited amount of information at one time, and that we chunk that information into meaningful packages in order to overcome processing limitations.

MicroCODIL knowledge bases consist of items of information (for example, the name of a property) in a simple hierarchical structure, but individual items can be linked to others by association and inference, thus establishing a set of complex statements and relationships. It is this grouping of items into interlinked subsets that allows MicroCODIL to handle poorly structured data, and is a key distinction between it and a relational database.

MicroPROLOG is an earlier and obvious competitor to MicroCODIL, but the latter has certain advantages for secondary education. It is a relatively simple language, and goals can be reached without getting too involved in syntax. In this sense it is in tune with other school-oriented developments based around LOGO. The ability of the software to cope with data which are not rigidly structured also contributes to this feeling of ready accesssibility.

A number of departments are now introducing POP-11 to undergraduates as their first programming language, and AlphaPOP makes good use of the facilities of the Apple Macintosh in providing an acclaimed system. Stephen Payne (1988) describes it as coming 'close to providing an all-purpose Psychologist's programming system, that can be used for both modelling and for running experiments'. The positive features of this package are usability and flexibility.

MICRO-
CONTROLLED
INTERACTIVE
VIDEO
TECHNIQUES

There is as yet very little indication of interactive video techniques being used to support psychology teaching. It is simply too soon for discs related to psychology to be available, and until support materials are produced there will be little investment in the hardware. Materials are starting to appear, however, and the educational opportunity by this interactive, multi-media technology will be too great for us to ignore.

Interactive video (IV) burst onto the educational scene a few years ago with the release of the BBC's Domesday disc, supported by the Phillips player which was in turn controlled by the BBC Master microcomputer or by the RML Nimbus. This new technology presents the user with an integrated package combining still and moving pictures, text, graphical representations and/or sound. It is interactive in that the users can select material as they choose but they can also operate on information held in this multi-mode database. For example, data held on the Domesday disc can be graphed in a variety of different ways and sub-sets of data can be isolated for further analysis. This integration of the means of presenting information and the high quality of the pictorial material are two reasons for education's interest in IV. A further perceived advantage is that use of IV encourages a non-formal learning situation in which students navigate themselves through the subject matter held on the disc.

Imagine, for instance, teaching an integrated laboratory and statistics class supported by IV. Using only one IV disc we could start with a demonstration of the phenomenon to be investigated, move to our own design of the experiment investigating the phenomenon and watch how the effect changes, and when we have agreed upon a design we can run the subjects through the experiment. We would then be given options for the analysis of our own data, and be given illustrations of the alternative treatments which are available. The analysis would be an integral part of the laboratory, but the laboratory would not be so intrusive as to get in the way of the statistics. Each would be given a purpose in this 'tutored exploration' environment in which the student would be able to interact with the materials on the IV disc to test optional designs and optional analyses with much reduced personal time cost in comparison with the traditional off-line laboratory.

After the initial euphoria of Domesday the educational penetration of IV has been disappointingly small. The reasons for this are not difficult to recognize. The cost of a complete Domesday system (disc, player and micro) was roughly £3,000 to £4,000, depending on the choice of micro, and initially there was only the one disc available: a disc whose content might be useful but whose internal structuring was so poor that it left many would-be users crying in despair. Quickly following on from the Domesday project came other initiatives such as IVIS (interactive video in schools) project but this used 'industry standard' disc players, unlike Domesday. Would-be users were yet again faced with the problem of non-compatibility of rival systems, the bug-bear of micro-technology both in teaching and in business.

Out of this gloom, however, more hopeful signs are beginning to emerge. Costs of IV systems have tumbled in the last year and there are a number of projects in hand to produce discs for the 'industry standard' players. We know of no disc specifically designed for psychology teaching, but there are relevant developments of interest in the field of medicine and health. Of particular interest is the disc produced by St Bartholomew's Hospital (Ingram and Jones, 1989) under the auspicies of the Marie Curie Foundation. The disc, software and documentation which make up this educational package run on an IBM-compatible PC and an 'industry standard' player (not the Phillips/Domesday system). The package is designed for use by general practitioners and district nurses to assist in promoting improvements in the care of cancer patients in the community. The disc is divided into seventeen 'chapters', each of which deals with a specific aspect of treatment and aims to provide a minimum of one hour of courseware. The diagnostic and pharmacological sections may be of little interest to psychologists but the sections on counselling and therapy, which include modules on 'Answering the hard questions', would be valuable additions to clinical and social psychology courses at undergraduate level, and possibly A-level as well.

The authors of this IV disc on the care of cancer patients have been surprised at the level of interest in their disc expressed by workers in para-medical and associated fields. It is not difficult to see why this resource has generated so much interest. The frank interviews with patients talking through their experiences, including their perceptions of medical care available to them, plus the medical professions' perceptions of the issues and problems they face in this field, provide a wealth of material for discussion and analysis for anyone interested in the sociopsychological issues of health care.

The disc is not yet on general release, but more information can be obtained from the first author at St Bartholomew's Hospital. Although the use of IV does involve considerable investment, the costs have reduced sufficiently to make their use in a school, college or large department feasible. What is needed now is a sufficient number of discs to make the hardware purchase worthwhile. Ingram and Jones's disc is a start.

Information It should be very clear that we have not used all of the software mentioned here ourselves. Part of the reason for this is the reluctance that software producers have in letting potential users try their products. In preparing this review we wrote to the producers of each package which we have mentioned and which is untried by us, requesting the opportunity to run it ourselves. Not only did *no* software producer send anything, even though a handful did promise review copies, but many of them did not even send promotional brochures. One software publisher responded to our request for information and sight of a review copy by sending a rather pompous letter which formally gave us permission to mention their program in this chapter! The generous conclusion is that business is so brisk that producers do not need to bother with this kind of advertising. However, it does point to the need for perseverance, and this is supported by a hint mentioned by one of the respondents to our questionnaire. When producers say one thing and then do another (in this specific case, failing to produce a back-up copy), then the route to success is through persistent complaining.

Updates on new releases of software for psychologists, and evaluations of software packages can be found in the invaluable 'Computer Column' of *The Psychologist* (monthly), and also in *Behavior Research Methods, Instruments, and Computers* (bimonthly), and in *Computers in Human Behavior* (quarterly). (*Behavior Research Methods, Instruments, and Computers* also publishes articles by psychologists who are sometimes prepared to make their programs generally available for copying fees.) An extensive summary of currently available software which can be used in psychology teaching has been prepared by Stoloff and Couch (1988). The new Computers in Teaching Initiative Centre in Psychology at the University of York will be providing a software information service and also publishing news-sheets containing software and courseware evaluations.

Acknowledgements. Thanks are due to all those who took time to complete and return questionnaires. Extensive comments on specific software packages, and on an early draft of this chapter, have been provided by Graham Beaumont, Mike Burton, Chris Darwin, Nick Hammond, Steve Newstead, Tony Roberts and Sarah Wilson, and we are especially grateful to them for their patience in dealing with our persistent enquiries.

References   BETHELL-FOX, C. (1889) Eysenck personality profiler. *The Psychologist*, 2, 30–31.

BEAUMONT, J.G. (1982) System requirements for interactive testing. *International Journal of Man-Machine Studies*, 17, 311–320.

BURTON, M. (1988) Knowol+ and ESIE. *The Psychologist 1*, 280–281.

BUSHNELL, I.W.R. and MULLIN, J.T. (1987) *Experimental psychology: A computerized laboratory course* and *Cognitive Psychology: A computerized laboratory course*. Hove: Erlbaum Associates.

CHAMBERS, W.V. and GRICE, J.W. (1986) Circumgrids: A repertory grid package for PCS. *Behavior Research Methods, Instruments and Computers 18*, 468.

HAY, D. (1989) SAMP survey sampling. *The Psychologist*, 2, 75.

Directory of Research in Automated (Psychological and Psychiatric) Testing (DRAT) from Dr S.L. Wilson, Research Department, The Royal Hospital and Home, Putney, West Hill, London SW15 3SW.

INGRAM, D. and JONES, R. (1989) Cancer patients and their families at home – an educational package for general practitioners and district nurses, based on a videodisc. Paper presented at the CAL 89 Symposium on Computer Assisted Learning, University of Surrey, April 1989. (Information about this specific IV disc can be obtained from: Dr D Ingram, The Medical College of St. Bartholomew's Hospital, West Smithfield, London EC1A 7BE.)

JOHNSON, C. (1988a). Test Plus. *The Psychologist*, 1, 150.

JOHNSON, C. (1988b). Spectrum-1. *The Psychologist*, 1, 413.

LEHMAN, R.S. (1986) Macintosh statistical packages. *Behavior Research Methods, Instruments and Computers 18*, 177–187.

McCLELLAND, J.L. and RUMELHART, D.E. (1988a) *Explorations in parallel distributed processing: A handbook of models, programs, and exercises.* Cambridge, Mass.: M.I.T. Press.

McCLELLAND, J.L. and RUMELHART, D.E. (1988b) A simulation-based tutorial system for exploring parallel distributed processing. *Behavior Research Methods, Instruments, and Computers*, 20, 263–275.

NASON, S. and ZABRUCKY, K. (1988) A program for comprehensive monitoring of text using HyperCard for the Macintosh. *Behaviour Research Methods, Instruments, and Computers* 20, 499–502.

PAYNE, S. (1988) AlphaPOP. *The Psychologist 1*, 454–455.

SEGALOWITZ, S.J. (1987) IBM PC tachistoscope: Text stimuli. *Behavior Research Methods, Instruments, and Computers 19*, 383–388.

STOLOFF, M.L. and COUCH, J.V. (1988) *Computer Use in Psychology: A directory of software*, 2nd ed. Arlington, Va.: American Psychological Association.

SYKES, B. (1987) BIOGRAM II. *Bulletin of The British Psychological Society* 40, 137.

THOMPSON, J.A. and WILSON, S.L. (1982) Automated psychological testing. *International Journal of Man-Machine Studies*, 17, 279–289.

WATTS, K. and BADDELEY, A. and WILLIAMS, M. (1982). Automated tailored testing using Raven's Matrices and the Mill Hill Vocabulary tests: A comparison with manual administration. *International Journal of Man-Machine Studies*, 17, 331–344.

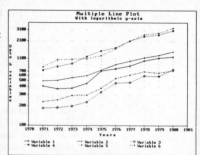
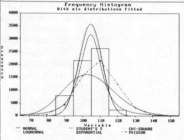
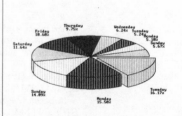
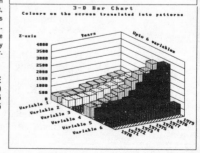

APPENDIX: MICROCOMPUTER USE AT A-LEVEL AND GCSE

Geoff Haworth

There are, I believe, special considerations to be borne in mind when looking at micro use at A-level and GCSE – for example, the unavailability of any existing micros on a permanent basis; the limited budget for the purchase of hardware and software; and the constraints on teaching time given the breadth of the syllabus at these levels. However, the presence of Artificial Intelligence (AI) on the A-level syllabus and the effect of TVEI across the curriculum have meant an increase in interest in microcomputer applications and a growing demand for information and software from psychology teachers in institutions of further education and schools. In the course of co-ordinating information on micro use for the Association for the Teaching of Psychology (ATP), I have become increasingly aware of teachers' needs and the problems we face in this particular area. I am therefore concentrating in this section on aspects of microcomputer use that I hope will be of most interest and practical use to anyone who teaches pre-degree level psychology.

HARDWARE: WHICH MICRO? As Underwood and Underwood point out in the previous section, there is no advantage in looking at the electronic wizardry of the microcomputer – though those who wish to do so might care to look at McKnight (1984). However, whilst teachers of psychology at A-level and GCSE do not need to be well versed in the finer points of how computers work or fluent in the jargon of the computer buff, there is some basic information that anyone who wishes to begin or increase the use of micros in their courses will find helpful.

Teachers who do not have regular access to their own micro and are considering buying one (or several) – a familiar occurrence since the advent of TVEI – are faced with the problem of deciding which micro to get. This decision is made all the more difficult for those who are not guided by college or departmental policies and who have little or no knowledge of computers. Initially it is worth talking to someone in the IT or computing department before dashing out and buying, say, a BBC B or Master because you know these have been popular machines in many schools and colleges. As always, be wary of High-Street sales staff who may well try to sell you something that suits their profits rather than your needs.

Basically, you will want a machine that can run the software that is suitable for psychology teaching now and in the future. Hence a word of caution about the BBC B and Master series: most schools and colleges have some BBC micros available, and because of their popularity there is a good deal of available software, some of which is directly relevant to psychology teaching (for example UnderStat and BIOGRAM II). However, these machines are fairly limited in their use because of their small memory capacities – some software is just too demanding of memory to run on them. You can tell the memory capacity of a micro by finding out how many K (kilobytes) it has. Most now have at least 512K (½ a megabyte of memory) whereas the BBC B has only 32K and the Master only 128K. In addition, most existing BBC machines in schools and colleges are fairly old and/or well-used and may experience maintenance problems in the long term. I would think carefully before buying a BBC B or Master, although you may be able to get a good deal on a second-hand machine for use in the short term.

It is not possible to recommend a particular machine since different teachers will probably have individual requirements. However, most colleges are now standardizing on IBM machines or those that are IBM PC compatible (for example, Nimbus, Opus, Compaq and Amstrad – not the PCW8256/8512). The big advantage here is that these machines are capable of running the same software by virtue of the fact that they use the same operating system called MSDOS (or simply DOS). However, this is not always the case (especially where programs use graphics) and before you buy any software you should check that it will actually run on your machine, or better still, see it running before you pay for it. Some micros, for example Nimbus, have what is called a BBC Basic interpreter which will translate some programs written for BBC machines to run on that particular micro – but you should check the copyright before you do this. Probably the best person to help you with problems of running software is the technician in the IT department and, if you have one, it is well worth getting to know him or her. The ATP also offers (non-professional) advice to teachers. Whilst at present most of the software in use by teachers up to A-level is written for the BBC, this will probably change in the future as demand increases for software that will run on ıвм-compatible machines.

Several pieces of software that are commercially available and aimed at pre-degree courses are now briefly reviewed. These fall predominantly into two camps – statistical packages and experiments/demonstrations.

STATISTICAL PACKAGES

The previous section examines some of the more powerful statistical packages that are available and widely used at both research and undergraduate levels (for example, spss PC+ , UNISTAT II and Minitab). There are, however, several packages that have been written specifically for the A-level market and designed to run on a variety of machines. I will look at two of these in some detail and mention others that are available.

StATPak

Concorde Informatics Ltd have produced sTATPak – a statistics program designed to analyse the results of A-level practicals. The program offers seven significance tests including parametric and non-parametric tests for a comparison of means, correlation and a chi-square test of association – the basic tests that are needed by students at this level. sTATPak will run on the Amstrad wordprocessor (PCW8265 and PCW8512) and ıвм-pc-compatible machines, which makes it particularly useful for those who do not have BBC machines.

sTATPak is fairly user friendly, although a thorough reading of the rather sketchy accompanying literature and several trial runs will be needed for the uninitiated. In its Amstrad pcw guise, sTATPak couldn't be simpler to load – just place the disc in the drive and away you go. In the ıвм-compatible version, this operation is slightly more complicated since it runs from within msdos and so the operating system first has to be supplied. The operations are very simple and instructions are supplied.

Once loaded, sTATPak offers the user the choice of entering data, running statistical tests or seeing what data files are available. The program conducts tests in three categories, depending on whether the data is from correlated samples, independent samples or is nominal data. One very useful feature is that the user can enter up to 20 sets of scores which are then stored on disc so that various statistical tests may be conducted without having to re-enter the data on each occasion. The user interacts with the program by responding to a series of questions, such as 'Which test do you want to use?' and this makes for ease of use. sTATPak will test the significance of the results from the given sets of data, tell the user if the results are significant, and say whether the null hypothesis is to be accepted or rejected at pre-selected significance levels for 1-and 2-tailed hypotheses. There is also a print-out option that gives very useful step-by-step calculations of the particular statistic chosen. In fact, stATPak will do all the things that most students will require in terms of inferential statistics for A-level work and is certainly cheap enough (£15 with reductions for ATP members) for some to want to buy their own.

UnderStat   TokSoft have developed UnderStat – a statistical package for the BBC (B and Master series) microcomputer which is specifically designed for students studying A-level psychology. The disc comes complete with a user's guide that includes an introduction to experimentation and the use of statistics that is valuable as a text for student use in its own right and is worthy of a few comments here. Not so much a user's guide, the TokSoft literature includes a comprehensive 22-page introduction that more or less covers the basic areas needed at A-level, from why we need statistics, through concepts such as sampling, variables, hypotheses, experimental design, levels of measurement, to significance testing and guidance on choosing and using statistical tests.The software itself offers programs for both descriptive and inferential statistics (14 different calculations in all), giving on-screen step-by-step calculation of results, plotting histograms and other graphs where appropriate and offering a print-out option. Such sophistication is reflected in the price, which is none the less still targeted at the school/FE-department budget, and is currently £50 (exclusive of VAT and p&p).

The UnderStat package is menu-driven and includes on-screen instructions and comprehensive supporting literature that make running the software a fairly simple operation. Data entry is straightforward and scores are stored in the computer's memory (not to disc as in stATPak) – making data temporarily available for use in a choice of tests without the need for it to be continually re-entered. Results can be seen on screen in tabular form and can easily be edited if mistakes have occurred. The software will use stored data to plot histograms and graphs (such as scattergrams for the correlation options) and will enable the user to obtain print-outs from the tables of results and graphs shown on the screen, provided that a suitable printer (such as the Epson FX or RX is connected – this is vital for the smooth running of the programs and the production of hard-copy.

UnderStat will perform a variety of statistical tests on data-entries and these are chosen from the menu by the selection of an appropriate key. Having completed the calculations, UnderStat shows the result on the screen, but requires the user to check for significance and interpret its meaning – a valuable exercise at this level. The supporting literature gives clear guidance on how to do this and statistical tables are provided in the Guide for users to consult. For the BBC-user, UnderStat will perform all the statistical calculations that are needed at A-level (and beyond) and provide hard-copy of tables and graphs for use in experimental write-ups. In addition, the introduction to statistics in the User's Guide is a valuable teaching and learning aid for A-level experimental and practical work.

Other statistics packages that are available for use at this level include 'Statistics for Psychology', an in-house production from South Kent College by myself and Shelley Gooding. This is a user-friendly menu-driven package written for the RML Nimbus machine. It offers a choice of nine tests for descriptive and inferential statistics, together with a 'help' option that guides unfamiliar users through the steps of choosing an appropriate statistic. Whilst 'Statistics for Psychology' is easy to use and does all that is necessary for the basic analysis of experimental data, it doesn't save data in the computer's memory or to disc, unlike UnderStat and STATPAK respectively, and doesn't go beyond the calculation of given statistics (the actual number-crunching), and users are left to check suitable tables for significance etc. The same authors have also produced a self-assessment program in experimental design and use of statistics – 'Tests in Psychology: Experiments and statistics'. This follows a simple question-and-answer procedure where users interact with the micro by typing in their responses which are then scored. The program is cheap (£6 to cover the cost of the disc and carriage), is easy to operate and deliberately has no copyright protection so that users can edit it to generate their own questions and answers. The program is written for the Amstrad PCW and could be useful for revision work, as well as for motivating students who are not too enamoured of this aspect of the A-level syllabus or the use of computers.

There is also a statistics disc with Andy Bell and Anthony Mellor's 'Experiments in Psychology', which is designed to run on the BBC B and Master series. This is the second disc of the package and comes with some detailed, yet difficult, user's instructions and worked examples. It is designed more as a student-centred learning aid which takes the user through various menu options that include a look at various aspects of experimentation, such as design, variables, hypotheses (together with some very useful self-assessment questions); samples, populations and the normal distribution (including some descriptive statistics); the concept of probability; and several options for the calculation of such inferential statistics as t-tests, correlation coefficients and 2x2 chi square. The package offers itself as a 'computerized companion' to Robson's (1983) 'Experiment, Design and Statistics in Psychology', and provides some guided examples and interesting graphics in relation to probability and significance testing. Consequently, the statistics disc has value as a tool for both classroom use and for distance learning but comes as a package together with the accompanying experiments disc (see below).

DEMON-
STRATIONS
AND
EXPERIMENTS

Both packages included here run on the BBC B and Master Series microcomputers and consequently offer some colourful and interesting graphics. They offer various demonstrations of visual phenomena and present ideas for computer-based experimental work in psychology that are suitable for use at both A-level and GCSE.

Dr George Mather of Sussex University has edited the programs for the ATP's 'Psychology Experiments and Demonstrations' disc, which is available at £10 to £17.50 (depending on format and ATP membership discount). The package (described as a 'suite of programs') is easily loaded and is menu-driven with users initially selecting from the demonstrations or experiments options. In the former, Dr Mather has put together ten visual demonstrations that include the Müller-Lyer illusion, the Hermann Grid, the Kanizsa Triangle and the Rubin Vase, and these are either presented in sequence or individually selected by pressing the appropriate key. The illusions and other visual phenomena are ideal for presentation on the BBC machine and provide some fascinating material to show to students of psychology at all levels. Each demonstration is preceded by a short on-screen description and the user moves easily through the sequence by pressing identified keys. The inclusion of supporting literature within the programs has meant that the user booklet is kept to an absolute minimum of a couple of pages and is simply written and extremely easy to follow.

In the experiments option, six examples suitable for A-level (and in some cases, GCSE) are presented. Users select from a menu of choices that include the Müller-Lyer illusion (with differing fin-angles from 15° to 75°), the Stroop Effect, and the primacy-recency effect in memory (with immediate recall and delayed recall conditions). In each case, there is simple supporting literature offering references to source material and on-screen details and instructions. The joy of using this disc is in the ease of running the various options – even the most computer-terrified user has nothing to fear! It offers a variety of programs that are useful for simple classroom demonstration purposes and others that have far more interesting applications in experimental work.

By contrast, the Bell-Mellor disc 'Experiments in Psychology' is accompanied by a weighty, well-documented 42-page User's Manual that supports some far more sophisticated software (reflected in the price of £99.50, which includes the statistics package discussed earlier). Users will have to take some time familiarizing themselves with all the possibilities that the package offers – 11 separate basic proposals for experiments, with options available within some of them – and reading the accompanying documentation.

Access to individual experiments is achieved through selections from the main menu which includes some familiar ideas, such as the Müller-Lyer illusion and the Necker Cube, but also some more obscure and interesting programs, such as congruency with self and visuo-spatial ability. Other selections include serial/parallel information processing, pitch and volume discrimination, memory tests and experiments in conformity. Some of the procedures in the package are fairly complex and constant reference to the User's Manual is needed. Indeed, most of the supporting material to help in the running of the package is contained within the Manual and there is not the wider use of on-screen information that characterizes the ATP disc. However, the Manual does follow step-by-step procedures and examples of on-screen presentations and this is a necessity given the sophistication of 'Experiments in Psychology'. Also contained in the Manual is some very useful background material for each experiment, with supporting references, that would enable the user to refer to wider sources for any practical write-up. The disc itself comprises a most comprehensive collection of programs for experimental work in psychology and could be a godsend for any A-level student who is struggling for ideas or any teachers wishing to make far more of their BBC with just one piece of software.

In addition to the software packages mentioned above, Synergy Software's BIOGRAM II (discussed by Underwood and Underwood in the preceding chapter) has useful applications for psychology at A-level and GCSE. it can be used in experimental work or demonstrations involving classical conditioning of galvanic skin responses (with due attention to ethical considerations, of course), as well as the documented uses in lie detection, phobia reduction and relaxation work. BIOGRAM II comes with electrodes that attach to the subject's fingers and connect to a small control box that plugs into the back of the BBC micro. It is easy to use and comes with clear and supportive accompanying literature.

A good deal of the software in use in the psychology departments of schools and FE colleges has been produced in-house and is not commercially available. In some respects this has the advantage over software that is bought in since it is usually tailor-made to suit the needs of the teacher concerned – and so tends to be unsophisticated and simple to use. Because it is highly probable that teachers in different institutions are duplicating each others useful software, the ATP is co-ordinating information on the uses of micro-computers for psychology teaching, and, in so doing, is trying to stimulate the production and use of psychology software in schools and colleges where there appears to be scope for development. Certainly one application that has not yet taken off is in distance learning where computer-based packages could become very popular and offer an alternative to the more traditional ways of studying psychol-ogy – the Bell-Mellor 'Experiment, Design and Statistics' disc is a step in this direction. Another possibility is the use of micros to help in the teaching of any artificial intelligence component of an A-level psychology course.

BBC TACHISTO-SCOPE PROGRAM

The previous section considers several programs and pack-ages that are commercially available and are believed to be of practical value to teachers of psychology. The following program is provided as a simple example to enable teachers to use their micro as a tachistoscope for demonstration or experimental purposes. It is very easy to use and aims to show those who are new to using micros what can be done with just a very simple program. For the advanced user, it might usefully add to your collection of commercial and in-house software, or provide the basis for the development of a more sophisticated program that you might write yourself or ask your IT department to write for you.

Instructions

The program will run on BBC Basic but can be used on machines other than the BBC (ie IBM compatibles) provided that you first load BBC Basic into the computer (you may be able to obtain a copy of BBC Basic from your computing department).

Once you have loaded BBC Basic, type in the following listing very carefully and press the **[ENTER]** key at the end of each line. Any mistakes will affect the smooth running of the program. Once you have done this type **Save "TACH"** and press the **[ENTER]** key. Next type **Run [ENTER]**. On subsequent occasions, once you have loaded BBC Basic and received the > sign, type **CHAIN "TACH"**. The word Tachistoscope will appear on the screen followed by a menu of 5 options.

The first thing you will need to do is to use option 1 to type in a word list. Then save this under a file name of 8 letters or less. This will be permanently saved to a disc until you erase it. You can load previously saved word lists from option 2. Once you have loaded a file you can display the words in that file on the screen. You do this by choosing option 3 and following the instructions on the screen. Words are presented in increments of 1/100th of a second every time the **[ENTER]** key is pressed and this continues until the space bar is pressed. The next word is then presented and the sequence continues until all words in the list have been shown.

You can now return to the menu and see the results by choosing option 4. Write these results down, as they are not saved, before moving on to the next subject or ending by choosing option 5. Once you receive the > sign you can remove the disc.

Listing

```
10   REM
20   MODE 3
30   PRINT TAB (30, 10) "TACHISTOSCOPE"
40   FOR N=1 TO 10000: NEXT N
50   REPEAT
60   PROCMENU
70   UNTIL FALSE
80   END
90   REM ***************************************************
100  REM PROCEDURE OPEN_FILE
110  REM ***************************************************
120  DEFPROCOPEN_FILE
130  CLEAR
140  CLS
150  PRINT TAB (10, 10) "HOW MANY WORDS
     WOULD YOU LIKE IN YOUR FILE";
160  INPUT N
170  CLS
180  PRINT TAB (10, 10) "PLEASE ENTER A NAME
     FOR YOUR WORD FILE AND PRESS RETURN"
190  INPUT N$
200  DIM W$ (N)
210  DIM T (N)
```

```
220   FOR J=1 TO N
230   CLS
240   PRINT "PLEASE ENTER WORD NUMBER   ";J
250   INPUT W$ (J)
260   NEXT J
270   X=OPENOUT (N$)
280   PRINT#X, N
290   FOR J=1 TO N
300   PRINT#X,W$ (J)
310   NEXT J
320   CLOSE#X
330   ENDPROC
340   REM ***************************************************
350   REM PROCEDURE GET_FILE
360   REM ***************************************************
370   DEFPROCGET_FILE
380   CLEAR
390   CLS
400   PRINT "PLEASE TYPE IN NAME OF FILE TO
      OPEN";
410   INPUT N$
420   X=OPENUP (N$)
430   INPUT#X, N
440   DIM W$ (N)
450   DIM T (N)
460   FOR J=1 TO N
470   INPUT#X, W$ (J)
480   NEXT J
490   CLOSE#X
500   ENDPROC
510   CLS
520   REM ***************************************************
530   REM PROCEDURE MENU
540   REM ***************************************************
550   DEFPROCMENU
560   CLS
570   PRINT TAB (5, 5) "1.  CREATE A FILE OF WORDS"
580   PRINT TAB (5, 7) "2.  OPEN A PREVIOUSLY
      SAVED FILE OF WORDS"
590   PRINT TAB (5, 9) "3.  DISPLAY WORDS"
600   PRINT TAB (5, 11) "4.  DISPLAY RESULTS"
610   PRINT TAB (5, 13) "5.  END PROGRAM"
620   PRINT TAB (5, 15) "TYPE IN YOUR CHOICE AND
      PRESS RETURN   ";
630   INPUT A
640   IF A=1 THEN PROCOPEN_FILE :PROCMENU
650   IF A=2 THEN PROCGET_FILE   :PROCMENU
660   IF A=3 THEN PROCDISP        :PROCMENU
670   IF A=4 THEN PROCRESULTS     :PROCMENU
```

```
680   IF A=5 THEN END
690   ENDPROC
700   REM ****************************************************
710   REM PROCEDURE DISP
720   REM ****************************************************
730   DEFPROCDISP
740   CLS
750   PRINT TAB (4, 4) "The file you have loaded is
      called " N$
760   PRINT TAB (4, 6) "It contains    ";N;" words "
770   PRINT TAB (4, 8) "Each of the words in the file will
      be displayed on"
780   PRINT TAB (4, 10) "the screen for an increasing
      period of time "
790   PRINT TAB (4, 12) "As soon as the word is
      recognised press the space bar "
800   PRINT TAB (4, 14) "When all the words have been
      recognised you will be given"
810   PRINT TAB (4, 16) "an opportunity to view the
      results "
820   PRINT TAB (4, 18) "Press RETURN to continue"
830   INPUT D
840   P=0
850   FOR X = 1 TO N
860   CLS
870   T=0
880   PRINT TAB (10, 10) "Press RETURN to display
      word"
890   PRINT TAB (10, 12) "As soon as word is
      recognised press space bar"
900   INPUT H
910   P=0
920   REPEAT
930   CLS
940   TIME=0
950   REPEAT
960   PRINT TAB (38, 12); W$ (X)
970   UNTIL TIME>T
980   CLS
990   T=T+1
1000  A=GET
1010  IF A=32 THEN P=999: T(X)=T: PRINT "WORD
      RECOGNISED Press any key to continue": h=GET
1020  UNTIL P=999
1030  NEXT X
1040  ENDPROC
1050  REM ****************************************************
1060  REM PROCEDURE RESULTS
1070  REM ****************************************************
```

```
1080    DEFPROCRESULTS
1090    CLS
1100    FOR X=1 TO N
1110    PRINT "WORD = "W$(X);"      ";T(X);"
        hundredths of a second"
1120    NEXT X
1130    PRINT "press any key to return to menu"
1140    H=GET
1150    ENDPROC
```

(*Note:* On some printers the # character is printed out as £.)

Acknowledgements. I am endebted to Robin Jones and Shelley Gooding of South Kent College for their help with various aspects of this appendix.

References

McKNIGHT, C. (1984) Microcomputers in psychology teaching. In D. Rose and J. Radford (Eds) *Teaching Psychology: A handbook of resources*. Leicester: BPS Books.

ROBSON, C. (1983) *Experiment, Design and Statistics in Psychology*. Harmondsworth: Penguin Books.

PSYCHOLOGICAL
APPARATUS

Aleph One Limited

The RELAXOMETER is a simple indicator of changes in autonomic arousal, capable of showing clearly the responses of the user to internal or external stimuli. Widely used clinically, its prompt and cogent feedback signal is unambiguous and easy to understand. All models have sound feedback; the Model Q has a meter and connection for external apparatus.

MYOELECTRIC instruments reveal activity in muscles via the somatic nervous system during, or in anticipation of, contractions.

The MYOLINK system passes signals from these types of instruments safely to a BBC Microcomputer and provides a variety of software for manipulating and displaying the signals.

The MYOLOG system extends these capacities to prolonged recording of autonomic and muscular and other signals from freely moving people in home, clinic and lab settings.

TEMPERATURE FEEDBACK apparatus reveals the effects of the autonomic nervous system on the peripheral circulation.

The ALPHA SENSOR provides auditory feedback for alpha activity with which the user can learn to alter their EEG pattern.

The BUG-IN-THE-EAR device allows an instructor discreetly to coach a trainee in interviewing or teaching situations.

Ask for details of the products of interest and for a List of Experiments.

ALEPH ONE Ltd. (O) The Old Courthouse Bottisham CAMBRIDGE CB5 9BA   Tel (0223) 811679   Fax (0223) 812713

UK Software Agents' and Suppliers' Addresses

Acorn Computers
Cambride Technopark
Newmarket Road
Cambridge CB5 8PD

Beebugsoft
Dolphin Place
Holywell Hill
St Albans
Herts AL1 1EX

Bell-Mellor
30 Forres Road
Sheffield
S. Yorks S10 1WE

Caxton Computer Systems Ltd
Little Brympton
Brympton d'Evercy
Yeovil
Som. BA22 8TD

Codil Language Systems
33 Buckingham Road
Tring
Herts HP23 4HG

Cognitive Applications
4 Sillwood Terrace
Brighton
E. Sussex BN1 2LR

Computer Concepts
Gaddesden Place
Hemel Hempstead
Herts HP2 6EX

Concorde Informatics Ltd
517 Leeds Road
Huddersfield
W. Yorks HD2 1YJ

Edward Arnold
Hodder & Stoughton Ltd
Mill Hill
Dunton Green
Sevenoaks
Kent TN13 2XX

ESM/Acornsoft
Duke Street
Wisbech
Cambs PE13 2AE

Elsevier-Biosoft
68 Hills Road
Cambridge CB2 1LA

Expert Systems International Ltd
9 West Way
Oxford OX2 OJB

Electronic Developments Co.
(W.C.R. & B.I. Withers Ltd)
Unit 37/E
Platt's Eyot
Lower Sunbury Road
Hampton
W. Mid. TW12 2HF

Forth Instrument Services
11 Brewster Square
Brucefield Industrial Estate
Livingston
West Lothian EH54 9BJ

Ivan Berg Software Ltd
Unit 8
James Cameron House
12 Castlehaven Road
London NW1 8QU

Lawrence Erlbaum Associates Software
27 Palmeira Mansions
Church Road
Hove
E. Sussex BN3 2FA

Leicester Computer Centre
9 Jarrom Street
Leicester LE2 7DH

Logotron Ltd
Dales Brewery
Gwydir Street
Cambridge CB1 2LJ

Lifeskills Associates
Clarendon Chambers
51 Clarendon Road
Leeds
W. Yorks LS2 9NZ

Longman Micro Software
Longman Resources Unit
33–35 Tanner Row
York YO1 1JP

McGraw-Hill Book Company (UK) Ltd
McGraw-Hill House
Shoppenhangers Road
Maidenhead
Berks SL6 2QL

MRH Systems and Software
20 Highfield Road
Kidderminster
Hereford & Worcester DY10 2TL

Precision Software
6 Park Terrace
Worcester Park
Hereford & Worcester KT4 7JZ

Serious Statistical Software
Lynwood
Benty Heath Lane
Willaston
South Wirral
Ches. L64 1SD

SPSS UK Ltd
9–11 Queens Road
Hersham Green
Walton on Thames
Surrey KT12 5LD

Synergy Software
7 Hillside Road
Harpenden
Herts AL5 4BS

The Test Agency
Cournswood House
North Dean
High Wycombe
Bucks HP14 4NW

TokSoft
20 Heatherdale Road
Camberley
Surrey GU15 2LT

Unisoft Ltd
PO Box 383
Highgate
London N6 5UP

*USA agents and suppliers of software
referred to in text*

Brainpower Inc
Suite 250
24009 Ventura Boulevard
Calabasas
California 91302

Clear Lake Research
5353 Dora Street No.7
Houston
Texas 77005

(Circumgrids is not available commercially, but W.V. Chambers can provide a listing of the Pascal program of Circumgrids for running on IBM PCs.)

Cricket Software
Suite 206 3508 Market Street
Philadelphia
Pennsylvania 19104

DataDesk Inc.
Box 4555
Ithaca
New York 14852

William V. Chambers
Department of Psychology
Wright State University
Dayton
Ohio 45431

Software Index

(Distributors are given in brackets after each item, and their addresses listed in the previous section.)

AlphaPOP
(Cognitive Applications)

BIOGRAM II
(Synergy Software)

Circumgrids
(William V. Chambers)

CLR ANOVA
(Clear Lake Research)

Cognitive Psychology: A
computerized laboratory course
*(Lawrence Erlbaum Associates
Software)*

DataDesk
(DataDesk Inc.)

DRAT
*(Dr S.L. Wilson, The Royal Hospital
and Home)*

Domesday
(Acorn Computers)

Experimental Psychology: A
computerized laboratory course
*(Lawrence Erlbaum Associates
Software)*

Experiments in Psychology
(Bell-Mellor)

Eysenck Personality Profiler
(Ivan Berg Software Ltd)

Knowol+
(Caxton Computer Systems Ltd)

Minitab
(Edward Arnold)

MicroCODIL
(Codil Language Systems)

Microtab
(Edward Arnold)

Psychology Experiments and
Demonstrations
*(Association for the Teaching of
Psychology)*

SAMP Survey Sampling
(Elsevier-Biosoft)

Spectrum-1
(The Test Agency)

SPSS PC+
(SPSS UK Ltd)

SPSSX
(SPSS UK Ltd)

Statistics for Psychology
(Geoff Haworth, South Kent College)

STATpak
(Concorde Informatics Ltd)

Statview
*(Brainpower Inc. and UK Macintosh
suppliers)*

StatWorks
*(Cricket Software and UK Macintosh
suppliers)*

Test Plus
(The Test Agency)

Tests in Psychology
(Geoff Haworth, South Kent College)

UnderStat
(TokSoft)

UNISTAT II
(Unistat Ltd)

UNISTAT III
(Unistat Ltd)

PSYCHOLOGY LABORATORY EQUIPMENT

Rosemary Westley

❑ *further information sources* ● *standard psychological laboratory equipment, including traditional, visual perception and unusual items* ● *electrophysiological equipment* ● *recording equipment* ● *suppliers' addresses and phone numbers*

There is a very wide range of equipment and materials used for psychology experimental work. This chapter deals with equipment most commonly found in psychology departments other than computers (which are covered in the chapter on microcomputers in this volume). It provides a guide to the equipment that is available together with a list of suppliers to contact for further information on specific items. The suppliers are all based in the UK although some of the equipment is manufactured elsewhere. A complete list of their addresses and telephone numbers is provided at the end of this chapter.

The chapter covers traditional psychology laboratory equipment such as tachistoscopes, mirror-drawing equipment and reaction time apparatus, electrophysiological equipment and a range of recording and monitoring devices. Not included in this chapter are:

1. *Tape recorders and accessories* – suppliers of tape recorders are so numerous that it is unneccessary to list them all. Your local *Yellow Pages* or *Thompson Directory* will provide a list of dealers in your area.

2. *Video equipment* – lists of suppliers' reviews of equipment and services can be obtained from:

Audio Visual Directory (published annually by EMAP McClaren Publishing) – contains details of equipment, dealers by region and production services.

Video Production Techniques (updated three times a year by Longman) contains reviews on equipment and information on production techniques.

Yellow Pages (British Telecom).

Most audiovisual departments in universities and colleges will have copies of one or more of these publications and staff are usually willing to give advice.

FURTHER INFORMATION SOURCES

Apart from the manufacturers and suppliers listed in the following pages, information, equipment and services can also be obtained from the following sources:

1. *Local education authorities* buy in large quantities a wide variety of educational equipment such as scientific apparatus, audiovisual equipment, video equipment and stationery. They will quite often supply other educational establishments with goods at very low prices.

2. *Local psychology departments* – in universities, polytechnics and colleges of further education. Academic and technical staff are usually very helpful in providing information concerning equipment, and are often prepared to lend apparatus for the occasional demonstration or for a class.

3. *Trade directories* – *Kelly's Manufacturers and Merchants Directory* has details of thousands of British companies and importers, listed under trade, product and service headings. Volume I of *UK Kompass Register* list products and services, while Volume II carries the names and addresses of British companies together with company information both alphabetically and by county. The directories may be found in your local library or central purchasing department. Their publishers' addresses are also listed at the end of this chapter.

4. *American and European suppliers* – in addition to the UK suppliers listed in the present chapter, numerous American and European companies supply scientific equipment. Further information can be obtained from the *Guide to Scientific Instruments* (American Association for the Advancement of Science).

Purpose-Built Equipment

Not all apparatus can be bought 'off the shelf', and you may need something special built. If you do not have access to technical assistance the problem can be approached as follows:

1. *Existing suppliers* – it is worth asking the companies listed in the following pages whether they are prepared to produce equipment to your specifications. They will often make adaptations or additions to equipment they already manufacture.

2. *Technical staff* – in universities, polytechnics and colleges

of further education build a great deal of 'one-off' apparatus. They may have what you want and be prepared to lend it to you. They can also advise you on what manufactured equipment could be adapted to meet your purpose.

3. *Consultancies* – there are many small local engineering firms that can build equipment for you. However they may require drawings and Martock Design will turn your ideas into a set of engineering drawings. Weylec also have a design and drawing service for electronic equipment. They are also electric battery consultants, and can provide useful advice on power supplies when designing portable equipment.

SECTION 1: STANDARD PSYCHO-LOGICAL LABORATORY EQUIPMENT

The standard equipment covered in this section has been used in GCSE, A-Level, and undergraduate courses for many years, but only a few companies now produce it, mainly in America. This type of equipment is very robust and does last for years. Also included is a list of less common items that have either been designed for teaching or may be relevant for project work. Items are in alphabetical order.

Aesthesiometer
▶ Used to measure sensitivity to touch.
There are four types:
1. Nylon filament – set of 20 individually mounted nylon filaments of equal length and varying diameter.
2. Dial – consists of a pointer with dial that measures forces within a 0-10 gram range.
3. Von Frey – consists of either a hypodermic-type tube and horse hair that can be varied in length, or a disc on which graduated nylon bristles extend.
4. Caliper – sliding caliper with two pointers. (See also the chapter in this book on DIY laboratory equipment.)

Audiometer
▶ Used to test hearing and may be used where hearing defects can affect the experiment, e.g. musical perception.
Models are available that test air condition, pure tone for thresholds in each frequency zone, tone decay for sensory adaption and detection of speech sounds.

Biofeedback equipment
See Section 2

Colour mixer
▶ Used to demonstrate a variety of perception phenomena. The equipment consists of a variable speed motor in a cabinet with circular disc mounted on the front. Stimulus materials such as black and white discs can be fixed to the front and spun at low speed to produce subjective colour

effects (Benhams tops), or coloured discs can be spun at high speed for colour-mixing experiments.

Depth perception apparatus
▶ For judgement of distance and perspective.
The subject, seated 20 feet from the apparatus, manipulates pull cords to align the moveable vertical rod with a stationary rod. Progression, overshoot and absolute accuracy can thus be determined and recorded.

Dispensers
▶ For reinforcement of subjects.
Electromechanical device for dispensing peanuts or Smarties to subjects as a reward.

Discrimination weights
▶ For psychophysics experiments.
Two series of identically sized weights are available:
1. With weight variations in 4– or 5–gram increments. The ranges are 50–86g; 75–125g; 175–225g, with a 100g or 200g weight as standard.
2. With a total range of 80–120 grams, in increments of ½g from 80–85g; 1g from 85–90g; 2g from 90–100g and 5g from 100–120g.

Dynamometer (hand)
▶ For measuring grip/pressures for strength of handedness experiments.
There are several designs:
1. Steel frame design – when frame is compressed by hand the pressure is indicated on a scale. Not very accurate.
2. Level design with scale that can measure maximal energy and fatigue rates. Measured range 0–100kg.
3. Pull type with double pointer calibrated from 0–272kg.

Flicker fusion apparatus
▶ The apparatus uses a single flashing lamp which can be set to flash between 10 and 110 times a second.

Grip tester
See Dynamometer

GSR meter
See Section 2

Labyrinth
See Maze

Maze
▶ Used for learning experiments.
1. Pencil maze – stencil of aluminium placed over paper to produce a permanent record of subject's performance.
2. Automatic tally maze – designed to be attached to an impulse counter or stopclock to save time in scoring the subject's performance.

Memory drum
▶ Can be used for numerous learning experiments.
A variety of stimuli can be presented: words, word groups,

figures, pictures or symbols. Stimuli are attached to a cylindrical drum mounted in a box with a viewing slit. The drum can be rotated to provide various exposure times between ¼ and 8 seconds.

Mirror-drawing apparatus
▶ Used for skill learning tasks or to demonstrate cerebal dominance.
1. Standard – paper patterns are attached to a board and traced from visual cues reversed and inverted in a mirror. (See also the chapter on DIY laboratory equipment in this book.)
2. Automatic scoring – metal base with non-conducting pattern flush with surface. Plate and tracing stylus can be connected to a battery and timer counter. Contact is made if the subject traces outside the pattern and a score is recorded on the counter.

Perimeter
▶ Apparatus for mapping the colour-sensitive areas of the retina.
Standard models consist of an arc approximately 8cm wide with a 33cm radius, which can be rotated 100° in each direction. Test stimulus which is projected onto the arc can be varied by size, colour (white, red, green, blue) and brightness. Measurements are recorded on charts which are supplied in pads of 100.

Phi phenomenon apparatus
▶ This apparatus demonstrates the phenomenon of apparent movement from one light to another.
The equipment has two individual light sources which are alternately illuminated; cycle times are variable.

Photic stimulator
▶ For experiments on perception, attention, vigilance etc.
This is basically a low-powered stroboscope.

Pursuit rotor
▶ For tests of speed and accuracy.
The equipment comprises a variable speed turntable with a target which the subject has to hit with a stylus as it rotates. Photoelectric versions exist which eliminate the necessity for any physical contact.

Reaction timer
▶ To measure the reaction time to a visual or auditory stimulus.
The equipment consists of a timer, a controller to activate the stimulus and start the timer simultaneously and a response key for the subject. Apparatus is available with either a single light or auditory stimulus or with up to eight visual stimuli (multiple-choice reaction) and with one to four response keys.

Rod and frame apparatus

▶ Designed for both research and teaching, applications include testing the subject's ability to perceive the orientation of his or her body in relation to a hypothetical axis of gravity.

The apparatus consists of an adjustable rod which the subject alters until it is apparently parallel to the true upright axis under conditions of reduced environmental cues.

Steadiness tester

▶ Used to measure psychomotor control.

The equipment comprises a block with nine holes of varying diameters, into which the subject is required to insert an electrical contact-making stylus without touching the sides. The apparatus is wired to a battery and counter.

Sound-attenuating chamber

▶ Although this type of apparatus is expensive, you may require a sound-attenuating chamber when external noise affects experimental procedures.

Tachistoscopes

▶ Can be used for investigating figural aftereffects, recognition thresholds, perceptual defence and visual acuity.

A tachistoscope displays a visual stimulus for brief periods. It may be a one, two or more field unit and use cards or slides to display stimuli.

1. Optical tachistoscopes have stimuli mounted on cards seen through a viewing hood. The field illumination and exposure times can be varied electronically. For more complex exercises, a sophisticated range of four-and six-field tachistoscopes is available and a pack tachistoscope for three-dimensional stimuli.

2. With projection tachistoscopes (projectors fitted with shutters and controllers) the stimuli are photographic slides. These are better for some tasks, for example group presentations. One- to four-field versions are available.

(See the chapter on microcomputers in this book for software for computer version.)

Tapping board

▶ Used to measure motor skills and fatigue rates.

This apparatus is a wooden board with metal plates at each end. The subject uses an electrical contact stylus to tap successively on the plates as rapidly as possible. Hits are recorded on a counter.

Timers, counters, tally counters, event recorders, frequency counters

See Section 3.

Tone generator ▶ For presenting audio stimuli.
The generator can present separate tones on a wide range of frequencies.

Tracing board ▶ This type of steadiness tester is used for a variety of motor tasks, for measuring speed and accuracy, as well as general performance under a variety of experimental conditions (for example, under stress, with alcohol, etc). This apparatus requires the subject to move a stylus between two wood-covered converging strips of metal without making contact. Contact closes the circuit, and an error is recorded on a counter system.

Visual illusions See Table 3.

White noise generator ▶ Used to mask out external noises or as a distraction device.

Table 1. Standard Laboratory Equipment and Supplier References

Equipment	*Supplier references**
aesthesiometer	
nylon filament	43
dial	43
Von Frey	9, 43
caliper	9, 43
audiometer	9, 43
biofeedback equipment *see* Section 2	
colour mixer	
machine	9, 12
discs	12
depth perception apparatus	9, 43
dispensers	
peanut	9
Smartie	9
discrimination weights	9, 43
dynamometer	9, 17, 43
flicker fusion apparatus	12, 43
grip tester *see* dynamometer	
labyrinth *see* maze	
maze	9
memory drum	15
mirror-drawing/mirror-tracing apparatus	9, 15, 43
perimeter	9, 24, 25, 27, 43
phi phenomenon apparatus	12
photic stimulator	45
pursuit rotor	9, 12, 15,
reaction timer	9, 12, 15, 17, 43
rod and frame apparatus	43
steadiness tester	9
sound-attenuating chamber	4, 22
tachistoscopes	
single-field	9, 43
two-field	9, 12, 15, 43
three-field	12, 43
six-field binocular	12
projection	
single-field	9, 15, 43
double-field	12, 15
three-field	12, 15
four-field	15
pack	12
accessories	9, 12, 15, 43
tapping board	9, 43
timers *see* Table 7	
tone generator	9, 43
tracing board	43
visual illusions *see* Table 3	
white noise generator	9

*The numbers given in the righthand column of this table and the six that follow refer to the relevant equipment suppliers, whose names and addresses are listed at the end of this chapter.

Table 2. Standard Laboratory Equipment Accessories and Supplier References

These accessories allow apparatus to perform more than one task and create more choice for experimental investigation. The items listed are only an indication of what can be obtained.

Equipment	*Supplier references**
automatic card changer (for 3-field tachistoscope)	12
blindfold goggles	9
computer interface (for the control of equipment)	9, 12
counter (electromechanical, 5-digit)	43
double-pulse generator (for 2-field tachistoscope)	15
electronic shutter (for converting projector into tachistoscope)	9, 12
footswitch or switch mats (for time reactions)	9, 15
four-field tachistoscope adaptor (converts 2 × 2-field tachistoscopes to 4-field)	12
headphones, stereo*	7, 15
interconnection cable	12, 15
microphone*	15
paper*	9
printed stars (for mirror drawing)	9
reaction time controller (simultaneously initiates tachistoscope display and reaction timer)	12
reed relay unit (adds to tachistoscope timer to provide central changeover for control of other experiments)	12
response keys (for time reactions)	12
shutter driver, 2 channel (drives a pair of electromagnetic shutters)	12
spare lens	12, 15
spare probes (for pursuit rotor)	15
tachistoscope stands: 2, 3 and 4 tiers	15
tape/slide synchronizer	9, 12
viewing hoods (for tachistoscopes)	12
voice-key/voice-activated relay (triggers equipment by a verbal signal)	9, 43
zoom lens (for projection tachistoscopes)*	12, 15

Items marked * can often be obtained more cheaply in High-Street shops than from specialist suppliers.

Table 3. Visual Perception Equipment and Supplier References

Experiments on the visual system are generally the most frequent in experimental psychology courses up to first-degree level. Table 3 contains an additional selection of equipment and materials which you may find useful for experiments on visual perception.

Equipment	*Supplier references*
cards	
coloured	37
Ishihara (for revealing colour blindness)	18
optical illusion	37
visual acuity and colour discrimination	18
eye test charts	24, 25
eye movement tracking equipment	43
eyetest cabinets (test for overall vision)	
colour vision	43
muscle imbalances	43
simple fusion	43
astigmatism	43
holograms	18
light discrimination apparatus	9
pinhole viewer	37
pseudo isochromatic plates (test colour blindness vs colour ignorance)	43
stereoscope (for viewing stereoptical cards and slides)	43
variable focus eye (demonstrates accommodation)	18
vision disc	37
vision tester	9
visual acuity box (demonstrates variations in visual acuity with intensity of illumination)	49
visual field plotter	24, 25
visual skills test set targets for fusion testing	49
vertical/lateral balance	49
colour blindness	49
depth perception	49
distant usable vision	49
near point usable vision	49

Table 4. Unusual Equipment and Supplier References

A list of less usual items of equipment that can be purchased and which psychology teachers may like to include in their laboratory courses. They may also find this type of equipment useful for project work.

Equipment	Supplier references
arm ergometer	18
back and leg dynamometer	9
bicycle ergometer	9
binaural amplifier (for demonstrating dichotic testing, lateralization of speed perception or auditory function)	43
bug-in-the-ear (a wireless earbug receiver for communications between teacher and student)	2
card-sorting box	9
finger ergograph	43
multi-sensor co-ordinator system (measures binocular/fusion, eye/hand co-ordination and spatial visualization)	9
rhythm tapping device (the device is used to determine a subject's ability to replicate various rhythm patterns under different spatial conditions)	9
sensitivity kit (measures sensitivity to lead – cold, touch and pressure)	9
tactile stimulator	9
treadmill	9
two-arm co-ordination test (a test of co-ordination of both arms working together to move a stylus around a six-pointed star)	9
wiggle chair	2

SECTION 2:
ELECTRO-
PHYSIO-
LOGICAL
RECORDING
AND
MEASURING
EQUIPMENT

Non-invasive physiological measurements are frequently used in psychology experiments to relate psychological and physiological variables. It is not likely that a complete physiological laboratory will be set up for teaching purposes. Table 5 lists the range of equipment that exists in this field from the very sophisticated evoked potential measuring equipment to single-channel recorders and meters. Recent interest in health education and advances in electronics have produced a range of cheaper devices that can be useful to students of psychology in their experimental work. Different manufacturers tend to use different names to describe their version of the same type of equipment, for example, equipment to measure heart rate or pulse is variously called: heart-rate monitor, pulsimeter, pulse-rate monitor, and electronic stethoscope. Table 6 contains a list of these devices arranged under function and suppliers' references.

Table 5. Electrophysiological Recording and Measuring
Equipment and Supplier References

Equipment	*Supplier references*
accessories	
chart paper	20, 45, 46
electrodes	9, 20, 45, 46
electrode gel	9, 20, 45, 46
transducers	9, 20, 46
ambulatory monitoring equipment	2, 8, 45
biofeedback systems	2, 8, 9, 48
biotelemetry systems	43, 45
evoked potential measuring equipment	8, 11, 32, 45, 46
oscillographs and preamplifiers	
(1-, 2-and multichannel for measuring)	
blood pressure	9, 20, 43, 45, 46
ECG (EKG)	2, 9, 20, 32, 43, 45, 46
EEG	8, 9, 20, 32, 43, 45, 46
EMG	2, 9, 32, 43, 45, 46
heart rate	2, 9, 20, 43, 45, 46
respiration	9, 20, 43, 46
skin resistance (GSR)	9, 20, 43, 46
temperature	2, 9, 20, 46
stimulators	
auditory	11
pattern reversal	11, 32, 46
photic and click	45, 46

Table 6. Single-Channel Physiological Monitors and Meters and Supplier References

Equipment	Supplier references
blood pressure	
blood pressure monitor	9, 44
electronic/digital sphygmomanometer	9, 48
sphygmomanometer	18
carbon monoxide smokerlyser	7
EEG	
alpha sensor	2
EMG	
EMG training system	9
myoelectric instruments	2
GSR and skin conductance	
GSR feedback unit	9, 48
GSR monitor	48
skin conductance meter	12
pulse/heart rate	
heart-rate monitor	9
heart-rate feedback monitor	
pulsimeter	48
pulse-rate monitor	18, 39, 44, 48
pulse stick	44
electronic stethoscope	9, 48
wristwatch pulse monitor	44, 48
relaxation units	
biofeedback relaxation system	
(temperature/GSR)	9
relaxometer	2
respiration	
breathing monitor	18
respiration feedback	2
spirometer	18, 20
temperature	
clinical thermometer (digital/electronic)	9, 44, 48
skin temperature meter	12
temperature feedback	2

SECTION 3:
RECORDING
EQUIPMENT

Table 7 covers a range of recording equipment that is often used with the apparatus mentioned in previous sections. Of course microcomputers are also very good recording devices (see chapter in this book on microcomputers). Also included in the list is equipment for the measurement of environmental variables such as noise levels, humidity, room temperature and light levels. This kind of information is necessary when carrying out experimental procedures such as psychological recording where levels of light, temperature and noise can affect the results.

Table 7. Recording Equipment and Supplier References

Equipment	*Supplier references*
counters	
tally (hand operated 4-digit, reset single or multiple unit)	5, 6, 9, 14, 18, 33, 43, 44
frequency	14, 19, 31, 40, 41, 42, 47
electromechanical (animal)	9, 43
timers	
Birkbeck	15
clocks	14, 40, 41, 42
interval	5, 6, 9, 16, 18, 33, 34, 35, 36
process	9, 16, 33
stopclock	5, 6, 9, 16, 33, 34, 35, 36
stopwatch	5, 6, 9, 14, 16, 33, 34, 35, 36, 40, 41, 42, 44
timer/counters	9, 12, 15, 43, 47
recorders	
event	9, 15, 19
chart	18
X/Y Y/t XY/t etc	1, 23, 33, 34, 35, 36, 40, 41, 42, 43
instrumentation	21, 38
physiological (*see* Tables 5 and 6)	
tapes *see* p.181	
environmental monitoring	
humidity recorder	14, 19, 33, 34, 35, 36, 44, 47
hygrograph	5, 6
hygrometer	16, 19, 34, 35, 36
light meter	40, 41, 42, 44
pH meter	13, 18, 33, 34, 35, 36, 44
sound level meter	19, 30, 40, 41, 42, 44
temperature recorder	18, 40, 41, 42, 44
thermohygrograph	16, 18, 33, 34, 35, 36
thermometer	
electronic	5, 6, 18, 33, 40, 41, 42
max.– min.	5, 6
wall	14
oscilloscopes	9, 14, 17, 34, 35, 36, 40, 41, 42, 47

Suppliers' Addresses

1. Advance Bryans Instruments
   14–16 Wates Way
   Mitcham
   Surrey CR4 4HR
   tel. (081) 6405624

2. Aleph One Ltd
   The Old Courthouse
   High Street
   Bottisham
   Cambridge CB5 9BA
   tel. (0223) 811679
   (agents for Farrell Instruments)

3. American Association for the
   Advancement of Science
   1515 Massachusetts Avenue NW
   Washington DC
   USA 20005

4. Amplivox Ltd
   13a Station Field Industrial Est.
   Kidington
   Oxford OX5 1LJ
   tel. (08675) 77977

5. BDH Apparatus (London & SE)
   (Baird & Tatlock)
   Freshwater Road
   Dagenham
   Essex RM8 1RZ
   tel. (081) 5977591

6. BDH Apparatus (Scotland)
   (MacFarlane Robson Ltd)
   Burnfield Avenue
   Thornliebank
   Glasgow G46 7TP
   tel. (041) 6372333

7. Bedfont Technical Instruments Ltd.
   Bedfont House
   Holywell Lane
   Upchurch
   Sittingbourne
   Kent ME9 7HN
   tel. (0634) 375614

8. Biodata
   10 Stocks Street
   Manchester M8 8QG
   tel. (061) 8332782

9. Campden Instruments Ltd
   186 Campden Hill Road
   London W8 7TH
   tel. (071) 2293442
   (agents for Lafayette Instruments)

10. Martock Design
    The Doctors Old House
    Water Street
    Martock
    Somerset TA12 6JN
    tel. (0935) 822870

11. Digitimer Ltd
    37 Hydeway
    Welwyn Garden City
    Herts AL7 1AF
    tel. (07073) 28347

12. Electronic Developments Ltd
    Unit 37/E Platts Eyot
    Lower Sunbury Road
    Hampton
    Middx TW12 2HF
    tel. (081) 9795047

13. EMAP Mclaren Ltd
    PO Box 109
    19 Scarbrook Road
    Croydon
    Surrey CR9 1QH
    Tel. (081) 7609690

14. Farnell Electronic Components Ltd
    Canal Road
    Leeds LS12 2TU
    tel. (0532) 63611

15. Forth Psychology Instruments Ltd
    11 Brewster Street
    Brucefield Industrial Estate
    Livingston
    W. Lothian EH54 9BJ
    tel. (0506) 418500

16. A. Gallenkamp & Co Ltd
    Belton Road West
    Loughborough
    Leics LE11 0TR
    tel. (0509) 237371

17. Gould Electronics Ltd
    Roebuck Road
    Hainault
    Ilford
    Essex IG6 3UE
    tel. (081) 5001000

18. Griffin & George
    Bishop Meadow Road
    Loughborough
    Leics LE11 0RG
    tel. (061) 9985221

19. Gulton Europe Ltd
    Maple Works
    Old Soreham Road
    Hove
    Sussex BN3 3EY
    tel. (0273) 778401

20. Harvard Bioscience
    Fircroft Way
    Edenbridge
    Kent TN8 6HE
    tel. (0732) 864003

21. Hewlett Packard
    Harman House
    1 George Street
    Uxbridge
    Middx UB8 1YH
    tel. (0895) 72020

22. ICI Acoustics
    PO Box 6
    Bessemer Road
    Welwyn Garden City
    Herts AL7 1HD
    tel. (07073) 23400

23. Lloyds Instruments
    Brook Avenue
    Warsash
    Southampton SO3 6HP
    tel. (048957) 4221

24. Keelers Instruments Ltd
    Clewer Hill Road
    Windsor
    Berks SLA 4AA
    tel. (07538) 57177

25. Keelers Instruments Ltd
    21 Marylebone Lane
    London W1A 4NS
    tel. (071) 9358512

26. Kelly's Directories
    Windsor Court
    East Grinstead House
    East Grinstead
    West Sussex RH19 1XB
    tel. (0342) 26972

27. Kodak Ltd
    PO Box 16
    Station Road
    Hemel Hempstead
    Herts HP1 1JN
    tel. (0442) 61122

28. Kompass Publishers Ltd
    Windsor Court
    East Grinstead House
    East Grinstead
    West Sussex RH19 1XB
    tel. (0342) 26972

29. Longman Group
    Longman House
    Burnt Mill
    Harlow CM2 0JE
    tel. (0279) 26721

30. Lucas Dawe Ultrasonics
    Western Avenue
    London W3 0SD
    tel. (081) 9926751

31. Malvern Electronics
    579 Kinston Road
    Raynes Park
    London SW20 8SD
    tel. (081) 5430077

32. Medelec Ltd
    Manor Way
    Old Woking
    Surrey GU22 9JU
    tel. (04862) 70331

33. Patterson Scientific
    M.J. Patterson (Scientific) Ltd
    Unit 2 Brookside
    Colne Way
    Watford
    Herts WD2 4QJ
    tel. (0923) 56177

34. Philip Harris
    (Southern England)
    618 Western Avenue
    Park Royal
    London W3 OTE
    tel. (081) 9925555

35. Philip Harris
    (Scotland)
    2 North Avenue
    Clydebank Business Park
    Clydebank
    Glasgow G81 2DR
    tel. (041) 9529538

36. Philip Harris
    (Northern England)
    Unit 4
    Parkway Four
    Trafford Park
    Manchester M17 1SN
    tel. (061) 8488800

37. Philips Scientific
    Test & Measurement Division
    Colonial Way
    Watford
    Herts WD2 4TT
    tel. (0923) 240511

38. Racal-Thermonic Ltd
    Hardley Industrial Estate
    Hyde
    Southampton SO4 6ZH
    tel. (0703) 843265

39. Ronotex Ltd
    Pine Street
    Stockport
    Cheshire SK3 OPF
    tel. (061) 4801206/7

40. RS Components (National)
    PO Box 99
    Corby
    Northants NN17 9RS
    tel. (0536) 201201
    (or London only (081) 3608600)

41. RS Components (North West)
    PO Box 12
    Kennedy Way
    Greelane Industrial Estate
    Stockport
    Cheshire SK4 2JT
    tel. (061) 4778400

42. RS Components (Midlands)
    PO Box 253
    Duddeston Mill Industrial Est
    Duddeston Mill Road
    Saltley
    Birmingham B8 1BQ
    tel. (021) 3594900

43. Scientific Marketing Association
    37 Mildmay Grove
    London N1 4RH
    tel. (071) 3595357
    (agents for Stoelting)

44. Solex International
    96 Main Street
    Broughton Astley
    Leics LE9 6RE
    tel. (0455) 283912

45. Specialized Lab Equipment
    15 Campbell Road
    Croydon
    Surrey CRO 2SQ
    tel. (081) 6890251

46. Stag Instruments Ltd
    16 Monument Industrial Park
    Chalgrove
    Oxon OX9 7RW
    tel. (0865) 891116
    (agents for Grass Equipment)

47. STC Instruments Services
    Dewer House
    Central Road
    Harlow
    Essex CM20 2TA
    tel. (0279) 29522

48. Surgicon Ltd
    84 Wakefield Road
    Brighouse
    W. Yorks HD6 1QL
    tel. (0484) 712147

49. Warwick Evans Optical Co.
    22 Palace Road
    Bounds Green Road
    London N11 2P6
    tel. (081) 8880051/2

50. Weylec
    5 Guildown Road
    Guildford
    Surrey GU2 5EW
    tel. (0483) 67287

Acknowledgement. Special thanks to Sue Nanji for her help in compiling this chapter.

Do-It-Yourself Laboratory Equipment

Rosemary Westley

❏ creating card materials ● developing apparatus from existing resources
● building your own equipment ● useful addresses

The previous chapter dealt with manufactured equipment and materials available for teaching. However, not all teachers of psychology will have the financial resources to equip classes with commercial apparatus, which can be very expensive if you need to have class sets. Neither will many classes at say GCSE, A/S or A-level be given specialist laboratories for their work. There is in any case a lot of equipment that cannot be purchased, regardless of resources.

The range of equipment and materials that can be used for psychology investigations is vast and this creates a problem in colleges where only one or two courses may be taught. Justifying expenditure on equipment that may be used only a few times a year, and then left to gather dust in a cupboard, can be difficult. Any equipment acquired must be flexible so that it can be used in many different studies.

Teachers will need both to encourage their students to test out the phenomena and processes taught and to be original and adventurous in their experimental work. They will have to provide a variety of materials and equipment to cope with the range of investigations that can be carried out.

Everyday Resources

Many teachers do cope very well with limited resources and a lot of imagination. Here are some of the ideas provided for A-level classes by Annette Cassells, a psychology teacher in Leicester.

Investigation	Materials
Interpersonal attraction	Wedding photographs from newspapers cut up and mounted on card and rated for attractiveness.
Depth perception – monocular vs binocular vision	Blu-tack, needle, ruler, A3 sheet of paper cut lengthways and sellotaped end to end, anglepoise lamp.
Stress	Large dot-to-dot pictures (with one dot missing), pulse-rate meter.
Effects of fatigue on performance	Several sheets of printed material for repeated tasks, stopwatch.
Memory	Lists of words randomly gathered, stopwatch.
Egocentrism	Lego space station, space people (alternative to Piaget three mountain task).
Effects of an audience	Pack of cards for sorting into suits or numbers, stopwatch for timing tasks with and without observers.
Perception of music	Tape-recorded extracts, personal stereo, written descriptions for comment or matching.
Divided attention	Two microphones, stereo cassette player, headphones.

It is clear that creating your own equipment has advantages because it is specifically designed to meet your needs and can be easily adapted.

There are some publications that do provide information on inexpensive, do-it-yourself apparatus such as the Association for the Teaching of Psychology *Newsletter* and their journal *Psychology Teaching*. The textbook for GCSE *Psychology: An introduction* by Nicky Hayes and Sue Orrell (1987), contains many useful ideas.

This chapter offers practical advice on the creation and acquisition of apparatus and materials that can be used for very little cost. It is intended to help teachers make the most out of whatever resources they may have.

There are three sections:
(1) creating card materials;
(2) developing apparatus from existing resources;
(3) building your own equipment.

SECTION 1:
CREATING
CARD
MATERIALS

The material for many experiments can be created out of paper and card. Students quite often create their own materials for investigation and it is a good idea to collect the efforts of the more artistic students, such as line drawings of everyday objects, which can be difficult to find in books and magazines and impossible to create if you can't draw, for use in next year's courses. Supplies of index cards, sheets of card, glue or staples and felt-tip pens are essential, as is sticky clear plastic or spray coating to preserve all the creative efforts. Many textbooks carry examples of materials which can be copied, such as the visual illusions below.

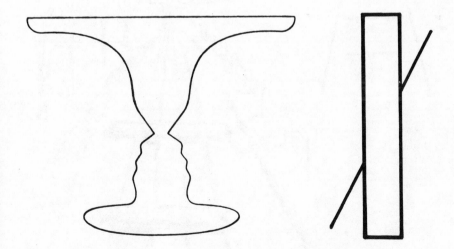

Rubin's vase   *Poggendorff illusion*

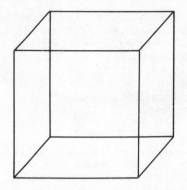

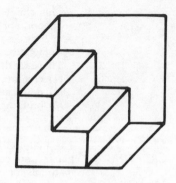

Necker cube   *Reversing figure staircase illusion*

Two versions of the Ponzo illusion

Two ambiguous figures

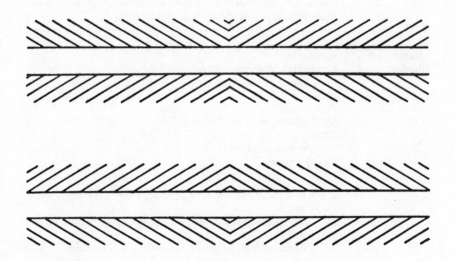

A variation of the Herring illusion

Archimedes spiral

Müller-Lyer illusion and Stroop effect cards are amongst those card materials that are used repeatedly, and are well worth making. Full instructions for these are given below, together with some ideas for other materials.

Müller-Lyer Illusion

MATERIALS:
1 large sheet thin white card
1 large sheet thick white card
Ruler
Protractor
Black felt-tip pen
Glue
Scissors or sharp knife
Graph paper

INSTRUCTIONS:
1. Cut a piece of thick card 220mm. long and 40mm. wide (card A)
2. Cut a piece of thin card 150mm. long and 125mm. wide (card B)
3. Place card A lengthways down the middle of card B.
4. Fold over edges of card B and glue to form a sheath (see Figure 1a).
5. Pull out card B and lay A and B end to end on a flat surface.

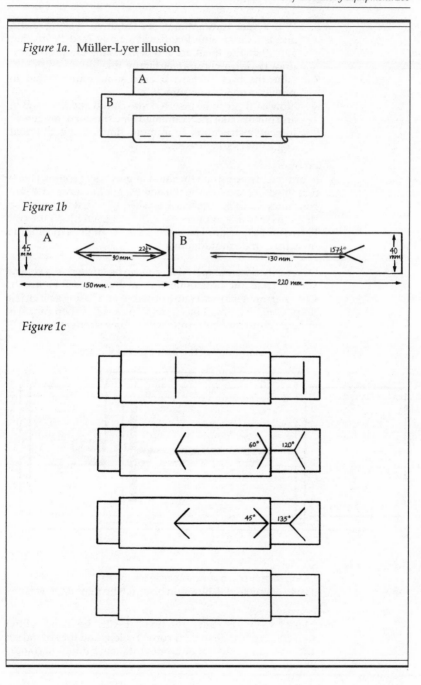

Figure 1a. Müller-Lyer illusion

Figure 1b

Figure 1c

6. With a ruler draw a 90mm. line lengthways along card A and a 130mm. line lengthways along card B, making sure that the lines are aligned. Using the protractor, draw two arrowheads (see Figure 1b).
7. Glue the back of card B onto some graph paper to provide a handy measure.
8. Now card A can be inserted into card B and then slid in and out to make the 'combined' line shorter or longer.
9. Repeat instructions four more times using different angle fins (see Figure 1c).

EXPERIMENT:
In order to demonstrate Richard Gregory's suggestion (1963) that the depth cues in the illusion trigger inappropriate size constancy scaling, subjects are asked to adjust the cards so that the black line appears to be the same length on the two halves of the illusion. The more acute the angle of the fins the more inaccurate the judgement.

Other experimental material can also be created in a similar way, such as the horizontal/vertical illusion (see Figure 2). Cut a narrow slit in the centre of card A and, using a black felt tip pen, mark a broad black strip on card B. When card B is slid in and out the central line will become shorter or longer.

Figure 2. A variation of the Müller-Lyer illusion

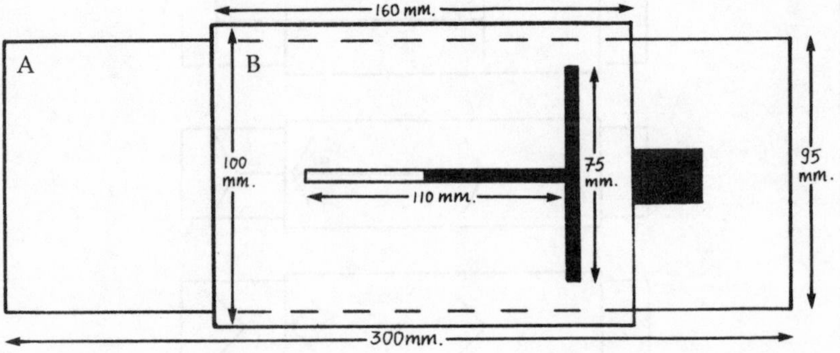

Stroop cards

MATERIALS:
96 Small plain cards (index cards are ideal)
1 each of green, red, blue and black felt-tip pens or pencils

INSTRUCTIONS:
Make two sets of cards, the first set with the names of the four colours written in their correct colour and the second set with the same colour words but written in a different colour, as follows:

SET I

12 cards with BLACK in black ink
12 cards with BLUE in blue ink
12 cards with RED in red ink
12 cards with GREEN in green ink

SET II

4 cards with RED in black ink
4 cards with BLUE in black ink
4 cards with GREEN in black ink
4 cards with BLUE in red ink
4 cards with GREEN in red ink
4 cards with BLACK in red ink
4 cards with RED in blue ink
4 cards with GREEN in blue ink
4 cards with BLACK in blue ink
4 cards with RED in green ink
4 cards with BLUE in green ink
4 cards with BLACK in green ink.

EXPERIMENT:

To demonstrate the Stroop effect each set of cards is shuffled and subjects are timed sorting each set into piles of colour by ink (not by name). It should take longer to sort set II as the name of the colour interferes with the processing of the ink colour. An explanation of the effect is given in Lindsay and Norman (1977).

Bruner or Concept cards

Concept cards are also easy to make. They consist of 81 individually different cards which feature symbols in red, green and black. The symbols are a cross, a circle or a square. There are one, two or three symbols. Each card has in black a one-, two- or three-line border. The 27 cards with black symbols are shown in Figure 3.

Figure 3. Concept cards

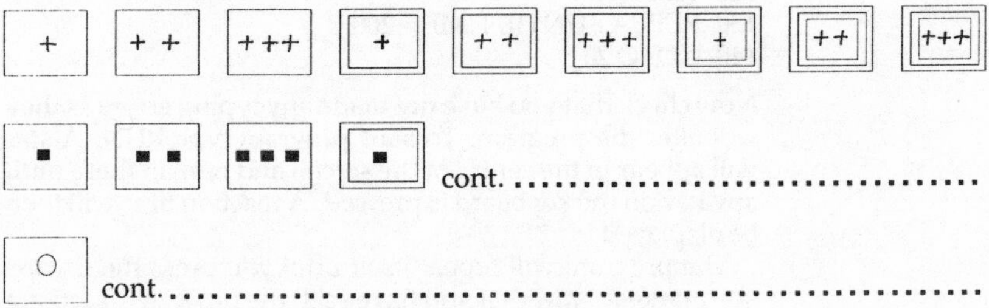

Repeat for red crosses; red squares, red circles; green crosses; green squares; green circles.

SUGGESTIONS FOR USE:
The cards can be used to demonstrate Bruner, Goodnaw and Austins' investigations of strategies used to learn new concepts. They are also very useful if you need a more complex card-sorting task.

SECTION 2:
DEVELOPING
APPARATUS
FROM
EXISTING
RESOURCES

In most institutions, departments other than psychology will use equipment that can be useful for psychology experiments.

Microcomputers are now widely used in psychology and colleges may have them to meet the needs of all departments. If you have programming skills, a microcomputer can be turned into a reaction timer, tachistoscope (a tachistoscope program is given Haworth, this volume), memory drum, pursuit rotor and used for statistical analyses. However, for those who find programming a little difficult you might like to use the following simple reaction time program to get you underway.

Reaction time program

The program is in BBC Basic, and enables you to measure reaction times to the nearest 10 milliseconds. Type in the following instructions:

```
10 MODE 7
20 CLS
30 TIME=0
40 REPEAT UNTIL TIME> 100+RND (100)
50 PRINT TAB (20, 12); "*"
60 *FX 15,0
70 TIME=0
80 r=GET
90 rt=TIME
100 CLS
110 PRINT "Reaction time was    "; rt*10;" milliseconds"
120 TIME=0
130 REPEAT UNTIL TIME> 200
140 GOTO 20
```

Now check that you have not made any typing errors as they will alter the program. To start program type RUN. A star will appear in the centre of the screen and remain there until any key on the keyboard is pressed. A reaction time will then be displayed.

The program will repeat itself until you press the Escape key marked. Now that you have seen the program in action I will explain what the instructions mean.

The numbers at the beginning of each line refer to the line

number of the program. They are set 10 lines apart so that additional instructions can be added if necessary.

10 MODE 7 Sets up screen (Teletext display 40 × 25 text)

20 CLS Clear screen

30 TIME=0 Computer timer is now set to zero

40 REPEAT UNTIL TIME> 100+RND (100)
Wait until time counted is greater than 100 centiseconds plus a random time in the range of 0 to 100 centiseconds

50 PRINT TAB (20, 12) "*"
Print a star on screen 20 characters across and 12 lines down

60 *FX 15,0 Clears keyboard buffer to prevent early response

70 TIME=0 Computer timing is now set to zero

80 r=GET Waits until any key is pressed

90 rt=TIME Reaction time is stored

100 CLS Clear screen

110 PRINT "Reaction time was "; rt*10" milliseconds"
Prints statement in quotes and the reaction time in centiseconds (milliseconds × 10)

120 TIME=0 Computer timer set to zero

130 REPEAT UNTIL TIME> 200
Wait until time counted is greater than 200 centiseconds

140 GOTO 20 Go to line 20 and repeat program.

This program can easily be altered to suit your needs; for example waiting times can be increased or decreased by changing the values in line 40 or 130 or the position of the star can be altered by changing the tab setting in line 50. You could also add an extra line 55 to display a second character.

Here are some additional instructions you could use as well:

```
 5   DIM REAC (10)
 7   FOR I=1 TO 10
42   X=RND (40)
44   Y=RND (25)
50   PRINT TAB (X, Y) "*"
90   REAC (I)=TIME
110  PRINT "Reaction time was";REAC (I)*10;"
120  TIME=0
130  REPEAT UNTIL TIME>200
140  NEXT I
145  CLS
```

Table 1. Other Departments' Resources

Equipment	Department	Used for:
pulse meters	PE; Biology	heart-rate monitoring
Ishihara cards	Biology	colour blindness
signal generator and headphones or speaker	Physics	generating tones (can be recorded for future use)
projector and shutter	Audiovisual; Physics	make a single field projection tachistoscope that can be used for single or group studies
dividers	Mathematics	used as aesthesiometers
record player	Audiovisual	spiral aftereffects or rotating illusion demonstrator
stroboscope	Physics; Design & Technology	a) greaseproof paper fitted over lamp to reduce glare – photo stimulator b) with black card with small aperture fitted over lamp – flicker fusion
mirror bosses, clamps and stands	Physics; Chemistry	mirror-drawing equipment
timer/counters	Physics	to measure reaction times
radio or television	Audiovisual	tuned to hiss between stations for white noise. Output can be recorded onto a tape recorder
metre rule	Physics	time reaction ruler

You may also find that your Works or Estates departments has a sound level meter or light meter.

```
147  T=0
150  FOR J=1 TO 10
160  PRINT "TRIAL ";J" RT=";REAC (J)*10
170  T=T+REAC (J)
180  NEXT J
190  PRINT
```

The position of the stimulus (star) will now be displayed randomly and the program will run 10 trials, store the data, display the 10 reaction times and calculate the average.

There are, of course, a number of other pieces of equipment that are often used in biology, physics, chemistry, physical education, design and technology and audiovisual departments which you may be able to use. Table 1 provides a few ideas.

Reaction time rulers

MATERIALS:
A metre rule

INSTRUCTIONS:
The subject is asked to hold the thumb and forefinger about one and a half inches apart at waist height. The experimenter holds the metre rule with the 0mm. mark exactly level with the subject's thumb and forefinger. At the given signal the experimenter drops the rule and the subject responds by closing the thumb and finger to stop its fall. The table below gives a read off of reaction time (to the nearest 10 milliseconds, which is accurate enough) in terms of millimetres measured to the point at which the subject stops the rule.

Reaction time (ms.)	Distance travelled (mm.)	Reaction time (ms.)	Distance travelled (mm.)
10	0.4905	260	331.578
20	1.962	270	357.5745
30	4.415	280	384.552
40	7.848	290	412.5105
50	12.2625	300	441.45
60	17.658	310	471.3705
70	24.0345	320	502.272
80	31.392	330	534.1545
90	39.7305	340	567.018
100	49.05	350	600.8625
110	59.3505	360	635.688
120	70.632	370	671.4945
130	82.8945	380	708.282
140	96.138	390	746.0505
150	110.3625	400	784.8
160	125.568	410	824.5305

170	141.7545	420	865.242
180	158.922	430	906.9345
190	177.0705	440	949.608
200	196.2	450	993.2625
210	216.3105	460	1037.898
220	237.402	470	1083.5145
230	259.4745	480	1130.112
240	282.528	490	1177.6905
250	306.5625	500	1226.25

Maze

There are several methods of creating a finger or pencil maze. Figure 4 illustrates a typical branch maze but the instructions given below allow for any design to be made.

MATERIALS 1;
Thick card
Scissors or sharp knife

INSTRUCTIONS 1:
Cut out track wide enough to insert pencil. Place a sheet of paper under the maze to record errors made.

MATERIALS 2:
As number 1.

INSTRUCTIONS 2:
Cut slot wider so that the subject is able to follow track with their finger.

MATERIALS 3:
Plywood
Beading
Glue.

INSTRUCTIONS 3:
Glue beading to track to form a slot that can be followed with a finger.

SUGGESTIONS FOR USE:
Subjects trace the maze blindfolded. Learning curves can be compared under different conditions; noise or distraction against no noise; active vs passive practice; massed vs distributed practice. Other variables such as the effect of the sex of the subject can also be investigated with this apparatus.

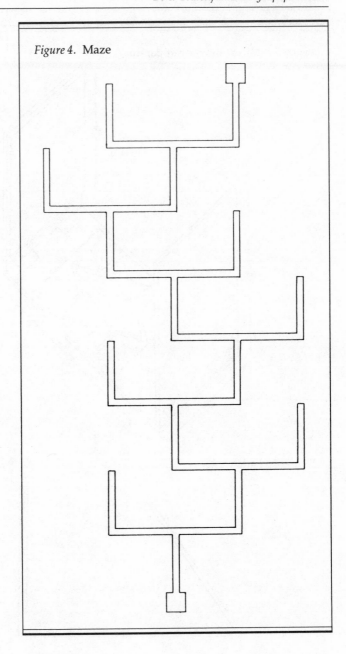

Figure 4. Maze

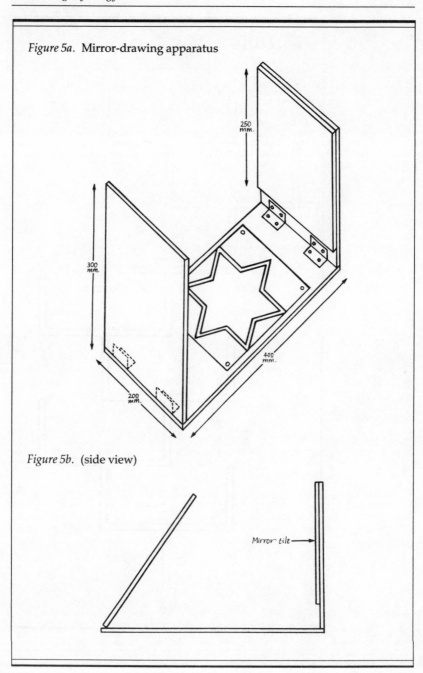

Figure 5a. Mirror-drawing apparatus

250 mm.

300 mm.

200 mm.

400 mm.

Figure 5b. (side view)

Mirror tile

Mirror-drawing apparatus

MATERIALS:
1 mirror tile
1 sheet of wood (plywood or chipboard, fibreboard – ideally plywood for side panel and fibreboard for base)
Glue or self-adhesive pads
4 hinges with screws.

INSTRUCTIONS:
1. Cut wood to sizes indicated in Figure 5a.
2. Glue, or fix with self adhesive pads, mirror tile to side panel B.
3. Fit a pair of hinges to each side panel A and side panel B then fit to board C.
4. Make photocopies of a five-or six-pointed star (see Figure 5c) or other shapes with a double border.

SUGGESTIONS FOR USE:
The subject, seated facing the mirror, draws round the star shape, between its double border, whilst looking at the star reflected in the mirror. Panel A prevents them seeing their hand directly.

The equipment is used to test the acquisition of visual motor skill on many variables such as massed vs distributed practice or learning by observation.

Note: After use the equipment can be folded flat for easy storage.

Figure 5c. Mirror-drawing shapes

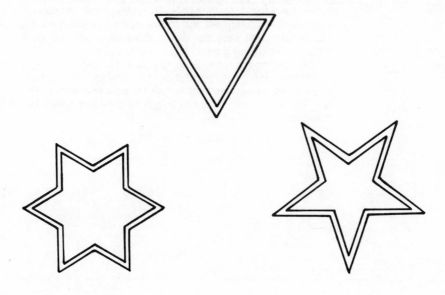

Depth perception apparatus

MATERIALS:
Sheet wood (plywood, chipboard) approximately 3/8in thick *or*
Very thick card
lengths of wood approximately 1in × ½in section (for reinforcing strips)
1 metre length of ¼in dowelling
½ metre rule
Wood glue
⅜in panel pins
Matt black paint.
Matt white paint.

INSTRUCTIONS:
1. Cut the wood to size as shown in Figure 6.
2. Assemble apparatus using glue and panel pins. Side reinforcing strips are only necessary if using card. The end strips are fitted to support the dowelling.
3. If you are using wood to make the viewing slit, drill two holes, one at each end of slit and cut out section in between using a fret saw.
4. Paint inside matt black.
5. Place ruler on floor of apparatus.

SUGGESTIONS FOR USE:
Illuminate apparatus by positioning an anglepoise lamp centrally above it and adjust to illuminate shadows. Suspend objects, such as 6-inch lengths of wire painted matt white, from the dowelling rails. The subject sees the objects through the viewing slit and indicates their position on the metre rule. Test subjects' depth discrimination first with both eyes open and then with one eye covered.

The equipment can also be used to test Gregory's prediction (1963) on the Müller-Lyer illusion. White wire versions of the Müller-Lyer halves are suspended from the rail. Instead of adjusting the length of the lines adjust the distance from the eye.

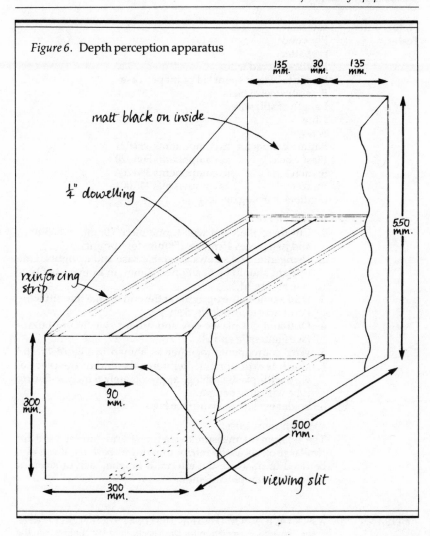

Figure 6. Depth perception apparatus

Motor Skills
Tester

MATERIALS:
Plywood
PP3 battery
Plastic-covered wire
Plastic tubing or spent ballpoint pen case
Brass or steel eyelets
Length of stiff wire
Glue
Screws
Battery connector   RS components 489 021
Plastic box   RS components 508 920
Switch   RS components 350 204
Buzzer   RS components 245 001
(audible warning device)

INSTRUCTIONS:
1. Cut three pieces of wood, one piece 70mm. × 565mm., and two pieces 45mm. ×150mm. for uprights.
2. Using glue and screws assemble base and uprights. One upright should be positioned 60mm. in from end of base (see Figure 7d).
3. Drill a hole in the uprights at the end to take the stiff wire. Bend wire to any desired shape.
4. Drill and cut plastic box and mount switch and buzzer (see Figures 7a and b).
5. Wire components together as shown in Figure 7c and attach box to upright. Reinforce the end of the piece of wire with plastic tubing, approximately 6 inches. Secure tube with glue or tape.
6. Solder eyelet onto wire (see Figure 7d).

SUGGESTIONS FOR USE:
The equipment measures steadiness and can be used for similar projects as the mirror drawing apparatus. It can also be used to measure the effects of fatigue, lack of sleep or drugs (for example caffeine).

References

ASSOCIATION FOR THE TEACHING OF PSYCHOLOGY *Psychology Teaching*. Association for the Teaching of Psychology, c/o the BPS.
GREGORY, R.L. (1963) Distortion of visual space as inappropriate constancy scaling. *Nature, 99*, 678–680.
HAYES, N. and ORRELL, S. (1987) *Psychology: An Introduction*. Harlow: Longman.
LINDSAY, P.H. and NORMAN, D.A. (1977) *Human Information Processing: An introduction to psychology*. 2nd edn. London: Academic press. 453–455.
STROOP, J.R. (1935) Studies of interference in serial verbal reactions. *Journal of Experimental Psychology, 18*, 643–662.

Figure 7 (a, b, c, d). Motor skills tester

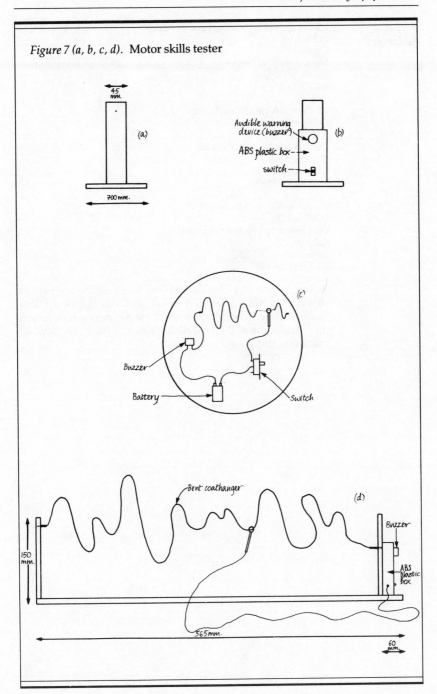

Useful
Addresses

RS Components (National and London)
PO Box 99
Corby
Northants NN17 9RS
tel. (0536) 201201
tel. (081) 3608600

RS Components (North West)
PO Box 12
Kennedy Way
Green Lane Industrial Estate
Stockport
Cheshire SK4 2JT
tel. (061) 4778400

RS Components (Midlands)
PO Box 253
Duddeston Mill Industrial Estate
Saltley
Birmingham B81 1BQ
tel. (021) 3594900

Acknowledgements. I would like to thank all the teachers of psychology who provided ideas and comments for this chapter. Also David Jordan and Pete Sanders who allowed me to use some of their excellent drawings from the previous volume of this book.

ETHICAL ISSUES

□ research with humans ● research with animals ● use of animals in teaching

RESEARCH
WITH
HUMANS

The following guidelines were approved by the Scientific Affairs Board of The British Psychological Society in March 1990.

Introduction

1.1 The principles given below are intended to apply to research with human participants. Principles of conduct in professional practice are to be found in the Society's Code of Conduct and in the advisory documents prepared by the Divisions, Sections and Special Groups of the Society.

1.2 Participants in psychological research should have confidence in the investigators. Good psychological research is possible only if there is mutual respect and confidence between investigators and participants. Psychological investigators are potentially interested in all aspects of human behaviour and conscious experience. However, for ethical reasons, some areas of human experience and behaviour may be beyond the reach of experimental, observational or other form of psychological investigation. Ethical guidelines are necessary to clarify the conditions under which psychological research is acceptable.

1.3 The principles given below supplement for researchers with human participants the general ethical principles of members of the Society as stated in The British Psychological Society's Code of Conduct (1985). Members of The British Psychological Society are expected to abide by both the Code of Conduct and the fuller principles expressed here. Members should also draw the principles to the attention of research colleagues who are not members of the

Society. Members should encourage colleagues to adopt them and ensure than they are followed by all researchers whom they supervise (e.g. research assistants, postgraduate, undergraduate, A level and G.C.S.E students).

1.4 In recent years, there has been an increase in legal actions by members of the general public against professionals for alleged misconduct. Researchers must recognize the possibility of such legal action if they infringe the rights and dignity of participants in their research.

General

2.1 In all circumstances, investigators must consider the ethical implications and psychological consequences for the participants in their research. The essential principle is that the investigation should be considered from the standpoint of all participants; forseeable threats to their psychological well-being, health, values or dignity should be eliminated. Investigators should recognize that, in our multi-cultural and multi-ethnic society and where investigations involve individuals of different ages, gender and social background, the investigators may not have sufficient knowledge of the implications of an investigation for the participants. It should be borne in mind that the best judges of whether an investigation will cause offence may be members of the population from which the participants in the research are to be drawn.

Consent

3.1 Whenever possible, the investigator should inform all participants of the objectives of the investigation. The investigator should inform the participants of all aspects of the research or intervention that might reasonably be expected to influence willingness to participate. The investigator should, normally, explain all other aspects of the research or intervention about which the participants enquire. Failure to make full disclosure prior to obtaining informed consent requires additional safeguards to protect the welfare and dignity of the participants (see Section 4).

3.2 Research with children or with participants who have impairments that will limit understanding and/or communication such that they are unable to give their real consent requires special safeguarding procedures.

3.3 Where possible, the real consent of children and of adults with impairments in understanding or communication should be obtained. In addition, where research involves all persons under sixteen years of age, consent should be obtained from parents or from those *in loco parentis*.

3.4 Where real consent cannot be obtained from adults

with impairments in understanding or communication, wherever possible the investigator should consult a person well-placed to appreciate the participant's reaction, such as a member of the person's family, and must obtain the disinterested approval of the research from independent advisers.

3.5 When research is being conducted with detained persons, particular care should be taken over informed consent, paying attention to the special circumstances which may affect the person's ability to give free informed consent.

3.6 Investigators should realize that they are often in a position of authority or influence over participants who may be their students, employees or clients. This relationship must not be allowed to pressurize the participants to take part in, or remain in, an investigation.

3.7 The payment of participants must not be used to induce them to risk harm beyond that which they risk without payment in their normal life style.

3.8 If harm, unusual discomfort, or other negative consequences for the individual's future life might occur, the investigator must obtain the disinterested approval of independent advisers, inform the participants, and obtain informed, real consent from each of them.

3.9 If longitudinal research, consent may need to be obtained on more than one occasion.

Deception   4.1 The withholding of information or the misleading of participants is unacceptable if the participants are typically likely to object or show unease once debriefed. Where this is in any doubt, appropriate consultation must precede the investigation. Consultation is best carried out with individuals who share the social and cultural background of the participants in the research, but the advice of ethics committees or experienced and disinterested colleagues may be sufficient.

4.2 Intentional deception of the participants over the purpose and general nature of the investigation should be avoided whenever possible. Participants should never be deliberately misled without extremely strong scientific or medical justification. Even then there should be strict controls and the disinterested approval of independent advisers.

4.3 It may be impossible to study some psychological processes without withholding information about the true object of the study or deliberately misleading the participants. Before conducting such a study, the investigator has a special responsibility to: (a) determine that alternative procedures avoiding concealment or deception are not available; (b) ensure that the participants are provided with sufficient information at the earliest stage; and (c) consult appropriately upon the way that the withholding of information or deliberate deception will be received.

Debriefing

5.1 In studies where the participants are aware that they have taken part in an investigation, when the data have been collected, the investigator should provide the participants with any necessary information to complete their understanding of the nature of the research. The investigator should discuss with the participants their experience of the research in order to monitor any unforeseen negative effects or misconceptions.

5.2 Debriefing does not provide a justification for unethical aspects of an investigation.

5.3 Some effects which may be produced by an experiment will not be negated by a verbal description following the research. Investigators have a responsibility to ensure that participants receive any necessary debriefing in the form of active intervention before they leave the research setting.

Withdrawal from the Investigation

6.1 At the onset of the investigation investigators should make plain to participants their right to withdraw from the research at any time, irrespective of whether or not payment or other inducement has been offered. It is recognized that this may be difficult in certain observational or organizational settings, but nevertheless the investigator must attempt to ensure that participants (including children) know of their right to withdraw. When testing children, avoidance of the testing situation may be taken as evidence of failure to consent to the procedure and should be acknowledged.

6.2 In the light of experience of the investigation, or as a result of debriefing, the participant has the right to withdraw retrospectively any consent given, and to require that their own data, including recordings, be destroyed.

Confidentiality

7.1 Subject to the requirements of legislation, including the Data Protection Act, information obtained about a participant during an investigation is confidential unless otherwise agreed in advance. Investigators who are put under pressure to disclose confidential information should draw this point to the attention of those exerting such pressure. Participants in psychological research have a right to expect that information they provide will be treated confidentially and, if published, will not be identifiable as theirs. In the event that confidentiality and/or anonymity cannot be guaranteed, the participant must be warned of this in advance of agreeing to participate.

Protection of Participants

8.1 Investigators have a primary responsibility to protect participants from physical and mental harm during the investigations. Normally, the risk of harm must be no greater than in ordinary life, i.e. participants should not be exposed to risks greater than or additional to those encountered in their normal life styles. Where the risk of harm is greater than in ordinary life the provision of 3.8 should apply. Participants must be asked about any factors in the procedure that might create a risk, such as pre-existing medical conditions, and must be advised of any special action they should take to avoid risk.

8.2 Participants should be informed of procedures for contacting the investigator within a reasonable time period following participation should stress, potential harm, or related questions or concern arise despite the precautions required by these Principles. Where research procedures might result in undesirable consequences for participants, the investigator has the responsibility to detect and remove or correct these consequences.

8.3 Where research may involve behaviour or experiences that participants may regard as personal and private the participants must be protected from stress by all appropriate measures, including the assurance that answers to personal questions need not be given. There should be no concealment or deception when seeking information that might encroach on privacy.

8.4 In research involving children, great caution should be exercised when discussing the results with parents, teachers or others *in loco parentis*, since evaluative statements may carry unintended weight.

Observational Research

9.1 Studies based upon observation must respect the privacy and psychological well-being of the individuals studied. Unless those observed give their consent to being observed, observational research is only acceptable in situations where those observed would expect to be observed by strangers. Additionally, particular account should be taken of local cultural values and of the possibility of intruding upon the privacy of individuals who, even while in a normally public space, may believe they are unobserved.

Giving Advice   10.1 During research, an investigator may obtain evidence of psychological or physical problems of which a participant is, apparently, unaware. In such a case, the investigator has a responsibility to inform the participant if the investigator believes that by not doing so the participant's future well-being may be endangered.

10.2 If, in the normal course of psychological research, or as a result of problems detected as in 10.1, a participant solicits advice concerning educational, personality, behavioural or health issues, caution should be exercised. If the issue is serious and the investigator is not qualified to offer assistance, the appropriate source of professional advice should be recommended. Further details on the giving of advice will be found in the Society's Code of Conduct.

10.3 In some kinds of investigation the giving of advice is appropriate if this forms an intrinsic part of the research and has been agreed in advance.

Colleagues   11.1 Investigators share responsibility for the ethical treatment of research participants with their collaborators, assistants, students and employees. A psychologist who believes that another psychologist or investigator may be conducting research that is not in accordance with the principles above should encourage that investigator to re-evaluate the research.

References   BRITISH PSYCHOLOGICAL SOCIETY (1978) Ethical Principles for Research with Human Subjects. *Bulletin of The British Psychological Society, 31,* 48–49.
BRITISH PSYCHOLOGICAL SOCIETY (1985) A Code of Conduct for Psychologists. *Bulletin of The British Psychological Society, 38,* 41–43.

RESEARCH   The Scientific Affairs Board of The British Psychological Society and
WITH   the Committee of the Experimental Psychology Society jointly
ANIMALS   propose the following guidelines to assist members of both Societies, and other investigators, in planning experiments on living animals. The guidelines are based on those published jointly by the Association for the Study of Animal Behaviour and the Animal Behaviour Society (1981). The Scientific Affairs Board of the BPS and the Committee of the EPS offer these guidelines as a checklist of points which investigators should carefully consider when planning experiments with living animals, and as a list of sources from which further information on particular issues can be obtained. [They should be seen as supplementing and not replacing the earlier statement by the Board published in the form of a Report of the Working Party on Animal Experimentation (*Bulletin of The British*

Psychological Society, 1979, *32*, 44–52.] These guidelines cannot exhaustively cover all points which may arise in the consideration of all possible experiments. Thus members of both Societies, and other investigators, are reminded of their general obligation to avoid, or at least to minimize, discomfort to living animals. To this end, when considering future research with animals, they are advised to discuss carefully details of any experiments which they propose with the local Home Office Inspector, and with colleagues who are experts on the topics which they propose to research. Investigators are also advised to seek, and to consider carefully, independent advice as to whether the likely scientific contribution of the work they intend justifies the use of living animals, and whether the scientific point they wish to make may not be made without the use of living animals (cf., for example Smyth, 1978). Investigators may also wish to consider the literature concerning the ethics of animal experimentation a short review of which is given by Dawkins (1980).

The Law For those resident in the United Kingdom references to the laws protecting animals is given in the Universities' Federation for Animal Welfare Handbook (UFAW, 1978). Failure to comply with these laws has resulted in prosecution. Members must make themselves aware of current legislation, and if in any doubt, should consult their local inspector, or the Home Office, Queen Anne's Gate, London SW1H 9AT. Workers outside the UK should acquaint themselves with the local requirements.

Ethical Considerations If the animals are confined, constrained, harmed or stressed in any way the investigator must consider whether the knowledge to be gained justifies the procedure. Some knowledge is trivial, and experiments must not be done simply because it is possible to do them. Alternatives to animal experiments should also be considered (Smyth, 1978).

Species Wherever research involves confining animals or the use of procedures likely to cause pain or discomfort the investigator should bear in mind that members of some species may be less likely to suffer than members of others. Choosing an appropraite subject usually requires knowledge of the species' natural history as well as its special needs.

Number of Animals Laboratory studies should use the smallest number of animals necessary. The number cannot be precisely specified, but careful thought to the design of an experiment is important. The number of animals used can often be greatly reduced through good experimental design and the use of statistical tests such as the analysis of variance and multiple regression that enable several factors to be examined at one time. If advice is needed a statistician should be consulted before an experiment is carried out. Hunt (1980) and Still (1982) both discuss ways of reducing the number of animals used in an experiment through alternative designs. The technical details can be found in Cox (1958) and Cochran & Cox (1966).

Endangered Species

Members of endangered species should not be collected or manipulated in the wild except as part of a serious attempt at conservation. Information on threatened species can be obtained from the Union for the Conservation of Nature, Species Conservation Monitoring Unit, 219C Huntingdon Road, Cambridge CB3 0DL, England. Lists of endangered species can be obtained by writing to the Office for Endangered Species, US Department of Interior, Fish and Wildlife Service, Washington, DC 20240.

Animal Suppliers

Animals should be obtained only from reputable suppliers and full records kept of their provenance and laboratory history. For workers in the UK advice may be obtained from the MRC's Laboratory Animals Centre, Carshalton, Surrey. The investigators should confirm that those responsible for handling the animals on route to the laboratory provide adequate food, water, ventilation and space, and that they do not impose undue stress. The investigators should also confirm that if animals are trapped in the wild this should be done in as painless and humane a manner as possible.

Caging and Social Environment

Caging conditions should take into account the social behaviour of the species. An acceptable density of animals of one species may constitute overcrowding for a different species. In social animals caging in isolation may have undesirable effects. Information as to the recommended requirements can be found in the UFAW Handbook (1978) and in the DHEW Publication No (NIH) 78-23 (1978).

Fieldwork

Fieldworkers should disturb the animals they study as little as possible. Even simple observations on wild animals can have marked effects on their breeding and survival. If animals are marked for identification or radio transmitters are attached, the animals may also be stressed by the capture and recapture. The stress involved varies greatly with the type of technique used and the species studied. Two useful sources of information are the books edited by Stonehouse (1978) and by Amlaner & Macdonald (1980).

Aggression and Predation including Infanticide   The fact that pain and injury may come to animals in the wild is not a defence for allowing it to occur in the laboratory. Huntingford (1984) has discussed the ethical issues involved, and recommends that, wherever possible, field studies of natural encounters should be used in preference to staged encounters. Where staged encounters are thought to be necessary the use of models or animals behind glass should be considered. The numbers of subjects should be kept to the minimum and the experiments as short as possible.

Motivation   When arranging schedules of deprivation the experimenter should consider the animal's normal eating and drinking habits and its metabolic requirements. It is not necessary to provide all species of animals with *ad libitum* food intake (as with household pets this may even be considered harmful in some cases). However, differences between species must be borne in mind: a short period of deprivation for one species may be unacceptably long for another. Moran (1975) discusses the tendency to rely on the exclusive use of food deprivation.

Aversive Stimulation and Stressful Procedures   Procedures that cause pain or distress to animals are illegal in the UK unless the experimenter holds a Home Office licence and the relevant certificates. The investigator should be satisfied that there are no alternative ways of conducting the experiment without the use of aversive stimulation. Lea (1979) discusses alternatives to the use of painful stimuli. If alternatives are not available the investigator has the responsibility of ensuring that any suffering is kept to a minimum and that it is justified by the expected scientific contribution of the experiment. Published papers are not always a good guide as to the minimum levels of electric shock that prove effective. A rat will avoid shocks that cause little if any overt distress. Information on the effects of different levels of shock in learning experiments is provided by Church (1972).

Surgical and Pharmacological Procedures   It is illegal to perform any surgical or pharmacological procedure on vertebrates in the UK without a Home Office licence and the relevant certificate. Such procedures should only be performed by experienced staff and it is a particular responsibility of senior staff to train and supervise others. Experimenters must be familiar with the technical aspects of anaesthesia (Myers, 1971; Barnes & Eltherington, 1973) and appropriate steps that should be taken to prevent post-operative infection in chronic experiments (Myers, 1971).

In pharmacological procedures, experimenters must be familiar with the literature on the behavioural effects and toxicity of the drugs being used. It is essential that low dosage pilot studies are done to determine behavioural effects and toxicities when new compounds are used or when a drug is being used for the first time in the particular laboratory. There are considerable differences in the way that different strains respond in the way that animals respond when in new environments.

Anaesthesia, Analgesia and Euthanasia

The experimenter must ensure that animals receive adequate post-operative care and that, if there is any possibillity of post-operative suffering, this is minimized by suitable nursing and the use of local anaesthetics where appropriate. Regular and frequent post-operative monitoring of the animal's condition is essential, and if at any time an animal is found to be suffering severe and enduring pain it must be killed. (This is also a requirement of the Home Office licence.) The UFAW Handbook should be consulted for methods of euthansia, which vary from species to species, and the recommended practices followed carefully.

Independent Advice

If an experiment is ever in any doubt about the condition of an animal, a second opinion should be obtained, preferably from a qualified veterinarian, but certainly from someone not directly involved in the experiments concerned.

Members with further questions or comments are encouraged to contact the Committee of the EPS or the Standing Advisory Committee on Standards for Psychological Research and Teaching Involving Animals of the BPS via the Leicester office of the Society.

References

AMLANER, C.J. and MacDONALD D.W. (1980) *A Handbook on Biotelemetry and Radio Tracking*. Oxford: Pergamon.
BARNES, C.D. and ELTHERINGTON, L.G. (1973) *Drug Dosage in Laboratory Animals*. Berkeley: University of California Press.
CHURCH, R.M. (1972) Aversive behaviour. In J.W. Kling and L.A. Riggs (Eds), *Woodworth and Schlossberg's Experimental Psychology*, 2nd ed. pp. 703–741. London: Methuen.

COCHRAN, W.G. and COX, G.M. (1966) *Experimental Designs*, 2nd ed. New York: Wiley.

COX, D.R. (1958) *Planning of Experiments*. New York: Wiley.

DAWKINS, M.S. (1980) *Animal Suffering*. London: Chapman & Hall.

Guidelines for the Use of Animals in Research (1981) *Animal Behaviour*, 29, 1–2.

HUNT, P. (1980) Experimental choice. In *The Reduction and Prevention of Suffering and Animal Experiments*. Horsham: RSPCA.

HUNTINGFORD, F. (1984) Some ethical issues raised by studies of predation and aggression. *Animal Behaviour*, 32, 210–215.

LEA, S.E.G. (1979) Alternatives to the use of painful stimuli in physiological psychology and the study of behaviour. *Alternatives to Laboratory Animals Abstracts*, 7, 20–21.

MORAN, G. (1975) Severe food deprivation: Some thoughts regarding its exclusive use. *Psychological Bulletin*, 82, 543–557.

MYERS, R.D. (1971) General laboratory procedures. In R.D. Myers (Ed), *Methods in Psychobiology*, vol.1, London: Academic Press.

SMYTHE, D.H. (1978) *Alternatives to Animal Experiments*. London: Scolar Press.

STILL, A.W. (1982) On the number of subjects used in animal behaviour experiments. *Animal Behaviour*, 30, 873–880.

STONEHOUSE, B. (Ed), (1978) *Animal Marking: Recognition Marking of Animals in Research*, London: Macmillan.

USE OF
ANIMALS IN
TEACHING

The use of animals in a teaching context is the subject of an Appendix to the Report of the Working Party on Animal Experimentation set up in 1976 by the Society's Scientific Affairs Board. The Appendix to the Report, which was published in 1979, is reproduced below.

There is legitimate public concern with the welfare of animals and questioning of the extent to which they can be permitted to experience discomfort, deprivation and suffering while serving man domestically, industrially, scientifically and recreationally. It is likely that repeated reference to animal experiments without comment desensitizes students to the ethical and scientific issues involved. As detailed rules cannot be given for what types of experiment are admissible on what species under what circumstances, it is in the general interest to inculcate a general scientific consciousness of the factors affecting animal welfare and of their ethical implications as well as a critical approach to claims of scientific benefit. Misunderstanding will be avoided if this scientific and ethical consciousness is shared by those who do and those who do not experiment with animals. Therefore all psychology research courses making substantial reference to research results from animals should attempt to make students aware:

1. That appropriate respect for animal species derives

from the understanding of their behavioural adaptations to their environments; that subjecting animals to highly restricted environments for the species concerned, to inappropriate diets, to enforced interactions with other species including humans, as may happen even with pets, can all cause suffering in varying degree.

2. That psychologists have greater access to this understanding than laymen and therefore have a greater than average social responsibility to lead public opinion in discriminating between what does and what does not constitute discomfort, deprivation or suffering for animal species, and to minimize unwarranted instances of any of these.

3. That different species have different effective environments and adapt to them in different ways, with the result that common factors to be discovered in the behaviour of different species may be abstract and emerge only when species differences such as relative importance of particular sense modalities are taken into account; that such differences can determine the degree of discomfort, deprivation or suffering that a procedure may cause to a particular species.

4. That some generalization between species including man may be possible when the relevant anatomy, physiology and behaviour patterns are considered. The decision to use a particular animal is often based on acceptance of a widely recognized 'animal model' for a particular type of behaviour or psychological phenomenon, where the ability to generalize to man is balanced against considerations of economy and husbandry.

5. That an experiment involving discomfort, deprivation or suffering in an animal should only be undertaken (and in general is only undertaken) with careful attention both to the scientific value of the knowledge likely to be gained and to the reduction in future discomfort, deprivation or suffering by man or other animals.

6. In courses involving practical work with animals, teachers should:

(a) Emphasize the positive contribution to the understanding of behaviour that can be made by experiments on non-articulate organisms where no discomfort, suffering or stress is involved.

(b) Emphasize the precautions necessary to minimize discomfort, deprivation or suffering and offer students the opportunity to discuss whether these as well as the educational or scientific objectives of the investigation have been met.

(c) Refer to the law preventing demonstration of invasive investigations on living animals and the requirement that experimental outcomes for such investigations should not be known in advance.

(d) Make maximum use of videotape or film where demonstration of any phenomena of problematic status (e.g. stress, fear, disability) may be essential.

FURTHER
ADVICE

Further advice can be sought from the Executive Secretary of the Society. Anyone contemplating research on animals should of course familiarise themselves with the legal situation. Information may be obtained from H Division, The Home Office, Queen Anne's Gate, London SW1H 9AT.

THE BPS CAREERS PACK

The **BPS Careers Pack** gathers together in one convenient package everything you need to know about studying psychology and jobs relating to psychology. The pack contains the following titles:

Thinking About Psychology?
Anthony Gale
Essential reading for all prospective psychology students and anyone interested in all that psychology has to offer.

Manage Your Own Career: A self-help guide to career planning
Ben Ball
Offers readers of all ages and at all stages in their careers a systematic way of preparing for changes in their working life.

Career Choices in Psychology: A guide to graduate opportunities
Detailed work profiles of professional psychologists.

Putting Psychology to Work
Will help both students and prospective employers recognize the value of an academic training in psychology.

How About Psychology?
For those contemplating a psychology degree or similar qualification.

These titles are available separately, or as part of the **Careers Pack** (which also includes two posters, and leaflets about psychology courses), price: **£21.50**

BPS
BOOKS

British Psychological Society
St Andrews House
48 Princess Road East
Leicester LE1 7DR UK

CAREERS AND COURSES

Ben Ball

❏ *careers for psychology graduates* ● *courses in psychology* ● *guidance resources*

The aim of this chapter is to provide an introductory overview of the main sources of information available to present and prospective students of psychology. It focuses primarily on the principal training and qualification routes and ends with a summary description of the career and educational guidance services provided for students in secondary, further and higher education. For a more detailed analysis, readers can refer to titles suggested in the references and further reading sections.

CAREERS FOR PSYCHOLOGY GRADUATES

Careers as Psychologists

Careers Choices in Psychology published by BPS Books gives a clear account of the main avenues in professional psychology in the UK. Qualification and training routes, the opportunities for career development, sample diaries of job holders are provided for each of the main specialisms: educational, occupational, clinical, criminological and legal, and teaching and research. A further source of information is provided by the range of booklets produced by the Association of Graduate Careers Advisory Services (AGCAS) which cover similar ground but link the work of psychologists with other professionals. Clinical psychology, for example, appears in *Health Care in the Public Sector.*

Competition for specialist training. It is perhaps important to point out that competition for training in the main specialist areas can be extremely severe. This is particularly true in the case of clinical psychology, where there were 750 applicants for 150 training places in 1987. In many cases, applicants will not only require a very good honours degree, but will also need some pre-entry experience prior to training.

The Appointments Memorandum is published monthly by The British Psychological Society (BPS) and is available to its members. It lists job vacancies, especially in the clinical, educational and academic areas. However, as Rose and Radford (1986) point out, over 75 per cent of psychology graduates will not qualify as professional psychologists, either because of limits on postgraduate training places and on public sector recruitment, or because of a wish to use their degree in other ways. So what happens to those who qualify at first degree level and who do not undertake professional training?

The General Labour Market In an earlier study, Ball and Bourner (1984) pointed to a range of options open to psychology graduates and in particular the diverse range of careers entered by cohorts of graduates in the early 1980s. Since then a number of studies have highlighted the particular employment difficulties experienced by psychology graduates in finding permanent work immediately on graduation. The Council for National Academic Awards' (CNAA) *Social Science Graduates: Degree results and first employment destinations* (1988), using statistical data for the period 1982–5, pointed to the comparatively high percentage of graduates unemployed (15.5 per cent for universities and 17.6 per cent for polytechnics in 1988). Retrospective analyses of this kind are obviously inadequate in not reflecting the current position. The last five years have seen, for example, rapidly improving graduate employment prospects, far fewer graduates unemployed and a graduate shortage in several key areas – a shortage which will be ever more apparent in the 1990s as, for demographic reasons, the supply of new graduates falls.

At the same time it is clear that changes in the labour market are influencing the choices of undergraduates:

– nearly 40 per cent of graduate jobs are open to graduates of any discipline

– the job growth in the services sector continues – 1 in 10 of all university graduates entering employment become trainee chartered accountants.

– poor pay and cuts in services have affected public sector recruitment.

In short, then, much has changed since the earlier studies were carried out. There are clear signs of a graduate shortage and the employment market for graduates of all disciplines is set to improve still further.

Psychology graduates can, with some ease, enter any number of commercial, industrial and public sector occupations.

Careers Outside Psychology

So what are the options open to psychology graduates who do not want to work as professional psychologists, but who would like to apply some or all of their specialist knowledge. In terms of career planning and development, much will depend on an individual's personal skills, values and interests, but the following provides a summary of some of the more obvious career routes.

Industry and Commerce. For those who like working in a commercial environment there are obvious applications of psychology in the field of advertising and market research. Consumer research – the planning of large-scale attitude surveys, carrying out in-depth studies of reaction to different products – provides an obvious example. But there are many other examples of the way graduates with statistical and data-handling skills can find an appropriate outlet in a commercial or industrial environment.

Working with people. Many students are drawn to psychology because of a basic interest in people and many graduates will enter work which requires high levels of interpersonal, and often helping skills. Counselling in educational settings or in statutory or voluntary agencies, careers guidance in schools and colleges, social work in its variety of specialist forms, teaching, particularly in special education, are obvious examples of areas in which psychology graduates will extend their professional training and be able to develop skills of diagnosis and person-centred intervention.

Research. For those graduates interested in developing their research skills there are a range of opportunities in industry as well as in higher education. Ergonomists, working on the human–machine interface, psychologists working in human factors research for the Ministry of Defence, can apply the methods of experimental psychology. But there are other kinds of research activity, for example, labour market research and manpower planning, which can take place in independent research consultancies and which rely on data-handling and problem-solving skills.

A review of the options open to those graduating in psychology is provided in *How about Psychology?* (1989) and in the various publications written by careers advisers that are listed in the further reading section.

Opportunities Overseas

Opportunities for both training and employment for psychology graduates exist overseas but the situation naturally varies widely from country to country.

Opportunities overseas are advertised in the general educational press, and on occasion in The British Psychological Society's *Appointments Memorandum.* Information may also be available through the British Council. It may be worthwhile enquiring of the cultural attaché of a country in which one is interested.

The USA is most likely to be of interest, being English-speaking and having far the largest psychological profession. The *APA Monitor,* published by the American Psychological Association, carries vacancies. The American Psychological Association also publishes *Graduate Study in Psychology and Associated Fields,* which annually covers some 600 programmes.

General advice is given in the following publications: *Scholarships Abroad,* (annual); *Work Your Way Around the World* (1989); *A Year Off . . . A Year On?* (1989) and *Working Overseas* (1988).

COURSES IN PSYCHOLOGY

The following notes will give an idea of the range of courses in psychology and serve as a guide to the sources of information available. They are illustrative rather than definitive.

GCSE, AS and A-level Courses and Exams

Most A-level psychology courses are offered by colleges of further education. In schools the amount of psychology teaching continues to increase, largely in the form of courses in child development, but there is comparatively little teaching at A-level. At present it is not possible to study psychology as an examination subject for Scottish highers or indeed for lower-level qualifications in Scotland. Further information about the extent of psychology teaching in schools and colleges of further education may be obtained from The Association for the Teaching of Psychology (ATP). The BPS Group of Teachers of Psychology is concerned largely with the teaching of psychology in higher education settings.

Two examining boards, The Joint Matriculation Board

(JMB) and the Associated Examining Board (AEB) offer psychology at A-level. The AEB also offers AS-level psychology, while the Northern Examining Association (NEA), the Midlands Examining Group (MEG) and the Southern Examining Group (SEG) all offer psychology examinations at GCSE-level in child development. There is also a 'higher level' psychology exam organized by the International Baccalaureate for students aged 16 to 18. (See useful addresses section for the boards' addresses.) To give just one example of the increasing popularity of psychology courses, the numbers of candidates for the AEB's A-level exam have almost doubled in the last four years. In 1988 there were over 6,000.

Details of all college course centres in the UK can be found in the *Directory of Further Education* and from individual local education authorities.

First Degree and Other Professional Courses

Recent evidence from the relevant admissions clearing houses reveals that psychology remains a popular subject of study. In its 1988 report the Polytechnic Central Admissions System (PCAS) pointed out that it handled 12,000 applicants (for psychology and related subjects) for 600 student places, a ratio of 20:1 applicants to places, one of the highest for any subject area.

Degree course information. The main sources of information concerning undergraduate programmes in psychology are obviously the prospectuses of individual institutions. However there are three separate compendia which list all courses in the principal sectors of higher education, and enable prospective students to compare the entry qualification required, length of course and so on. *The Polytechnic Courses Handbook* gives listings of all first degrees. *University Entrance: The official guide* provides information on all universities, their degree courses and precise details of entry requirements. *The Colleges and Institutes of Higher Education Guide* describes the small number of colleges which have psychology as a component in modular and social science degrees.

A detailed summary of existing psychology courses in the UK is found in the *Degree Course Guide* for psychology, which is updated every two years. This contrasts course content, selection procedures, assessment methods, recruitment numbers and departmental research interests. As well as single-honours programmes it also provides some information on joint-honours programmes or modular courses in which psychology may play a large part.

A range of other publications are available for the intending student – alternative prospectuses, 'good' university guides and so on. Existing students and staff provide an immediate source of information and when attending for interviews or open days, applicants need to make use of these 'primary sources'. Applicants may also want to check whether a particular degree programme gives the Graduate Basis for Registration as a Chartered Psychologist.

There are of course a range of study options in which psychology forms a major part. It is also possible, for example, to complete an undergraduate programme with the Open University (OU). To obtain Graduate Membership of the BPS students must undertake a range of full credit courses: social psychology, cognitive psychology and introduction to psychology as well as a selection from a range of other courses which include personality, development and learning, research methods in education and the social sciences.

Many vocational first degree courses, which form the basis of professional training, will also contain a significant psychology component. Programmes in education, nursing, social work, speech therapy and training for other paramedical careers are obvious examples.

Postgraduate Courses

Postgraduate study information. The Compendium of UK Postgraduate Studies in Psychology is compiled and published each year by the Department of Psychology at the University of Surrey. It comprises information supplied by departments of psychology on opportunities for research or graduate training. This usually includes a list of staff and their research interests. It does not necessarily include all courses in which psychology graduates may be interested and should be used in conjunction with *Graduate Studies*.

Graduate Studies is published yearly by Hobsons Press. It lists degrees by research and by taught course, and certificate and diploma courses, by subject, with institutions alphabetically within subject. Entry qualifications and content are specified for many of the courses. It aims to provide a comprehensive listing of postgraduate courses, representing all sectors of the higher education system. A range of freely available publications for undergraduates also summarize the main taught courses.

For those wanting to qualify in clinical psychology, the *Clearing House Handbook* covers all aspects of admission to the relevant postgraduate training courses. It is also worth remembering that a small number of postgraduate diploma courses provide a conversion course for graduates who have studied a first degree with a major psychology component. Successful completion of these courses enables students to apply for graduate membership of the BPS.

For anyone interested in teaching, *The* NATFHE *Handbook* is essential reading since it lists all forms of initial teacher training. It is perhaps worth noting that it is not possible to use psychology as a main subject specialization for the Postgraduate Certificate in Education.

The Postgraduate Bulletin published three times a year by the Central Services Unit lists immediate vacancies for graduate study, research and training across the entire range of disciplines.

For many students wishing to study further, the main problem is one of finding finance. All students are advised to read the relevant Research Council booklets, available in their Careers Advisory Services.

Other Specialist Courses

In addition to full-time courses lasting a year or more, there are other short, intensive courses which can be grouped under two broad headings. Firstly those concerned with *professional updating*, for example, short courses of introduction to new psychometric tests for occupational psychologists, workshops on counselling skills and approaches for those in the helping professions are examples of the vast range of short course provision.

There are also numerous *general interest* courses run under the auspices of university extramural departments or local authority adult education programmes which may provide a basic introduction to general psychology for people who have not studied the subject before.

A range of courses also exist under the OU's associate student programme, providing shorter professional updating courses and those designed to develop personal interests. Courses include: Introduction to Psychology, Biology, Brain and Behaviour, Cognitive Psychology.

GUIDANCE RESOURCES

Students about to complete their courses will want to make use of the guidance resources available to them in order to clarify their future educational or occupational decisions. In secondary schools the careers teacher will be the main focus for guidance activity, with possibly the additional involvement of the Head of Sixth Form. Local education authority officers will be closely involved in school-based guidance activity and, in particular, in one-to-one advisory interviews with pupils. In colleges of further education, there may be full- or part-time careers tutors to fulfil a careers guidance role. Once again, students will have access to their Local Education Authority Careers Service, whose careers officers will be trained in careers guidance, many of whom will have studied psychology at undergraduate level. In polytechnics, universities and colleges of higher education there will be institution-based careers advisory services staffed by small teams of careers advisers. They tend to operate on a self-referral basis – students and graduates use the services as and when they wish, but contact tends to be concentrated in a student's final year. An overview of careers guidance services in higher education is provided by Ball (1985). Careers advisers work on a counselling/advisory and information-giving model. Typically, students are offered counselling interviews, followed by an introduction to the information resources available to them. This may occasionally be supplemented with the results of psychometric test data, although this is not generally the pattern. Instead, many careers services will offer a programme of seminars by representatives of particular occupations, or subjects such as 'Applications and Interviews'. In some institutions, careers advisers have an educational role, and contribute to various courses of study on the subject of career and professional development. Careers advisers also maintain links with the graduate recruiters and engage in placement activity.

Computer-Based Guidance Systems

Computer-assisted career guidance systems (CAGS) are now increasingly used in the UK and the United States. In schools and some colleges, the most widely used are CASCAID and JIIG-CAL. Both encourage 'self-assessment' by finding a match between students' interests and occupational titles. The system most widely used in commercial and industrial settings is CAREER BUILDER which has a career-planning rationale, providing self-appraisal on the basis of personal skills, values and interests. The most comprehensive system to date, PROSPECT, has been designed initially for use in higher education, and funded largely by the Department of Education and Science. Users have the choice of completing one or more of four linked modules concerned with:

- self-assessment – appraising abilities, skills, interests and values;
- identifying options – searching and analysing occupations and employers;
- a decision aid to evaluate options;
- planning for entry and self-marketing.

While based largely on a career planning rationale, PROSPECT nevertheless retains a matching orientation – user profiles of skills and values for example are matched against over 200 graduate-level occupations.

Diagnostic Guidance and Vocational Guidance Agencies

A different model of guidance practice is provided by the private vocational guidance agencies which are mainly London-based in the UK. Here the emphasis is on diagnostic guidance. Psychometric test data from interest, aptitude and personality tests is used as a precursor to the one-to-one consultation, after which clients are provided with a written summary or report. Differential fee rates may be changed according to the kind of service offered. Initial career guidance, for example, may attract a lower rate of fee than a career review for those in mid-career. Some employing organizations now provide career guidance for employees, particularly at managerial level by using the services of external consultants. In particular, outplacement counselling for redundant executives is now provided by a number of consultancies, using psychometric testing, group discussion and/or individual counselling. For the majority of adults in the UK, there has been, however, no freely available national careers guidance provision since the closure of the Occupational Guidance Units in the early 1980s.

Educational Guidance

In the field of educational guidance for adults, there have been some new and exciting developments. There is now a burgeoning national network of educational guidance units, offering advice and information about education and training routes. Although not presently available in all geographical areas, it is clear that in future this will be the case. This initiative by the Unit for the Development of Adult and Continuing Education (UDACE) has been reinforced by the Training Access Point (TAP) initiative funded by the Training Agency which provides information about education and training opportunities via local computer terminals. There is therefore an attempt being made to provide freely available, up-to-date educational information supported in some cases by one-to-one advice and counselling. It is hoped that one result of the educational guidance initiative will be to improve access to existing educational opportunities, particularly in higher education. This will have obvious implications for intending students of psychology, in particular 'mature entrants' to further and higher education.

For teachers and lecturers in psychology one of the main challenges in the future will be to design and employ assessment methods that will enhance students' awareness of the way they can use their qualifications in psychology and develop basic practitioner skills. The Education for Capability and Enterprise Initiatives in Higher Education are designed with this aim in view. Developing students' self- and occupational awareness, for example, can be enhanced by appropriate teaching programmes. Guidance thus becomes an outcome of the teaching and learning process.

References   AMERICAN PSYCHOLOGICAL ASSOCIATION (APA) (annual) *Graduate Study in Psychology and Associated Fields*. Washington DC: APA.

ASSOCIATION OF COMMONWEALTH UNIVERSITIES (ACU) (annual) *University Entrance: The official guide*. London: ACU.

ASSOCIATION OF GRADUATE CAREERS ADVISORY SERVICES (1989) *Guidance, Counselling and Advisory Work*. Manchester: Central Services Unit.

ASSOCIATION OF GRADUATE CAREERS ADVISORY SERVICES (1989) *Health Care in Private Practice*. Manchester: Central Services Unit.

ASSOCIATION OF GRADUATE CAREERS ADVISORY SERVICES (1989) *Health Care in the Public Sector*. Manchester: Central Services Unit.

ASSOCIATION OF GRADUATE CAREERS ADVISORY SERVICES (1989) *Personnel and Employee Relations*. Manchester: Central Services Unit.

ASSOCIATION OF GRADUATE CAREERS ADVISORY SERVICES (1988) *Working Overseas*. Manchester: Central Services Unit.

BALL, B. (1987) Graduate and career guidance. *Guidance and Assessment Review*, 3, no. 3.

BALL, B. and BOURNER, T. (1984) The employment of psychology graduates. *Bulletin of The British Psychological Society*, 37, 37–40.

BRITISH COUNCIL (annual) *Scholarships Abroad*. London: British Council.

CAREERS RESEARCH AND ADVISORY CENTRE (CRAC) (1989) *A Year Off. . . A Year On?* Cambridge: CRAC/Hobsons Press.

CAREERS RESEARCH AND ADVISORY CENTRE (CRAC) (annual) *The Directory of Further Education*. Cambridge: CRAC/Hobsons Press.

CAREERS RESEARCH AND ADVISORY CENTRE (CRAC) (annual) *Graduate Studies*. Cambridge: CRAC/Hobsons Press.

CENTRAL SERVICES UNIT (triannual) *Postgraduate Bulletin*. Manchester: Central Services Unit.

CLEARING HOUSE FOR POSTGRADUATE COURSES IN CLINICAL PSYCHOLOGY (annual) *Clearing House Handbook*. Leeds: Clearing House for Postgraduate Courses in Clinical Psychology.

Colleges and Institutes of Higher Education see Standing Conference of Principals.

COMMITTEE OF DIRECTORS OF POLYTECHNICS (CDP) (annual) *The Polytechnic Courses Handbook*. London: CDP.

Compendium of UK Postgraduate Studies in Psychology see University of Surrey Psychology Department.

COUNCIL FOR NATIONAL ACADEMIC AWARDS (CNAA) (1988) Social science graduates: Degree results and first employment destinations. *CNAA Information Services Outcomes, Paper 1*. July.

Directory of Further Education see Career Research and Advisory Centre.

Graduate Study in Psychology and Associated Fields see American Psychological Association.

Graduate Studies see Career Research and Advisory Centre.

GRIFFITHS, S. (1989) *Work Your Way Around the World*. Oxford: Vacation Work.

HIGGINS, L.T. (1989) *How about Psychology?* rev. ed. Leicester: BPS Books.

HIGGINS, L.T. (1988) *Career Choices in Psychology*. Leicester: BPS Books.

NATIONAL ASSOCIATION OF TEACHERS IN FURTHER AND HIGHER EDUCATION (NATFHE) (annual) *The NATFHE Handbook: The handbook of initial teacher training*. London: NATFHE.

NEWSTEAD, S., MILLER, M. and FARMER, E. (1989) *Putting Psychology to Work*. Leicester: BPS Books.

Polytechnic Courses Handbook see Committee of Directors of Polytechnics.

Postgraduate Bulletin see Central Services Unit.

ROSE, D. and RADFORD, J. (1986) The unemployment of psychology graduates. *Bulletin of The British Psychological Society, 39*, 451–456.

Scholarships Abroad see British Council.

STANDING CONFERENCE OF PRINCIPALS (SCIP) (annual) *Colleges and Institutes of Higher Education*. Ormskirk: SCIP.

Univeristy Entrance: The official guide see Association of Commonwealth Universities.

UNIVERSITY OF SURREY PSYCHOLOGY DEPARTMENT (annual) *Compendium of UK Postgraduate Studies in Psychology*. Guildford: University of Surrey Psychology Department.

Further Reading

BALL, B. (1989) *Manage Your Own Career: A self-help guide to career choice and change*. Leicester: BPS Books and Kogan Page.

CANTER, S. and CANTER, D. (Eds) (1982) *Psychology in Practice*. Chichester: Wiley

CAREERS RESEARCH AND ADVISORY CENTRE (CRAC) (annual) *Graduate Employment and Training*. Cambridge: CRAC/Hobsons Press.

CENTRAL SERVICES UNIT (CSU) (annual) *Register of Graduate Employment and Training*. Manchester: CSU.

DAUNCEY, G. and MOUNTAIN, J. (1987) *The New Unemployment Handbook*. Cambridge: National Extension College.
(*A practical handbook with chapters on time use and survival strategies as well as job hunting.*)

MILLER, R.C.I. (1983) *Successful Job Hunting*. Oxford: Blackwell.

NEWPOINT PUBLISHING (annual) *Graduate Opportunities*. London: Newpoint Publishing.

NEWPOINT PUBLISHING (annual) *Which Degree?* London: Newpoint Publishing.
(*Provides information on all university, polytechnic and college of higher education first-degree courses.*)

PATES, A. and GOOD, M. (1986) *Second Chances: The guide to adult education and training opportunities*. Sheffield: Careers and Occupational Information Centre.

SYRETT, M. and DUNN, C. (1988) *Starting a Business on a Shoestring*. Harmondsworth: Penguin.

USEFUL ADDRESSES

American Psychological Association
1200 Seventeenth Street NW
Washington DC 20036
USA

Associated Examining Board
Staghill House
Guildford
Surrey GU2 5XJ
tel. (0483) 506506

Association of Graduate Careers
  Advisory Services
c/o Central Services Unit

Association of Heads of Psychology
  Departments
c/o Dr P.J. Barber
Department of Psychology
Birkbeck College
Malet Street
London WC1E 7HX
tel. (071) 5806622

British Association for the Advancement
  of Science
Fortress House
23 Saville Row
London W1X 1AB
tel. (071) 4943326

British Broadcasting Corporation
Insight Information
London W1A 1AA
tel. (071) 5804468

British Psychological Society
St Andrews House
48 Princess Road East
Leicester LE1 7DR
tel. (0533) 549568

Business and Technician Education
  Council
Central House
Upper Woburn Place
London WC1H OHH
tel. (071) 3876068

Careers Research and Advisory Centre
2nd Floor, Sheraton House
Castle Park
Cambridge CB3 OAX
tel. (0223) 460277

Central Services Unit for University and
  Polytechnic Careers and
  Appointment Services
Crawford House
Precinct Centre
Manchester MN3 9PE
tel. (061) 2734233

Council for National Academic Awards
344–354 Gray's Inn Road
London WC1X 8BP
tel. (071) 2784411

Department of Education and Science
Elizabeth House
38 York Road
London SE1 7PH
tel. (071) 9349000

Economic and Social Research Council
Cherry Orchard East
Kembrey Park
Swindon
Wilts SN2 6UQ
tel. (0793) 513838

Information and Resource Centre for
Teaching Psychology
Department of Psychology
East London Polytechnic
Romford Road
London E15 4LZ
tel. (081) 5907722

International Baccalaureate Office
18 Woburn Square
London WC1H ON5
tel. (071) 6371682

Joint Matriculation Board
Manchester M15 6EU
tel. (061) 2732565

Library of the British Psychological
Society
University of London
Senate House
Malet Street
London WC1E 7HU

Medical Research Council
20 Park Crescent
London W1N 4AL
tel. (071) 6365422

Midland Examining Group
c/o Oxford and Cambridge Schools
Examination Board
10 Trumpington Street
Cambridge CB2 1QB
tel. (0223) 64326

National Advisory Body for Local
Authority Higher Education
39–45 Tottenham Court Road
London W1P 9RD

National Foundation for Education
Research
The Mere
Upton Park
Slough
Berks SL1 2DQ
tel. (0753) 74123

Northern Examining Association
c/o Joint Matriculation Board

Open University Educational
Enterprises
The Open University
Walton Hall
Milton Keynes MK7 6AA
tel. (0908) 274066

Research Defence Society
Grosvenor Gardens House
Grosvenor Gardens
London SW1 OBS
tel. (071) 8288745

The Royal Society
6 Carlton House Terrace
London SW1Y 5AG
tel. (071) 8395561

Science and Engineering Research
Council
Polaris House
North Star Avenue
Swindon SN2 1ET
tel. (0793) 411000

Scottish Education Department
New St Andrew's House
St James Centre
Edinburgh EH1 3TB
tel. (031) 5568400

Society for Research into Higher
Education
University of Surrey
Guildford GU2 5XH

Special Group of Teachers of Psychology
c/o The British Psychological Society

Southern Examining Group
Central Administration Office
Stag Hill House
Guildford
Surrey GU2 5XJ
tel. (0483) 503123

University Central Council on
Admissions
PO Box 28
Cheltenham
Glos. GL50 35A
tel. (0242) 222444

INDEX

BPS BOOKS

THE BRITISH PSYCHOLOGICAL SOCIETY

From the series PROBLEMS IN PRACTICE:

Series editors: Glynis Breakwell, David Fontana and Glenys Parry

Each title in this new series focuses on a common problem across a number of different professions - industry, education, medicine, the police and other public and social services. The focus of each book is on practical skills and insights of relevance both to the workplace and outside. For simplicity of style, each book has a single author but the range of problems and situations addressed draws on the expertise of all three series editors.

Coping with Crises

Glenys Parry

There are few professionals who do not come into contact with people in crises, whether a nurse caring for the victim of a road accident, a teacher trying to reach an unhappy pupil, a manager announcing redundancies or a health visitor breaking bad news. This is a book for anyone who works with people in crisis. Professional help should go hand-in-hand with the person's own resources; the aim is to 'enable' rather than 'disable' the person's own coping mechanisms. In order to do this, you need to understand the psychology of coping and of how people seek and accept help.

Paperback 0 901715 81 6 **£5.99**   Hardback 0 901715 82 4 **£16.99**

Facing Physical Violence

Glynis Breakwell

Physical assault is a large and growing problem, particularly for nurses, social workers and other carers, but also in teaching and other public services.

Why do such attacks occur? Is it true that some people seem to invite attacks whilst others escape? How might one deal with violent situations? These and other questions are examined using a number of questionnaires and problem scenarios. **Facing Physical Violence** strikes a careful balance between giving practical guidance and a full consideration of the issues, making it of equal interest to practitioners and policymakers.

Paperback 0 901715 95 6 **£5.99**   Hardback 0 901715 96 4 **£16.99**

Managing Stress

David Fontana

Stress in professional life is a much discussed problem nowadays. Clearly, people under too much stress (or too little) do not work at their best. **Managing Stress** demonstrates the importance of identifying exactly what stresses you, including both external factors in the environment and factors within yourself. Using non-technical language, and with an emphasis upon practical and easily mastered strategies, David Fontana takes the reader step-by-step through the things that can be done to enhance stress resistance and to increase professional efficiency.

Paperback 0 901715 97 2 **£5.99**   Hardback 0 901715 98 0 **£16.99**

Interviewing

Glynis M. Breakwell

Whether you are dealing with clients, patients or students, interviewing skills are employed in any situation where information is exchanged and evaluated: recruitment, appraisal, teaching skills, allocating resources, planning changes, dealing with the media. So what makes a good interview? There is more to it than asking and answering questions. Breakwell describes interviews from both perspectives - that of interviewer and interviewee - since to be effective you need to understand what is happening from both sides. Exercises and guidelines throughout the book are designed to promote self-assessment, to uncover stereotypes and misconceptions, and to try out the methods and skills described.

Paperback 1 85433 000 4 **£5.99**   Hardback 1 85433 001 2 **£16.99**

Social Skills at Work

David Fontana

Social Skills at Work explores the ways people relate to each other in their working lives and considers how people can achieve greater control over and satisfaction from them. Fontana emphasizes that true social skill is founded on self-knowledge: knowing how you feel about your exchanges with others and understanding what you want from them, as well as considering what other people want from their relationships with you. With the aid of practical examples, exercises and case studies readers are encouraged to analyse what makes them dissatisfied with current habits of relating to others, and suggests how beneficial change can be effected. Self-management thus comes to be seen as an integral part of social skill.

Paperback 1 85433 015 2 **£5.99**   Hardback 1 85433 016 0 **£16.99**

BPS BOOKS THE BRITISH PSYCHOLOGICAL SOCIETY

The **Psychology in Action** series

Psychology has a great deal to say about how we can make our working lives more effective and rewarding: the way we see other people, how they see us, and our abillity to communicate with others and achieve what we want from a situation. Starting from actual practice in the classroom, the police station, the surgery or the interviewing room, **Psychology in Action** looks at the everyday working methods and concerns of particular groups of people and asks: where and how can psychology help ?

CLASSROOM CONTROL
David Fontana

'should be required reading' **Parents' Voice**

'A sound introduction in its area for education students' **TES**

'Wise, detached, pragmatic, sensible ... thoroughly useful' **Education**

Classroom Control investigates the causes of disruptive classroom behaviour and presents strategies based on insights into both the behaviour of pupils and the teacher's own behaviour. These strategies focus on commonly occurring situations such as inattentiveness, hyperactivity, lack of interest, defiance, rudeness, bullying and classroom violence.

Teachers are encouraged to examine their own response to classroom challenges and their concept of the role of the teacher. How are teachers for instance. to cope with the stress which threats to their self-image produce? This practical approach addresses areas of urgent concern to student and serving teachers and educationalists. It is equally applicable to both primary and secondary schools.

David Fontana has an international reputation as an educationalist and psychologist with extensive firsthand classroom experience as teacher and as observer and examiner of students in training. He has written a number of books on education.

1985; 192 pages
0 901715 39 5 pb **£6.50**   0 901715 42 5 hb **£20.00**

BPS BOOKS
THE BRITISH PSYCHOLOGICAL SOCIETY

Thinking About Psychology ?   Anthony Gale

Anything that people are, or people do, or people think, can be studied by psychologists.

● But how exactly do they do this? What methods do they use?
● What does a course in psychology entail? How do you choose between different courses?
● What is the use of psychology and which careers does it lead to?

These and many other practical questions are explored in this lively introductory guide. Detailed appendices provide comparative information about first-degree courses.

May 1990; 128 pages ; 1 85433 031 4   **£5.99**

Manage Your Own Career: *A self-help guide to career planning*
Ben Ball

This book offers readers of all ages and at all stages in their careers a systematic way of preparing for changes in their working life. By reviewing past experiences, pinpointing present interests, skills and values and setting goals for the future, readers can take control of their own careers and improve their motivation and confidence.

January 1989; 112 pp; 1 85091 861 9   **£5.99**

British Psychological Society
St Andrews House
48 Princess Road East
Leicester LE1 7DR UK

THE ASSOCIATION FOR THE TEACHING OF PSYCHOLOGY

is an independent, non-profit making organization for those involved in teaching psychology at any level. Membership is open to anyone interested in the teaching of psychology.

Publications include the twice-yearly journal of the ATP, **Psychology Teaching**, and our quarterly **Newsletter**, both of which are free to members. The ATP is actively involved in publishing teaching materials, and also maintains an expanding bank of resource materials.

Conferences and workshops, including the annual ATP Conference, are regularly organized and sponsored by the ATP.

Local groups affiliated to the ATP meet regularly in several parts of the country.

Membership is £10, with a special rate for students. To join, or for further information, write to:
The Secretary, The ATP, c/o The British Psychological Society, St Andrews House, 48 Princess Road East, Leicester LE1 7DR.

BPS BOOKS
THE BRITISH PSYCHOLOGICAL SOCIETY

Sense and Nonsense about Hothouse Children
A Practical Guide for Parents and Teachers

Michael J. A. Howe

Are geniuses made or born? This book makes practical sense of the various contradictory messages frequently aired by media 'experts'. While refuting some of their more extreme claims, Michael Howe's research shows that the proponents of 'hothouse' training are essentially correct about the achievement potential of the 'average' child. He considers some of the difficult questions that arise from this:

○ If a child's early progress can be accelerated, how much can parents and teachers realistically hope to achieve? And how much *should* they hope to achieve?

○ What kind of learning activities should be offered, and how can they be adapted to the needs of the individual child?

○ What are the emotional, psychological and social costs of intensified early learning? How can accelerated intellectual achievement be combined with healthy personal development?

Combining recent research, case histories and down-to-earth practical guidance, this book will be invaluable to anyone concerned with the education of young children.

Michael Howe is Reader in Human Cognition at the University of Exeter. He has written a number of well-known books on exceptional abilities in young people, and over 70 journal articles.

August 1990; 112 pp
1 85433 039 X paperback   approx £6.00

British Psychological Society
St Andrews House
48 Princess Road East
Leicester LE1 7DR UK